The People Are Holy

The History and Theology of Free Church Worship

The People Are Holy
The History and Theology of Free Church Worship

by
Graydon F. Snyder
and
Doreen M. McFarlane

[handwritten inscription: To Bryon on your birthday, with appreciation. Grady]

MERCER
UNIVERSITY PRESS

ISBN 0-86554-952-4   MUP/P301

The People Are Holy:
The History and Theology of Free Church Worship
    Copyright ©2005
    Mercer University Press, Macon, Georgia USA
    All rights reserved
    Printed in the United States of America
    First edition, December 2005

The paper used in this publication meets the minimum requirements
    of American National Standard for Information Sciences—
    Permanence of Paper for Printed Library Materials,
    ANSI Z39.48-1984.

Library of Congress Cataloging-in-Publication Data

Snyder, Graydon F.
    The people are holy : the history and theology of Free Church worship
/ by Graydon F. Snyder and Doreen McFarlane.—1st ed.
    p.   cm.
    Includes bibliographical references (p.) and indexes.
    ISBN-13: 978-0-86554-952-4 (pbk. : alk. paper)
    ISBN-10: 0-86554-952-4 (pbk. : alk. paper)
    1. Free churches—Liturgy—History. 2. Free churches—Liturgy—
Theology.
    I. McFarlane, Doreen.   II. Title.
BX4817.S59 2005
264'.09—dc22

                                                            2005028638

Contents

Preface

What follows is a theological/biblical description of the "Free Church" as it comes together for worship. In no way can this be called a "manual of worship," although, hopefully, readers may gain insights that could inspire new procedures. We intend to show what worship would be like if the pattern of the early church was taken seriously and if the particular theology of the Free Church was integrated into the life of the church.

The authors come from lifelong involvement in the Free Church. Graydon F. Snyder has been professor of New Testament and dean of two Free Church seminaries: Bethany Theological Seminary and Chicago Theological Seminary. Doreen McFarlane earned her Ph.D. at Chicago Theological Seminary and has been pastor of Free Church faith communities. She is now pastor of the Flagg Road United Church of Christ, West Hartford, Connecticut.

We thank the staff of Mercer University Press for their encouragement in this project. We think particularly of Marsha Luttrell, production manager extraordinaire; longtime friend Edd Rowell, senior editor; and Marc Jolley, director.

We also express deep appreciation to our spouses, Michael McFarlane and Lois Snyder, not only for their patience, but for their deep interest and experience in our subject: Free Church worship.

November 2005   *Graydon F. Snyder and Doreen M. McFarlane*

To our primary covenant partners

Michael and Lois

Introduction

Paul speaks of the assembly of those who follow Jesus as "the body of Christ." The term "body of Christ" is more than a metaphor. It describes and embodies the sense of the church as a gathered community. Such a community is by nature nonhierarchical and composed of a company of equals, although each member will be given differing gifts and responsibilities. Throughout this book we focus on the vital importance of group participation, shared leadership, and community decision making. In order truly to "be the church" the equality and participation of each member must be maintained. Such is the nature of the Free Church, at least in its definitive form. When every local church member sees himself or herself as a part of the "body of Christ" in this way, worship, seen as community formation, becomes central to the life of the church. In addition, and importantly, such full participation of every member of "the body" will more likely result in actions that bring about harmony, peace, and justice in community, nation, and world.

This book offers the reader a glimpse of worship in the Free Church. It comes from decades of participation in congregational life. Yet, what we offer here is not simply a description. We have joined our experience with the practice of the early church and a "body of Christ" theology. The result is a form of worship we believe signifies the Free Church.

Chapter 1

Characteristics of the Free Church

Unfortunately, the topic of worship in the Free Church tradition is not one of the most-debated topics of the twenty-first century. Normally authors would want to tell readers this is the best book on a subject of utmost significance to the readers. While the issue discussed in this book may be very important, it has indeed remained at a subterranean level in Western Christianity. We do not often discuss the form of worship, preaching, or teaching in churches that are primarily congregational in their organization and conviction.[1] As authors we are confounded by this situation. In the United States, congregational style churches may be in the majority. While not every denomination categorized as congregational will act in a Free Church manner, in this study we are thinking in general of Baptists, United Church of Christ, Disciples of Christ, Churches of Christ, Churches of God, Quakers, Mennonite, and Church of the Brethren.[2] We mention these churches because they have officially met under the rubric "Believers' Church."[3] In

---

[1]Significant studies that include the Free Church tradition come from James F. White. His *Introduction to Christian Worship*, 3rd ed. (Nashville: Abingdon Press, 2000) is almost a model for this study. His history of worship has extensive material on the early church and then continues to the present time with constant reference to the Free Church: *A Brief History of Christian Worship* (Nashville: Abingdon, 1993).

[2]D. H. Williams lists the following as "Free Churches": Hutterites, Mennonites, Quakers, Baptists, Congregationalists, Evangelical Free, Methodists, Nazarene, Disciples of Christ, Brethren, Church of God, Adventist, and Independent churches. See his *The Free Church and the Early Church: Bridging the Historical and Theological Divide*, ed. D. H. Williams (Grand Rapids MI: Eerdmans, 2002) vii.

[3]There have been several conferences of denominations that identify themselves with the appellation "Believers' Church." The first significant conference was held in 1967 at the Southern Baptist Theological Seminary in Louisville, Kentucky. See *The Concept of the Believers' Church*, ed. James Leo Garrett, Jr. (Scottdale PA: Herald Press, 1969). Another was held at Chicago Theological Seminary in 1970. See "Believers' Church Conference 1970," *The Chicago Theological Seminary Register* 60/6 (1970). In 1975 another conference was held at Pepperdine University, Malibu, California. See the *Journal of the American Academy of Religion* 44

cluded in our discussion are the Methodists, though they have not officially participated in the Believers' Church conferences. We will reference many independent churches, Pentecostals, and most African-American congregations as also inherently Free Church in their attitude and organization.[4]

Given the ecclesiastical potpourri we have just mentioned, nomenclature becomes an impossible task. The term "Believers' Church" was coined by Max Weber (1864–1920) to designate those Christians who wished to join a "community of personal believers of the reborn and only those." Church historian George Williams (1914–2000) defined the Believers' Church as "the gathered church of committed disciples living in the fellowship of mutual correction, support, and abiding hope."[5] Most of us object to the term Believers' Church because we wish to speak of a congregational style, not a quality of faith. *Believers'* Church implies that anyone outside the aforementioned denominations must be nonbelievers. Nothing could be farther from the truth. Belonging to a Believers' Church does not ensure faith any more than belonging to any other group implies faithlessness. We started with the term Free Church, a term that does refer to structure rather than quality of faith. When the term Free Church was first coined it referred to those churches that insisted on the separation of church and state.[6] While the term may still be pertinent in some areas of the world, it is not especially helpful in the United States. The United States Constitution strictly forbids the governmental promotion of any given religion. Every church, synagogue and mosque in the United States could properly be called "Free." So we ask our readers' indulgence. We will use the term Free Church to name the denominations we have in mind. We will sometimes use the term "congregational" to signify the form of the churches found in the Free Church.[7]

(March 1976). There have been eight such conferences with differing constituencies and a variety of topics. For a complete list see Merle D. Strege, ed., *Baptism and Church: A Believers' Church Vision* (Grand Rapids MI: Sagamore, 1986) 207-208.

[4]For the impact of the charismatic movement on worship see John R. K. Fenwick and Bryan D. Spinks, *Worship in Transition: The Liturgical Movement in the Twentieth Century* (New York: Continuum, 1995) 105-14.

[5]George H. Williams, *Wilderness and Paradise in Christian Thought* (New York: Harper & Brothers, 1962) 214. See also his *The Radical Reformation* (Philadelphia: Westminster Press, 1962) xxviii-xxxvi.

[6]Franklin H. Littell, *The Free Church* (Boston: Starr King Press, 1957) 1-14.

[7]George H. Williams discusses the implications of nomenclature in "The Believers' Church and the Given Church," in *The People of God: Essays on the Believers' Church*, ed. Paul Basden and David S. Dockery (Nashville: Broadman

In any case there are certain characteristics that mark the congregational style church.[8] They are:

Separation of church and state

The church was pluralistic from the very beginning. There was no uniform organization or belief during the first three centuries. Though scholars differ on the forms of early Christianity, one suspects the very earliest Jesus organization was based on his prophetic wisdom found in documents like Q (*Quelle*, sayings of Jesus).[9] Another type would have been the Hellenistic church of the Apostle Paul based on the good news of reconciliation and redemption.[10] Yet another was the Johannine tradition—Jesus revealed ultimate Truth.[11] By the second century these various Jesus communities became separate great urban centered traditions: Antioch, Ephesus, Jerusalem, Alexandria, and Rome.[12]

After the conversion of Constantine the church became the only legal religion and eventually, under Charlemagne, church and state were united as the Holy Roman Empire. There appeared to be one Christianity, though actually there were always dissenters.[13] While the Reformation again offered Christians a choice, it did not promote or allow geopolitical plural-

---

Press, 1991) 325-32. The terms "Gathered" (Free Church) and "Given" (mainline or territorial church) avoid undesired implications, but have not gained general usage by Free Church historians.

[8]Above all see Donald Durnbaugh, *The Believers' Church: The History and Character of Radical Protestantism* (New York: Macmillan, 1968) esp. 209-99. Also Calvin Redekop, *Mennonite Society* (Baltimore: Johns Hopkins University Press, 1989) 52-54. John Howard Yoder sees the origin of Free Church characteristics in the ethos of Judaism at the time of Jesus. See Yoder, *The Jewish-Christian Schism Revisited*, ed. Michael G. Cartwright and Peter Ochs (Grand Rapids MI: Eerdmans, 2003) 133-42.

[9]John S. Kloppenborg Verbin, *Excavating Q: The History and Setting of the Sayings Gospel* (Edinburgh: T&T Clark, 2000) 166-213.

[10]Wayne A. Meeks, *The First Urban Christians: The Social World of the Apostle Paul* (New Haven CT: Yale University Press, 1983) 164-92.

[11]Raymond E. Brown, *The Community of the Beloved Disciple* (New York: Paulist Press, 1979) 45.

[12]B. H. Streeter, *The Primitive Church* (New York: MacMillan, 1929) 31.

[13]As documented by an important forerunner of the Free Church, Gottfried Arnold, in his *Unpartheyische Kirchen- und Ketzer-Historie, vom Anfang des Neuen Testaments bis auf das Jahr Christi 1688* (Franckfurt am Mayn: Thomas Fritschens sel Erben, 1728).

ism to exist. Though there were now different nation-states, the religion of
the prince, or state, was still the only acceptable religion for the people.

This strict alliance of church and state had not gone unchallenged.
Followers of Peter Waldo (Waldensians) and Jon Hus (Hussites) insisted
on the freedom to meet and worship without political interference. When
a little group of dissenters met in Zürich, on January 21, 1525, and baptized
each other, the medieval state/church system began to disintegrate. The first
Anabaptist group called for a religious freedom that would allow them to
carry out the will of God as they saw it, not as dictated by any particular
political system.

Once the separation of church and state occurred, it spread rapidly.[14]
The Anabaptists were followed by other Teutonic groups such as the
Hutterites (1527), Mennonites (1539), and Brethren (1708). Eventually all
Hutterites, Brethren, and most Mennonites (except some Dutch) immigrated to the United States and Canada. About the same time changes
occurred in England. Influenced by the continental Reformation, especially
Calvin, Puritanism ("pure" biblical authority) developed as a critique of the
state church. While some Puritans wished to reform the Church of England,
others (Dissenters and Nonconformists), stressing biblical authority,
believed separation was necessary.[15]

From this movement came the English Free Churches.[16] Some insisted
on the authority of the congregation, hence Congregationalists (1640).[17]
Others, Baptists, influenced by the Dutch Anabaptists, stressed adult
immersion (perhaps 1615). One radical group, the Quakers, rejected
ecclesiastical authority and all sacraments (1652). Another movement,

[14]Above all see Durnbaugh, *The Believers' Church*, 64-161. Also Ross Thomas
Bender, *The People of God: A Mennonite Interpretation of the Free Church
Tradition* (Scottdale PA: Herald Press, 1971) 27-58.

[15]Horton Davies, *The English Free Churches* (London: Oxford University
Press, 1952) 41-62. Davies lists Congregationalists, Baptists, and Methodists as
Free Churches indigenous to England. The fourth church, Presbyterians, derived
from Switzerland and sought to be among conforming Puritans.

[16]Ernest A. Payne, *The Free Church Tradition in the Life of England* (London:
SCM Press, 1944) 44-49.

[17]G. F. Nuttall, *Visible Saints: The Congregational Way, 1640–1660* (Oxford:
Blackwell, 1957) 71. Erik Routley, *The Story of Congregationalism* (London:
Independent Press, 1961) 23. On New England Congregationalists (not Separatists!)
see Edmund S. Morgan, *Visible Saints: A History of the Puritan Ideal* (New York:
New York University Press, 1963) esp. 64-65.

Methodism, was more influenced by continental Pietists than by Anabaptists. John and Charles Wesley associated with dissenting English religious societies until the conversion that occurred at Aldersgate on May 24, 1738. The Wesleys attempted to avoid sectarianism by remaining an *ecclesiola in ecclesia* (Pietism),[18] but in 1749 the Methodist associations or societies moved toward a separate church.

Once in America, immigrants from the continent and England joined with new Free Churches in an environment that encouraged (even demanded) separation of church and state. For example, led by the Campbells, a major new American Free Church that stressed adult immersion, the Disciples of Christ, began in 1811–1812.[19] The United Church of Christ came into being much later (1957), but combined the old traditions of the Reformed Church (Calvinism), Evangelical Church (Lutheranism), and Congregationalism (British Separatism).[20]

Adult baptism

While infant baptism need not go hand in hand with the state church, historically it has. The child, without its own decision or consent, enters, by baptism, the *established* society of Christendom. When the established church practices infant baptism, then freedom of choice, a multiplicity of faith responses, and the adult decision to join a faith family are all denied. For the Free Church these elements are sine-qua-non aspects of the Christian faith. In fact, Anabaptism takes its derogatory name from its practice of rebaptizing adults who wished to make an adult decision.[21]

To be sure, adult baptism would be necessary in order to avoid the union of church and state created by infant baptism. However, the first debates in the sixteenth century involved more than just the church/state conflict. The Anabaptists rejected baptism as a sacrament. While the Reformers also rejected most sacraments they could not deny the sacramen-

---

[18]Frank Baker, *John Wesley and the Church of England* (Nashville: Abingdon Press, 1970) 106, 116-17.

[19]Lester G. McAllister and William E. Tucker, *Journey in Faith: A History of the Christian Church (Disciples of Christ)* (St. Louis: Bethany Press, 1975) 117-19.

[20]*Reformation Roots*, ed. John B. Payne. *Living Theological Heritage of the United Church of Christ* 2, Barbara Brown Zikmund, series ed. (Cleveland: Pilgrim Press, 1997) 1-29.

[21]Miroslav Volf speaks of it as the "privatization of decision" over against social decision. See his *After Our Likeness: The Church as the Image of the Trinity* (Grand Rapids MI: Eerdmans, 1998) 14.

tal nature of baptism and the eucharist. So the early Reformers and those of the so-called Radical Reformation split over the issue of baptism—not only because of separation of church and state, but also over a theology of sacraments.[22]

In addition to these two concerns—separation of church and state and sacramentalism—there was yet another reason to insist on adult baptism. While both the Reformation and the Free Church rejected the theological and ecclesiastical authority of medieval tradition, the Radical Reformation insisted on the primary authority of Scripture in church practice. Anabaptists maintained infant baptism was a later tradition, not a New Testament practice. The New Testament knew only baptism of adults.[23] Zwingli argued that the New Testament evidence was not that clear. Zwingli was probably correct, as we shall see, but even so adult baptism became a symbol for the Free Church position on the separation of church and state, sacramentalism, and the use of Scripture over against Tradition.

No force in religion

Separation of church and state automatically implies that neither the state nor any other social structure can force a person to accept a specific faith, or any faith for that matter. Though from the beginning (sixteenth-century) congregational types protested the right of the prince to determine which faith was correct, eventually objections to the use of force became more universal. Many objected to the use of military force by the state. Most objected to the use of violence to create unwanted conformity. Many congregational types are inevitably pacifistic to some extent. At the same time they are also reluctant to let the state force moral and faith decisions on society as a whole.

---

[22]On the sixteenth-century debates see Rollin S. Armour, *Anabaptist Baptism: A Representative Study* (Scottdale PA: Herald Press, 1966) 27-30. The "Radical Reformation" is also known as the "Left Wing of the Reformation" or the "Third Reformation." In general, it includes all reforming elements not identified with the Magisterial Reformation (Luther, Calvin). Three radical groupings are included: Anabaptists (from which evolved the Free Church tradition), Spiritualists, and Evangelical Rationalists.

[23]Phyllis Rodgerson Pleasants, "*Sola Scriptura* in Zürich?" in *The Free Church and the Early Church*, 80-84.

The Free Church slogan has been "freedom of conscience."[24] Freedom of conscience affects deeply the social message of these faith communities. For example, while many congregational types today would frown on abortion, at the same time most Free Churches would be reluctant to allow the state to force that position on society as a whole. That is, a woman has the "freedom of her own conscience to make a choice." The state cannot take that away. Or again, many would likely opt for a strong Sunday observance, but would be slow to enact blue laws. That is a matter of conscience, not law.

The issue of conscience is complex. At first glance it might appear that "freedom of conscience" leads to anarchy. Whatever a person firmly believes is permissible. That is not a useful understanding of "conscience."[25] The term was coined by the Apostle Paul to describe how deep convictions were formed and maintained. The Greek term *suneidesis* was first used by Paul in 1 Corinthians 8:7 to describe those who were converting to the new faith. He said they had a weak conscience because they were unable to adapt as quickly as others. Conscience is not an individual matter, nor is it a God-given guide for moral behavior. The conscience is created by interaction with family and community.[26] It is the psychic attachment to one's group. Pangs of conscience occur when the individual breaks that attachment. The break can be massive, such as attacking someone in the family, or it can be very slight, such as eating with the wrong utensil. To have a clear conscience means no break with the formation community has occurred.

In Corinthians Paul tried to protect the recent convert's conscience until such a time as the Christian community had transformed it.[27] For example, a person taught not to eat idol meat, needed time to understand that the gods represented by idols did not exist. The same is true for the Free Church. Individuals should not be forced to act in a way that is contrary to their formation or basic convictions. Changes will eventually occur as the individual participates in the faith community. At the same time neither

---

[24]Carl F. Bowman, *Brethren Society: The Cultural Transformation of a "Peculiar People"* (Baltimore: Johns Hopkins University Press, 1995) 5, 78, 353-56.

[25]See Krister Stendahl, "The Apostle Paul and the Introspective Conscience of the West," *Harvard Theological Review* 56 (1963): 199-215.

[26]Donald E. Miller, *The Wing-Footed Wanderer: Conscience and Transcendence* (Nashville: Abingdon Press, 1977) 15-16.

[27]Graydon F. Snyder, *First Corinthians: A Faith Community Commentary* (Macon, GA: Mercer University Press, 1992) 125-28; 233-34.

state nor church has the right to force on a faith group outward assent to religious convictions not acceptable to its corporate conscience. Free Church people call that "freedom of conscience."

Mutual assistance

A primary mark of the early Jesus movement was its care for the other. Caring became so natural it occurred unconsciously. In the parable of the sheep and the goats the sheep did not know when and to whom they had given assistance.

> Then the righteous will answer him, "Lord, when was it that we saw you hungry and gave you food, or thirsty and gave you something to drink? And when was it that we saw you a stranger and welcomed you, or naked and gave you clothing? And when was it that we saw you sick or in prison and visited you?" And the king will answer them, "Truly I tell you, just as you did it to one of the least of these who are members of my family, you did it to me."   (Matt. 25:37-40)

Love was material and political because love was covenantal. Love is far more than a feeling. Love even extends social covenants to the enemy.

> "If you love those who love you, what credit is that to you? For even sinners love those who love them. If you do good to those who do good to you, what credit is that to you? For even sinners do the same. If you lend to those from whom you hope to receive, what credit is that to you? Even sinners lend to sinners, to receive as much again. But love your enemies, do good, and lend, expecting nothing in return."
>
> (Luke 6:32-35)

Such love has its roots in the Hebrew Scriptures. Though there are many rich words for love in Hebrew, we think primarily of *chesed* or "steadfast love" (RSV, NRSV). God has steadfast love for the people, as affirmed, for example, in a marriage analogy:

> And I [God] will take you [Israel] for my wife forever; I will take you for my wife in righteousness, and in justice, in steadfast love [*chesed*], and in mercy.   (Hosea 2:19)

In return Israel is asked "to love [*chesed*] the Lord your God with all your heart, soul, and might" by doing what God has commanded (the Ten Commandments [Deut. 6:4-9]). The Lord does not seek sacrifice but asks us "to do justice, and to love [*aheb*] kindness [*chesed*] and walk humbly with God" (Micah 6:8). Such love is communal and social, in contrast to modern individualistic love.[28] The early church was noted for its caring. For example, they strongly opposed infanticide and they cared for persons infected during plagues.[29]

It would be inappropriate to suggest that Catholics and Reformers did not care about people while the Radical Reformers did. As early as 1522 the Lutheran Reformer Carlstadt issued a tract entitled *On the Putting Away of Pictures and That There Should Be No Beggars among Christians*. The Wittenberg town council then forbade begging and, subsequently, established a Common Chest to help the poor, needy, and sick. This was the first official Protestant attempt to deal with poverty. The issue here is one of ultimate definition. Catholics characterized the church as "one, holy, catholic, and apostolic." The true catholic faith was "what has been believed everywhere, always, and by all" (Vincent of Lérins, ca. 450 CE). Luther found the church wherever "the Word of God is rightly preached and the sacraments properly administered." (Calvin added "proper discipline.") The Radical Reformation stressed more a church that witnessed to its faith, served others as well as each other, and formed a close fellowship.[30] William Penn described the Quakers as ones who formed community and loved one another.[31]

Through the centuries since the Reformation the Free Churches have continued to assist one another. More radical groups, like the Hutterites and the Society of Brothers, followed the model of the first church in Jerusalem:

> All who believed were together and had all things in common; they would sell their possessions and goods and distribute the proceeds to all, as any had need.
>   (Acts 2:44-45)

---

[28]Wolfgang Stegemann, "The Contextual Ethics of Jesus," in *The Social Setting of Jesus and the Gospels*, ed. Wolfgang Stegemann, Bruce Malina, and Gerd Theissen (Minneapolis: Augsburg Press, 2002) 45-61.

[29]See Rodney Stark, *The Rise of Christianity* (Princeton NJ: Princeton University Press, 1996) 73-94.

[30]*Every Need Supplied: Mutual Aid and Christian Community in the Free Churches, 1525–1675*, ed. Donald F. Durnbaugh (Philadelphia: Temple University Press, 1974) 3.

[31]William Penn, "Preface: A Summary Account of the Divers Dispensations of God to Men," in *A Journal or Historical Account of the Life, Travels, Sufferings, Christian Experiences, and Labour of Love, in the Work of the Ministry, of that Ancient Eminent, and Faithful Servant of Jesus Christ, George Fox* (Philadelphia: Friends' Bookstore, 1892) xxix-xxx.

Even though most did not practice community of goods, still mutual aid was prominent. Those who live in Mennonite or Amish territory will be well aware of such mutual assistance as "barn raisings." Barn raisings not only help a member of the community, but also serve as important, enjoyable social occasions. Occasionally a popular movie, like *Witness* (Paramount Pictures, 1985), will offer to the public a fairly accurate reenactment of such mutual assistance. While these may be dramatic instances for public viewing, less obvious are programs of financial assistance, care for families that have lost major sources of income, care for the chronically ill, communities for the elderly, support for objectors to war, and many others. From the very beginning, given the separation of church and state, the churches have taken over programs that might have otherwise been expected of the state. The state depends on those programs of mutual assistance.

At the turn of the twentieth century mutual assistance shifted to universal service. In 1920 a group associated with the Mennonite Central Committee sent a shipment of relief material to Beirut. The twentieth century then saw a rapid increase of organizations dedicated to making mutual aid a universal caring: the American Friends Service Committee, the Brethren Service Committee, the Methodist Commission on Overseas Relief, and others. Eventually, significant aid programs emerged from these efforts, such as the Heifer Project, CROP (Christian Rural Overseas Project), and, above all, Church World Service.[32]

Congregational types are driven toward communal life, but that normally takes the form of mutual assistance rather than common ownership of property. While capitalism may have emerged from Protestantism, especially Calvinism, socialism and communism took inspiration from the early Free Church practice of mutual aid.[33]

No oaths and no creeds

The issue of creedalism and taking oaths is a subsection of separation of church and state. Free Church Christians do not oppose public statements of faith, but they do oppose giving final allegiance to any political or

---

[32]Graydon F. Snyder, *Health and Medicine in the Anabaptist Tradition: Care in Community* (Valley Forge PA: Trinity Press International, 1995) 73-89.

[33]Richard Henry Tawney, *Religion and the Rise of Capitalism: A Historical Study* (London: J. Murray, 1926) 271-73. Max Weber, *The Protestant Ethic and the Spirit of Capitalism* (New York: Scribner's, 1958; orig. 1930) 144-54. See Durnbaugh, *Every Need Supplied*, 15.

religious formulation that would make some people unwanted dissidents. Objection to creeds does not derive from a difference of opinion regarding faith, but from a belief that no entity, political or ecclesiastical, has the right to define a common faith for people who meet to serve Jesus. Free Church types also oppose any action (such as oath taking) that makes the state the arbiter of truth.

Essentially there are no creeds in the Bible. The faith of the biblical people was covenantal. Covenants describe correct action (orthopraxy) rather than right thinking (orthodoxy) about God. The Hebrew Scriptures have no commandment about correct belief. The single faith statement in the Hebrew Scriptures, the Shema, calls on the Jew to love the one God:

> Hear, O Israel: The LORD is our God, the LORD alone. You shall love the LORD your God with all your heart, and with all your soul, and with all your might. Keep these words that I am commanding you today in your heart. Recite them to your children and talk about them when you are at home and when you are away, when you lie down and when you rise. Bind them as a sign on your hand, fix them as an emblem on your forehead, and write them on the doorposts of your house and on your gates.
>
> (Deut. 6:4-9)

The subsequent Ten Commandments then expand on the covenant with God (first four commandments) and the covenant with others (second six commandments). The commandments of the Hebrew Scriptures describe the correct way to keep these relationships. They never describe right thinking. The Jesus tradition continues the covenant tradition and adds "neighbor" to the Deuteronomic Shema:

> He said to him, "What is written in the law? What do you read there?" He answered, "You shall love the Lord your God with all your heart, and with all your soul, and with all your strength, and with all your mind; and your neighbor as yourself." And he said to him, "You have given the right answer; do this, and you will live."   (Luke 10:26-28)

There are no creedal statements in the New Testament. The closest would be Paul's short summary in 1 Corinthians:

> [Y]et for us there is one God, the Father, from whom are all things and for whom we exist, and one Lord, Jesus Christ, through whom are all things and through whom we exist.   (1 Cor. 8:6)

Even this is a Paulinized Christocentric version of the Jewish Shema.[34] Instead of creedal statements (beginning with "I believe . . . ") we find simple confessions of faith ("Jesus is . . . "). Directed toward Jewish audiences the followers of Jesus spoke of Jesus as "Christ" (Messiah). Speaking to Hellenistic audiences the followers of Jesus spoke of Jesus as "Lord."[35]

The so-called *kerygma* (proclamation of the gospel) found in 1 Corinthians 15:3-7 was passed on to Paul by the first Christians as a summary of the good news, but not as a credo.[36] By the end of the second century the *kerygma*, expanded to include the Trinity, was used as an interrogatory baptismal confession (as can be seen in Hippolytus, *Trad. ap.* 21:12-18). These Trinitarian confessions gave rise to creeds like the "Apostles' Creed," a statement of the faith taught, not the faith confessed.

"Faith" or "belief" (*pisteuo*) was for the most part a verb, not a noun. In the Gospel of John there is no noun at all for "belief" (*pistis*), only the verb. On the other hand, while he spoke of "faithing" Paul frequently made reference to faith as the condition of trusting or believing (for example, Rom. 1:17, 1 Cor. 13:13, passim). The church of the first centuries had no uniform creed. As we have seen, there were multiple faith communities and several major Christian centers (see p. 5). No center could have established a catholic creed.[37] Only after Constantine did the church formulate a statement of faith that should be held by all Christians everywhere ("The Nicene Creed," 325 CE).

The function of creeds plagued debates between the Reformation and the Radical Reformation. Both rejected the authority of every church council, but neither was willing to dismiss the early councils such as Nicaea.[38] Following the conflicts around the Council of Trent both Reformers and Radicals tended to make Scripture the only source of God's revelation.[39] Making *sola scriptura* an inviolable "creed" did considerable

---

[34]So Vernon H. Neufeld, *The Earliest Christian Confessions* (Grand Rapids MI: Eerdmans, 1963) 44. Oscar Cullman, *The Earliest Christian Confessions*, trans. J. K. S. Reid (London: Lutterworth, 1949) 50-51.

[35]Vernon H. Neufeld, *The Earliest Christian Confessions*, 68, 146.

[36]C. H. Dodd, *The Apostolic Preaching and Its Developments* (Chicago: Willett, Clark & Company, 1937) 1-49.

[37]For a list of N.T. and Early Church incipient faith statements see Everett Ferguson, "Confession of Faith," *Encyclopedia of Early Christianity*, 222-23.

[38]D. H. Williams, in *The Free Church and the Early Church*, ix (preface).

[39]D. H. Williams, "Scripture, Tradition, and the Church," in *The Free Church and the Early Church*, 118-24.

damage to Western Christianity. It caused to a large extent the confessional rigidity of modern Fundamentalism.[40] To escape scriptural rigidity or intense biblicism, it will be necessary for the Free Churches to deal with tradition and the creeds in a more evenhanded way. One formulation that might relax the rigidity would be to accept the early creeds and confessions to the extent that they reflect and rightly adapt the apostolic tradition.[41] Even more critical is the continued placement of scriptural interpretation in the hands of the congregants.

Because of the radical separation of church and state, members of the Free Churches avoid all oaths of fealty. While they accept citizenship and generally support the state, they cannot offer uncontested allegiance to any political entity. For someone not raised in this tradition, the depth of this characteristic may be difficult to comprehend. It is not simply a rule; it is a deeply rooted attitude. Congregational types simply do not make decisions on the basis of the *bonum publicum*. They cannot make the "general good" a top priority.

Perhaps to the surprise of some, the same attitude holds true for the church as an institution. A church that has been identified with the state (often called a "mainline" church) usually defines the *bonum publicum* by creedal statements, ordinances, and political allegiances affirmed by all members. Persons who do not subscribe to the creeds and ordinances do not belong, or may be declared heretical.[42] In a state church, disagreement with the creed was an open invitation for religious persecution and/or political exile. Taking an oath, then, is a serious matter.

In the Jesus tradition the followers of Jesus are not to take oaths:

> "Again, you have heard that it was said to those of ancient times, 'You shall not swear falsely, but carry out the vows you have made to the Lord.' But I say to you, Do not swear at all, either by heaven, for it is the throne of God, or by the earth, for it is his footstool, or by Jerusalem, for it is the city of the great King. And do not swear by your head, for you cannot make one hair white or black. Let your word be 'Yes, Yes' or 'No, No'; anything more than this comes from the evil one." (Matt. 5:33-37)

---

[40]Martin Marty et al., *Fundamentalism Observed*, vol. 1 (Chicago: University of Chicago Press, 1991) ix-x.

[41]E. Glenn Hinson, "The Authority of Tradition: A Baptist View," in *The Free Church and the Early Church*, 141-61.

[42]A major reason for rejecting the authority of creeds. See William Tabbernee, "Alexander Campbell and the Apostolic Tradition," in *The Free Church and the Early Church*, 168.

The admonition does have multiple meanings. In Judaism oath taking was discouraged. It may have been a concern of the third commandment. Specific discussions about oath taking occur in Sirach (Ecclesiasticus) 23:9-11 as well as in *Shebuoth* (*Oaths*) in the *Mishnah* (Jewish commentary on Torah, Genesis–Deuteronomy). The attachment to the oath-taking passage in Matthew (5:37) doesn't address taking oaths, but truth telling. Telling the truth was also a concern of the Ten Commandments ("false witness") since falsification would confound the functions of the covenant. The wisdom writer of James (5:12), though concerned more about personal integrity, reflects the same double concern found in Matthew 5:33-37.

Historically the issue of oath taking has gone in yet another direction. The Matthew text forbids taking an oath to any religious or secular power—including one's own self-fulfillment. Early Christians were asked to take an oath of allegiance to the emperor or to the gods of the empire. The early Fathers of the church (Tertullian, Origen, Gregory of Nazianzus, and Chrysostom) of course opposed such allegiance to the state and to idolatry. Martyrdom resulted. At the time of the Reformation all Radical groups refused to take oaths of allegiance. Refusing to take an oath of allegiance became a visible mark of the Free Church much like baptism of adults.

Oath taking today varies according to a denomination's view of the state. Those denominations that historically were attached to the state have no problem with taking oaths and vows of allegiance (Roman Catholic, Anglican, even Reformed). It is the genius of Lutheranism that the individual stands in the conflict between church and state. To take an oath of allegiance to state places the Lutheran in an ontological conflict between the two kingdoms that is solved only by the grace of God.[43]

Some Free Churches are so intensely separated from the state that matters of the state do not directly concern them. Like Lutherans, there are two kingdoms, but the follower of Jesus belongs to only one. Consequently an oath of allegiance to the state has no value. Hutterites, Amish, Society of Brothers, older Mennonites would make that two-kingdom separation.[44]

---

[43]Hans Windisch, *The Meaning of the Sermon on the Mount*, trans. S. MacLean Gilmour (Philadelphia: Westminster Press, 1951) 185. Robert Benne, *The Paradoxical Vision: A Public Theology for the Twenty-first Century* (Minneapolis: Fortress Press, 1995) 91-96.

[44]Donald Kraybill and Carl F. Bowman, *On the Backroad to Heaven: Old Order Hutterites, Mennonites, Amish, and Brethren* (Baltimore: Johns Hopkins University Press, 2001) 79.

Some Free Churches, on the other hand, understand their purpose involves reformation of the state. They will not necessarily take an oath of allegiance to the state, but they will strive to create a state that makes adherence possible (for example, Disciples, United Church of Christ, Methodists, Church of the Brethren).[45]

Communitarian

The biblical people are a *covenant* people. The people are "holy."[46] From the beginning the Jews were the people of God (Exod. 19:4-6), destined to be a great nation that would eventually make all people children of God (Gen. 12:1-3). The final book of the Bible describes that time when, indeed, that universal community will have been formed (Rev. 21:1-4). Meanwhile, biblical writers narrate that process of becoming God's people.[47]

As part of that process the Jesus tradition portrays Jesus as someone highly inclusive in his actions and proclamations.[48] He associated with sinners and tax collectors (Luke 7:34; Mark 2:15-17). While he may have healed out of compassion, the persons healed, otherwise rejected as unclean, became members of the Jesus community. For example, the woman with the flow of blood became a daughter of the church (Mark 5:34); Peter's mother-in-law became a deacon in the church (Mark 1:31); the Gerasene demoniac became a proclaimer of the good news (Mark

---

[45]For a still-useful description of these differences see H. Richard Niebuhr, *The Social Sources of American Denominationalism* (New York: Henry Holt, 1929). Niebuhr speaks of the communal Free Churches as the "disinherited," 26-76, esp. 48-49; middle-class churches are individualistic and rational, 77-105. Free Church academicians have long identified their tradition with Niebuhr's "Christ against Culture" in his *Christ and Culture* (New York: Harper & Brothers, 1951) 45-82.

[46]"Holy" in the sense of set apart, dedicated, for the service of God. In 1792 the founders of the Methodist movement named a covenant group the "Holy Club." See *Listening to the Spirit: A Handbook for Discernment*, ed. William Paulsell (St. Louis: Chalice Press, 2001) 6.

[47]Nils Dahl, *Das Volk Gottes: Eine Untersuchungen zum Kirchenbewussteins des Urchristentums* (Oslo: J. Dybwad, 1941) 2-5.

[48]Stanley Hauerwas says the church is the kind of community that tells rightly the story of Jesus. See his *A Community of Character: Toward a Constructive Social Ethic* (Notre Dame IN: University of Notre Dame Press, 1981) 81-82. And in *The Peaceable Kingdom: A Primer in Christian Ethics* (Notre Dame: University of Notre Dame Press, 1983) 100, Hauerwas writes that the church "must never cease from being a community of peace and truth in a world of mendacity and fear."

5:20).[49] Jesus called out disciples, his immediate community, who also preached, healed, and cast out demons (Mark 3:14-19). At the same time Jesus stood out as a unique individual in a society that placed ultimate value on submission to the will of the collective (Mark 1:21-22).

The aggressive formation of an inclusive People of God occurred after the Easter event. Paul gathered Jews and Gentiles, males and females, slaves and masters (Gal. 3:28). While new converts to the Jesus movement became part of a collective, led by the Spirit (1 Cor. 12:4), at the same they received distinct gifts and functions:

> Now there are varieties of gifts, but the same Spirit; and there are varieties of services, but the same Lord; and there are varieties of activities, but it is the same God who activates all of them in everyone. To each is given the manifestation of the Spirit for the common good. To one is given through the Spirit the utterance of wisdom, and to another the utterance of knowledge according to the same Spirit, to another faith by the same Spirit, to another gifts of healing by the one Spirit, to another the working of miracles, to another prophecy, to another the discernment of spirits, to another various kinds of tongues, to another the interpretation of tongues. All these are activated by one and the same Spirit, who allots to each one individually just as the Spirit chooses.
>
> For just as the body is one and has many members, and all the members of the body, though many, are one body, so it is with Christ. For in the one Spirit we were all baptized into one body—Jews or Greeks, slaves or free—and we were all made to drink of one Spirit.   (1 Cor. 12:4-13)

Paul's body analogy, with arms and legs, but no head, has become a manifesto for congregational types. At first the earliest churches remained congregational. For example, Paul could not force his will on the Corinthian church, so he had to send a mediator (2 Cor. 1:23-2:11). John the Elder of Ephesus could not compete with the congregational power of Diotrephes (1 John 9-10).[50] Congregational members elected the leaders of their church. Itinerant authorities, not members of a congregation, were suspect, perhaps not even welcome (*Didache* 11:3-6). In any case, to be elected a leader of a congregation, a bishop or minister, had only local sig-

---

[49]Donald Senior and Carroll Stuhlmueller, *Biblical Foundations for Mission* (Maryknoll NY: Orbis Press, 1983) 149-51.

[50]Ernst Käsemann, "Ketzer und Zeuge: Zum johanneischen Verfasserproblem," *ZTK* 48 (1951): 292-311.

nificance. A leader could not transfer that position to another congregation.[51]

As we have suggested, the early Free Church rejected the authority of
the single magistrate (Roman Catholicism) as well as authoritative leadership by commissions or boards (for example, among Protestants, synods or
presbyteries). The first Anabaptists insisted on congregational authority.
When authority to make decisions, determine policy, and select particular
workers belongs to the congregation, then the members must interact on an
open basis. That kind of community lies at the heart of the Free Church.
Congregational types do have leaders, but such leaders ordinarily represent
the community, not a hierarchy.

The primary virtue for congregationalists is submission to the will of
God, the Spirit, and the direction of the community rather than obedience
to leadership. Consequently, individual, authoritarian leadership qualities
are not encouraged. Normally the Free Church movement forms persons
who expect a high sense of community and a low sense of individuality. In
contrast to creedal groups, where a wrong idea can be heretical, among the
Free Churches heretics are those with private idiosyncrasies. Ecclesiasti-
cally Free Churches speak of "the priesthood of all believers" in order to
stress that, as in the New Testament, the *charisma* ("gift") of ministry does
not belong with either the bishop or the priest.[52]

While Free Church people would base their congregationalism on the
form of the church in the New Testament, there is much more at stake than
restitutionism. Anthropologically speaking humans are formed in community. Responsiveness to that fact lies at the heart of our existence. Modern
sociologists have recognized that most people of the world act communally
while only Western civilization will promote intense individualism.[53]

---

[51]Everett Ferguson, "The 'Congregationalism' of the Early Church," *The Free
Church and the Early Church*, 129-40.

[52]James Leo Garrett, Jr., "The Biblical Doctrine of the Priesthood of the People
of God," in *New Testament Studies*, ed. Hubert L. Drumwright and Curtis Vaughan
(Waco TX: Baylor University Press, 1975) 137-49. Luther himself had argued that
a shoemaker, a smith, a farmer—all are eligible to act as priests.

[53]Richard L. Rohrbaugh, "Ethnocentrism and Historical Questions about
Jesus," in *The Social Setting of Jesus and the Gospels*, 27-43. Bruce J. Malina, *The
New Testament World: Insights from Cultural Anthropology* (Louisville: West-
minster/John Knox Press, 1993) 51-60.

Reflections on the theology of community are scarce. There aren't many "Free Church theologians" in any case.[54] Most academic types assume the validity of community, so deal primarily with issues of authority and ethics. Theologically or ontologically speaking, social collectivity would be rooted in ultimate reality, for example, the Trinitarian nature of God.[55]

Discernment

Although the various Free Churches differ regarding the function of Scripture and Tradition, almost always they use the Bible as the source for congregational faith and life.[56] The Bible is used as the basis for preaching, teaching, worship, and community decision making. Free Church people seldom refer to a Church Father, like Augustine, or a founding leader, like Calvin or Luther. None of the Free Churches assume the experience of the Holy Spirit alone is the ultimate authority, though that would be true of some groups, like the Quakers, who relate well with Free Churches. The Bible is the authority, but its authority does not depend on infallibility. Free Church people do not worry much about literal interpretation of Scripture or concern themselves with seeming contradictions. At the same time, as we shall see, Scripture can be called inspired, but verbal inspiration plays no role in Free Church thinking. The inspiration may occur when, led by the Spirit, the faith community reads and studies the Bible together.

Discernment depends as much on perceiving the sense of the meeting as knowing the source and meaning of biblical history. Failure to discern

---

[54]Dwight A. Moody, "Contemporary Theologians within the Believers' Church," in *The People of God: Essays on the Believers' Church*, 333-54. Also James Wm. McClendon, *Systematic Theology: Ethics* (Nashville: Abingdon Press, 1986) 20-26. McClendon rightly notes Free Church theology is and should be narrative and ethical in nature rather than propositional or creedal (34-39).

[55]So Miroslav Volf, in *After Our Likeness: The Church as the Image of the Trinity* 217-20. For the theological basis for community see also James Wm. McClendon, *Systematic Theology: Ethics*, 43; and Thomas Finger, *Self, Earth, and Society: Alienation and Trinitarian Transformation* (Downers Grove IL: InterVarsity Press, 1997) 8-11.

[56]Luke Timothy Johnson, *Scripture and Discernment* (Nashville: Abingdon Press, 1996) 112. Ruth Fletcher, *Take, Break, Receive: The Practice of Discernment in the Christian Church (Disciples of Christ)* (Indianapolis: Div. of Homeland Ministries, n.d.).

what is happening in the community, especially at worship, can be devastating. Paul says people are dying (being alienated) because of that:

> Whoever, therefore, eats the bread or drinks the cup of the Lord in an unworthy manner will be answerable for the body and blood of the Lord. Examine yourselves, and only then eat of the bread and drink of the cup. For all who eat and drink without discerning the body, eat and drink judgment against themselves. For this reason many of you are weak and ill, and some have died.   (1 Cor. 11:27-30)

If prayer, singing, and congregational interaction, have appropriately prepared the community, then, when the Scripture is studied and presented, it may sense the leading of the Spirit. The presence of the Spirit at that time affirms the inspiration of the passage. This happens constantly in the Free Church tradition. Usually there is no specific name for it: Bible study, worship, prayer meeting, adult church school, or whatever. The Disciples of Christ call it *discernment*. After preparation to receive the text, it is read or studied in terms both of the original context and the study group's present context. Not everyone will come to the same opinion about the passage, but the group will wrestle with the text until there is discernment about its meaning. Consensus would be a desirable, but not necessary, result.

Because discernment can lead to consensus, the Free Church often seeks unanimity in its decision making. Operating by majority rule can create conflicts between two or more groups. While building full accord may have its difficulties, such as failure to act at all, many groups recognize its validity. In 2002 the World Council of Churches decided to work on the consensus model. A consensus is reached when one of the following occurs:

(1) all are in agreement (unanimity);
(2) most are in agreement and those who disagree are content that the discussion has been both full and fair and that the proposal expresses the general "mind of the meeting"—the minority therefore gives consent;
(3) the meeting acknowledges that there are various opinions, and it is agreed that these be recorded in the body of the proposal;
(4) it is agreed that the matter be postponed;
(5) it is agreed that no decision can be reached.[57]

---

[57]Janice Love, "Can we all agree?" *The Christian Century* (6-19 November 2002): 8.

Whatever the system, it is crucial that everyone is relatively satisfied with the decision making. Otherwise, since there is no higher authority, fragmentation will eventually occur.

Nonconformity or simplicity

Sociologists of denominational groups have long noted that the Free Church types come primarily from the middle class or even the lower class. Such analyses have not stood the test of time, yet there is sufficient truth in the observation to consider it a characteristic of the Free Church. Historically congregationalists have been nonconformists. They not only fail to act as society expected, but sometimes deliberately reject societal expectations. One thinks of the Quaker unwillingness to do gestures of obeisance toward royalty. Several Free Churches are reluctant to use titles such as Doctor, Sir, Lady, President, General, Reverend, and other titles of honor. Of course, there are several reasons for reluctance to show honor. On the one hand, Free Church people tend to assume we are all children of God and therefore equal. Submitting to people of higher rank destroys that sense of equality in the sight of God. Furthermore the reverse is true: accepting the obeisance of another person will take us all back into the "spirit of slavery" (Rom. 8:15). There is only one Lord and Master. The Jesus word stresses the faith necessity to recognize that:

> But you are not to be called rabbi, for you have one teacher, and you are all students. And call no one your father on earth, for you have one Father—the one in heaven. Nor are you to be called instructors, for you have one instructor, the Messiah. The greatest among you will be your servant. All who exalt themselves will be humbled, and all who humble themselves will be exalted.   (Matt. 23:8-12)

For those faith communities seeking to restore the life of the early church, there can be no question about nonconformity. Jesus not only asked his disciples to dissociate themselves from the hierarchical class structure, but he asked them to ignore those regulations that created special classes. He severely attacked the kosher (clean and unclean) regulations (Mark 7). In the Beatitudes he redefined those who did not belong (poor, meek, hungry) as the very ones who would receive the joy of the Kingdom (Matt. 5:3-11, or more clearly Luke 6:20-23). The disciple of Jesus does not meet the expectation of society. The disciple of Jesus does not conform. The disciple of Jesus has only one Lord.

Paul does not stress nonconformity as much as does the Jesus tradition. Still, one cannot doubt that Paul failed to satisfy both Jewish and Roman societal norms:

> Five times I have received from the Jews the forty lashes minus one. Three times I was beaten with rods. Once I received a stoning. Three times I was shipwrecked; for a night and a day I was adrift at sea; on frequent journeys, in danger from rivers, danger from bandits, danger from my own people, danger from Gentiles, danger in the city, danger in the wilderness, danger at sea, danger from false brothers and sisters; in toil and hardship, through many a sleepless night, hungry and thirsty, often without food, cold and naked. And, besides other things, I am under daily pressure because of my anxiety for all the churches.
>
> (2 Cor. 11:24-28)

And he does call for followers of Christ not to be conformed to this age, but free of this world's mindset, to discern the will of God—whatever is good, acceptable, and perfect (Rom. 12:2).

Many associate nonconformity with simple living. That is, rejection of wealth and conspicuous consumption constitute the essential element in nonconformity. The Jesus tradition makes that abundantly clear:

> "No one can serve two masters; for a slave will either hate the one and love the other, or be devoted to the one and despise the other. You cannot serve God and wealth." . . .
>
> "Do not store up for yourselves treasures on earth, where moth and rust consume and where thieves break in and steal; but store up for yourselves treasures in heaven, where neither moth nor rust consumes and where thieves do not break in and steal. For where your treasure is, there your heart will be also." . . .
>
> "Therefore I tell you, do not worry about your life, what you will eat or what you will drink, or about your body, what you will wear. Is not life more than food, and the body more than clothing? Look at the birds of the air; they neither sow nor reap nor gather into barns, and yet your heavenly Father feeds them. Are you not of more value than they?"
>
> (Matt. 6:24, 19-21, 25-26)

Regardless of the association between nonconformity and simple living,[58] the church of the first two centuries did reject the social standards of the Roman Empire. They refused to worship the emperor because they

---

[58]Vernard Eller, *In Place of Sacraments: A Study of Baptism and the Lord's Supper* (Grand Rapids MI: Eerdmans, 1972) 13-16.

had only one Lord. They were cautious about going to the baths. They did not participate in pompous dinners, but consumed primarily simple forms of bread and fish. They did not attend violent or off-color spectacles. Perhaps above all, because Jesus was their only patron, they rejected the patron-client system, a rejection that eventually permanently altered Roman society.[59]

After Constantine, after Christianity became the formal religion of the Empire, the nature of nonconformity altered. While the new Christianity did not return to the extravagance of the earlier Romans, it was those who rejected developing Roman Christianity that now practiced nonconformity. The history of those who rejected the culturalization of Christianity unfortunately cannot be satisfactorily reconstructed. Ernst Troeltsch argued that Christianity moved along three discrete paths: the church, that included all the people in the Empire; the sects, that included those who rejected the cultural accommodation; and the mystics whose relationship to God involved neither accommodation nor rejection.[60] Traces of the nonconformists lead us to such pre-Reformation groups as the Waldensians (ca. 1179) and the Hussites (1467). Following the Reformation many such faith communities emerged. First were the Anabaptists (1525). Their influence appeared in other European groups: the Hutterites, the Amish, the Brethren, and more directly the Mennonites.

It would be inappropriate to say that medieval Catholicism retrieved the pomposity of Roman life. It would be most inappropriate to say that Lutherans and Calvinists promoted a luxurious lifestyle vis-à-vis Catholicism. At the same time the Left Wing of the Reformation did live a simple lifestyle that did not conform to the level of European society. Their sense of equality without allegiance to any ruler except Jesus, the Lord, rightly made them appear as radical Separatists. The same was true of the British Separatists: Puritans, Quakers, Congregationalists, and Methodists.

Some groups still maintain clear nonconformity. The Amish are the most obvious: prescribed clothing from the seventeenth century, horse-and-buggy transportation, no electricity. Others, like the Hutterites, the Society of Brothers, and Old Order Mennonites, have remained simple with nonconformist dress codes.[61] While most Free Church people today seem

---

[59]Peter Lampe, "Paul, Patrons, and Clients," *Paul in the Greco-Roman World*, ed. J. Paul Sampley (Harrisburg PA: Trinity Press International, 2003) 488-523.

[60]Ernst Troeltsch, *The Social Teachings of the Christian Churches*, trans. Olive Wyon (New York: Harper, repr. 1960; orig. 1931) 2:993-94.

[61]Esther Fern Rupel, *Brethren Dress: A Testimony of Faith* (Elgin IL: Brethren

to conform to society, one can see a distinction. Church buildings are almost never cathedral types. They are built to be efficient for the members, not to serve society as a whole. There is little art or ornamentation in these churches. The congregation may be well dressed on Sunday, but seldom extravagant. There are not many Cadillacs (no Porsches) in the church parking lot. Niebuhr is right to that extent: free Church people do tend to be middle or lower class. Why? Poor business managers? No inheritance resources? Or does ostentation destroy one's faith? Driving a new Cadillac or a Porsche signals you may have left the Free Church.

Understanding nonconformity and simple living does not come easy. Even though the first Anabaptists may have been primarily peasants, even though many early Left Wing Christians lived communally,[62] even though ostentation was considered evil, still there are wealthy Free Church members. Living simply and being parsimonious has its rewards. With the resources saved, Left Wing families do prosper. For example, in 1975 U.S. Mennonite families had a twenty-nine percent higher income than the national average. About the same time it was estimated there were 700 Mennonite millionaires—out of a North American membership of about 350,000. A 1981 Canadian survey shows that Baptists, Hutterites, Mennonites, and Pentecostals earned an income only slightly lower than Lutherans, Presbyterians, and those of the United Church of Canada. On a comparative basis such persons were hardly poverty stricken.[63]

Through time the Free Church understanding of simplicity has altered. For most the issue has become one of idolatry. Simplicity no longer refers to wealth or ostentation. It refers to what has become primary in our lives, be it fortune, cars, fame, family, or anything else. Unless Jesus Christ is primary then we are serving some other master. Jesus, then, calls his disciples to reject commercialism or excessive consumption and to exist simply on what is needed.

As we shall see, faith communities with these Free Church characteristics would expect and use forms of worship, Bible study, and preaching that reflect their congregational heritage.

Encyclopedia, 1994) 4-15.

[62]The Radical Reformation was sometimes considered to be the historical source for Socialism and even Communism. See Redekop, *Mennonite Society*, 7.

[63]Redekop, *Mennonite Society*, 198-200.

Chapter 2

Context for Worship

The Free Church Builtform

The first meeting places for Mediterranean Christians were houses (Acts 16:19; Rom. 16:5; Philem. 2; Col. 4:15). There were other places of meeting like halls (Acts 19:9), or a room in an apartment (Acts 20:7-8). We know from other sources they also met in warehouses, back rooms, open fields and even baths. There were no builtforms[1] constructed as churches. At least we know of none. The house-churches for meeting tended to be square rooms with flat roofs. In wealthier homes the meeting might have occurred in the open peristyle with the triclinium serving as the locus for the Agape. In either case the architecture reflected the nature of the church—a family where brothers and sisters met to worship the Parent. The Son, Jesus, was present in their midst. The leaders were fellow family members.

We do have archaeological evidence for some third-century meeting places. The most famous is that of Dura-Europos, a town in Syria destroyed by an opposing army (256 CE). Anticipating the destruction of the city, the defenders of Dura-Europos stacked protective dirt against the inside of the town wall. That defensive action saved for later archaeologists a half of a house church and a half of a synagogue—each a stunning treasure. Other meeting places include a back room behind a shop in the church of *SS Giovanni e Pauli* in Rome, and perhaps the house of Peter in Capernaum. To the best of our knowledge, before Constantine there were no structures built to house a church. The first might well be *S. Crisogono* in Rome. It was a plain, flat, rectangular building with no seats, no chancel, and no apse.[2]

It wasn't until after Constantine that church buildings became rectangular halls, with, perhaps, a nave, side aisles and a clerestory. The

---

[1]A "builtform" (often as two words, "built form") is a structure designed for a specific use, for example, a library builtform, a schoolhouse builtform, a dwelling/residence builtform, or a *church builtform*.

[2]L. Michael White, *The Social Origins of Christian Architecture*, 2 vols. (Valley Forge PA: Trinity Press International, 1996) 1:102-39. Graydon F. Snyder, *Ante Pacem: Archaeological Evidence for Church Life Before Constantine*, rev. ed. (Macon GA: Mercer University Press, 2003) 150-52.

change in architecture reflected a change in theology.[3] The church was now
an organization which, when gathered, faced the divine presence located in
the apse. Acknowledgement of and appropriation of this divine presence
was made possible by persons selected or appointed for worship leadership
(that is, priests). The priests stood in front of the altar and faced the apse.
Architecturally, the Roman Christian church had become an elongated
rectangle built on a central axis. The square flat room, symbolizing the
presence of God in the community, disappeared.

At the Reformation everything changed. The medieval churches now
came under control of different Christian groups. The Roman Catholic
churches remained the same for a time, but eventually did away with the
chancel and its altar directed toward the front or apse. Catholic liturgy
became more inclusive of the assembled congregation. The chancel became
more of a platform or stage and the priest faced the congregation as the
mass was said. Since the Lutherans tended to reject that which was not
biblical, they kept the medieval church, but adapted it for the preaching of
the Word. Calvinists were more likely to construct new builtforms or, at
least, do severe rearrangement of the interior. They moved the altar(s) into
a medial position where the congregants could gather at the communion
table for the Eucharist. They made the pulpit central for the preaching of
the Word. Again, with the congregation so central, Calvinists tended
toward flat ceilings, and, so that the congregation could come closer to the
service of the Word, they added balconies.[4]

Some religious builtforms may be simply accidental or functional. For
the most part, however, there is a theological implication. Domes stress the
experience of the transcendent divinity. Rectangular naves stress the
eschatological journey of persons and society. Square, flat builtforms stress
the presence of God with the community.[5]

The interior of a Free Church will normally be quite simple. At the
front will be a raised dais with a central pulpit. The central pulpit signifies

---

[3]For useful diagrams see John E. Skoglund, *Worship in the Free Churches*
(Valley Forge PA: Judson Press, 1965) 109-15.

[4]James F. White, *A Brief History of Christian Worship*, 138-40. Also White,
Protestant Worship and Church Architecture (New York: Oxford University Press,
1964) 81-82.

[5]Graydon F. Snyder, "The Aesthetic Origins Of Early Christian Architecture"
in *Text And Artifact: Judaism And Christianity In The Ancient Mediterranean
World*, ed. Stephen G. Wilson and Michel Desjardins (Waterloo ON: Wilfrid
Laurier University Press, 2000) 289-307.

the importance of the scripture and its exposition to the congregation. Liturgical functions do not share that central importance. Communion is shared from a special table that might be placed before the pulpit. For those who baptize adults, the baptistery will be nearby, perhaps even directly behind (underneath) the pulpit. While the major church ordinances, baptism and communion, may occur at "center stage," their importance will be subordinate to the pulpit with its Bible in place. Some Free Churches do have the split chancel. Worship is directed from one side and preaching from the other. Seldom do the two lecterns terminate side aisles.

It would be extremely difficult to characterize accurately Free Church use of space. There is little uniformity. Some churches are still square and flat. Arched ceilings do occur, but they tend to be less frequent than flat ceilings. Some more imaginative churches have built semicircular or even round sanctuaries. An excellent example is the Flagg Road United Church of Christ in West Hartford, Connecticut. It consists of a round structure with a spire. Loring Sabin Ensign, pastor at the time the church was built, said:

> Thinking of ourselves as a people of God gathered around the table of our Lord, to be fed by his varied grace, to render thanksgiving, praise, and gifts, we had to have a multicameral sanctuary of a round nature. . . . Everyone gathered is a participant; no one can be a mere spectator. Pastor, choir, and any other liturgists are all part of the gathered congregation, with no one set apart in some "holy" space. . . . Everyone is equal at the foot of the cross. There is thus no chancel, no nave.[6]

That does indeed fit the community-centered Free Church tradition: most buildings are square with a center aisle, or perhaps two "center" aisles. The formative Pennsylvania Dutch "meetinghouse" was rectangular with one door opening between the long sides and two windows to the right and left.[7] In the interior the congregation sat on benches with no backs. Despite massive adaptations to mainline architecture, very few Free Church buildings have a nave, two side aisles, and a clerestory.[8]

---

[6]"Experimentation in Ritual," *Architectural Digest* (1965): 141-44.

[7]White notes the similarity of the American Anabaptist church house with the Quaker meetinghouse. *Protestant Worship and Church Architecture*, 110-11. See his floor plan.

[8]John L. Ruth, " 'Only a House . . . Yet It Becomes': Some Mennonite Traditions of Worship Space," *The Mennonite Quarterly Review* 73 (1999): 235-56.

Likewise very few Free Churches would have towers over a nonexistent transept. A tower would only occur as an incidental architectural ornament. The spire is another issue. Perhaps the most romantic picture of an American church consists of a frame building with a spire nestled among the trees. Usually that would be a Free Church. The spire started in the twelfth century as a pyramid on the tower. Quickly it became a marvelous pinnacle for the cathedral. Nineteenth-century Americans, especially Puritan types, picked up the spire as an ornamentation and bell tower over the front or entrance of the church.

Artistic enhancement

We assume synagogues at the time of Jesus would not have been decorated. We have no archaeological remains from that time, but the assumption matches what we know. In the earliest sites one can find symbols such as the menorah or the ethrog and lulab.[9] Like the earliest church, the earliest synagogue decorated with frescoes has been preserved in Dura-Europos. The artists have portrayed various biblical scenes. Floor mosaics, of an astrological nature, have been uncovered in the early Palestinian synagogues *Beth Shean* and *Beth Aleph*.

Our earliest known church house, at Dura-Europos, is also decorated with a few frescoes. These frescoes include *The Good Shepherd*, *Jesus Walking on the Water*, *The Woman at the Well*, *The Healing of the Paralytic*, *Adam and Eve*, *David and Goliath*, and *The Women at the Tomb*. The importance of this archaeological discovery cannot be overestimated. Most of the early Christian art and decorations occur in the catacombs. Consequently some have concluded that early Christian art occurs only in funereal contexts. Dura-Europos proves otherwise. After Constantine, churches were consistently decorated with mosaic art. Prior to Constantine, in addition to Dura-Europos, there are slight indications the meeting places were decorated: frescoes in the meeting room in *SS Giovanni e Pauli* in Rome, and some mosaics on the early floor of the church in Aquilea.[10]

Why was church art so late in appearing? Some argue the prohibition against images kept the first Christians from using art. They believe the

---

[9]While there are many decorations in Judaism, there are only five definitive identity symbols: the *menorah* or seven-pronged candelabra, the *shofar* or ritual horn, the *ethrog* or citrus fruit used at Sukkoth, the *lulab* or palm used at Sukkoth, and the *torah shrine* itself. See Jacob Neusner, *Symbol and Theology in Early Judaism* (Minneapolis: Fortress Press, 1991) 210.

[10]Snyder, *Ante Pacem*, 68-75.

first Christians were aniconic proto-Protestants.[11] That is not widely accepted, especially since there are too few extant churches to demonstrate the thesis. But then, had the first Christians decorated their house churches with Christian symbols, archaeologists may have discovered some of them. Perhaps the first Christians did decorate their meeting places, but their nascent culture had not yet sufficiently impacted the Hellenistic world to create a new symbol system. Only by the end of the second century did Christian material (inscriptions, symbols, pictorial art) begin to appear. So we may have the archaeological remains of earlier house churches, but have no way to recognize them as Christian.[12] Others argue the first Christians were too poor to engage expensive artisans.[13] We don't know how the first Christians engaged artisans to portray biblical symbols previously unknown to them.

While the modern Free Church sanctuary will be tastefully painted and decorated, there will be no art per se. There will be no sculptures, no pictures of biblical heroes. No pictures of church saints and founders. There may be stained glass windows and these might have portrayals of biblical symbols: the good shepherd, fish, a cross. There will be no crucifixion or suffering Jesus. If Jesus is included in the windows, it will be a nondescript, even insipid, portrayal. There is no congruent Free Church Jesus symbol. In fact, there is no recognizable Free Church symbol at all. Consequently, there is no inherent reason for art to appear in the sanctuary.

In many Free Church sanctuaries one finds banners. Banners signal changes of the church seasons and special events. Sometimes they simply inspire congregational worship much like the music. Banners are not traditional art. That is, they do not recall the tradition of the congregation, they do not recall the history of the church, and they do not portray biblical scenes. Banners encourage worship at the moment.

The lack of art, that is, iconoclasm, has puzzled many. It is often defended as the logical extension of the second commandment that forbade images of God. Jews extended the second commandment to include art in general, so that very few ancient synagogues have portrayals in them (except Dura-Europos, of course). Early Christians used art in catacombs and eventually in all churches. One cannot cogently argue that the early

---

[11]See the discussion by Robin Margaret Jensen, *Understanding Early Christian Art* (London: Routledge Press, 2000) 15.

[12]Snyder, *Ante Pacem*, 3.

[13]Paul Corbey Finney, *The Invisible God: The Earliest Christians on Art* (New York: Oxford University Press, 1994) 108-10.

church followed the second commandment and avoided art (see Finney). The attack on art primarily occurred with such iconoclasts as Cromwell who knocked off the heads of statues in British churches (for example, in the Ely Cathedral). Inheritors of the British Reformation in New England avoided art. Consequently most Free Church, Puritan, and Calvinist-type church buildings lack significant artistic portrayals. The rejection of prior medieval Catholicism has been fairly thorough.

Theologically speaking, the second commandment should be taken seriously. Portrayals of God and/or Jesus can do much damage. God dare not be created in human form. For the most part Jewish and Christian artists have avoided the humanization of God. In some early instances, primarily the *Sacrifice of Isaac*, God did appear as a hand. Very occasionally God was portrayed like a Roman God.[14] Jesus was another matter. Jesus had appeared in human form. Some argued that failing to portray Jesus denied the Incarnation. So Jesus was portrayed as a man and his divinity appeared in his miraculous actions (healing, multiplication of the loaves and fishes, and turning water into wine).[15] Of course, Jesus the Christ (risen Lord) can be Caucasian, African, Oriental, male, female. But to portray the historical Jesus as an insipid non-Jew can do damage to those who absorb the truth visually.

Nevertheless, it is not likely the second commandment really prompted Free Church iconoclasm. The Free Church builtform started as a meeting-house, often square-like and simple. People gathered there for many reasons. The meeting place itself is not holy. The people are holy. To be sure, art, architecture, and music contribute to the inspiration of the congregation. To be sure, there are precious memories associated with the narthex and the pews. Still, the meeting place is not holy. The people are holy. To use art in such a way as to suggest otherwise will finally undermine the life of the congregation.

Music

In preparing for the hearing of the text, no element of worship is more important than the music. Music sets the theme and engages the psychic level of the congregation as it prepares for the sermon. Music and dance serve as a "technology of bonding."[16] Theologically speaking, music is a

---

[14]Snyder, *Ante Pacem*, 64-66.
[15]Robin Jensen, *Understanding Early Christian Art*, 94-129.
[16]*The Origins of Music*, ed. Nils L. Wallin, Björn Merker and Steven Brown (Cambridge MA: MIT Press, 2000). See esp. Walter Freeman, "A Neurobiological

form of gift or sacrifice of ourselves to God, for in music the congregation communes with God. Listeners as well as those singing or playing an instrument ideally are at one with each other through sound, rhythm, and words. Although the musical presentation may resemble a performance in that it is done to the best of one's abilities, in the church setting music is worship. It provides a way of giving to God while also preparing the body of Christ for the presence of the Spirit.

From the beginning, music played a crucial role in the worship of the faith community. Christians inherited from Judaism a music-oriented liturgy.[17] The Psalms so often remind us of that fact:

> Praise the LORD!
> How good it is to sing praises to our God;
>> for he is gracious,
>> and a song of praise is fitting. . . .
>
> Sing to the LORD with thanksgiving;
>> make melody to our God on the lyre. . . .
>
> Praise the LORD!
> Praise God in his sanctuary;
>> praise him in his mighty firmament!
> Praise him for his mighty deeds;
>> praise him according to his surpassing greatness!
> Praise him with trumpet sound;
>> praise him with lute and harp!
> Praise him with tambourine and dance;
>> praise him with strings and pipe!
> Praise him with clanging cymbals;
>> praise him with loud clashing cymbals!
> Let everything that breathes praise the LORD!
> Praise the LORD!   (Psa. 147:1, 7; 150:1-6)

Music can also be worshipful even if in the form of lament.[18] Because many of the opening words of the lament Psalms relate to the musicians, various instruments, and singers, we can assume these too were part of

---

Role of Music in Social Bonding," 411-24.

[17]William L. Holladay, *The Psalms through Three Thousand Years: Prayerbook of a Cloud of Witnesses* (Minneapolis: Fortress, 1993) 113-33.

[18]Claus Westermann, *Praise and Lament in the Psalms* (Atlanta: John Knox Press, repr. 1981; orig. 1965) 165-94.

Second Temple worship. Each of the Psalms that follow is addressed "To the chief musician":

How long, O LORD?
Will you forget me forever?
    How long will you hide your face from me? . . .

My God, my God, why have you forsaken me? . . .

O God you have cast us off,
    you have scattered us.
You have been displeased. . . .

O LORD God of Hosts,
    how long will you be angry
        with your people's prayers?   (Psa. 13:1; 22:1; 60:1; 80:4)

In recent years, there has been a significant rise in the popularity of contemporary "praise music." This new music has become a vital and vibrant part of the worship of much of the Free Church. Music of lament has perhaps declined as praise music has increased. A combination of the words and music of praise and lament might better reflect the human condition and enhance worship. Examples of lament music that continue to be used in Free Church include any number of spirituals, petitionary prayer hymns, as well as choral anthems. Some favorite laments would be "Nobody knows the trouble I've seen," "Come, ye disconsolate," and "Precious Lord, take my hand."

At the time of Jesus, singing was done in unison. The richness of the music was created by pitch and rhythm rather than harmony. Given the power and ubiquity of singing, one is surprised that singing by the first Jesus movement is mentioned so seldom. The only recorded description of a Jesus celebration would be the Last Supper, where following good Jewish practice they "sang a hymn and went out" (Mark 14:26; Matt. 26:30). In later descriptions of emerging Christian worship, the congregants sing psalms and hymns (1 Cor. 14:15; Col. 3:16; Eph. 5:19). When Paul and Silas were jailed in Philippi, they led the other prisoners in a service of worship in which they prayed and sang hymns to God (Acts 16:25).[19]

Early Christian literature consistently refers to singing in the church though seldom to any specific music.[20] Ignatius writes:

---

[19]Stephen G. Wilson, "Early Christian Music," in *Common Life in the Early Church* (Harrisburg PA: Trinity Press International, 1998) 390-401.

[20]*Music in Early Christian Literature*, ed. James W. McKinnon (Cambridge

Therefore it is fitting that you should run together in accordance with the
will of your bishop, as indeed you do. For your justly renowned presbytery, worthy of God, is attuned to the bishop as the strings are to the harp.
Therefore in your concord and harmonious love, Jesus Christ is sung. And
now you all become a choir, that being harmonious in love, you may
receive the pitch of God in unison, and you may with one voice sing to the
Father through Jesus Christ, so that He may both hear you, and perceive
by your works that you are indeed the members of His Son.

(IgnEph 4.1-2)

In the early church there must have been groups of singers (choirs).
Pliny, in his letter to Trajan wrote that Christians met early in the morning
and sang antiphonally a hymn to Christ as if to a god (*Ep.* 10.96.7). Mention is made of women singers, and boy's choirs. The only objection to
music comes from Fathers who feared church music derived primarily from
pagan music.[21] Even in a church setting its prior use would evoke non-
Christian memories.

Augustine, for example, enjoyed the music of the church, perhaps too
much. He wondered if it weren't more pleasure than worship.[22] During the
first centuries of the church there was distrust of both instrumental music
and "the forms and types of music connected with the great public
spectacles such as festivals, competitions, and dramatic performances, and
also the music of intimate and convivial occasions."[23] Converts had to be
weaned from anything connected with their pagan pasts. Despite the
problem of pagan antecedents, however, early Christian services of
worship, modeled after Jewish synagogue services, included vocal music
based on the Psalms.

The situation at the Reformation brings consternation to both theologians and practitioners. Martin Luther was an admirer of Netherlands
polyphony, and believed in the educational and ethical power of music.[24]
Luther wanted the entire congregation to participate in church music.
Because there were many local congregations, the results varied from the

UK: Cambridge University Press, 1987) 12-27. Edward Foley, *Foundations of
Christian Music: The Music of Pre-Constantinian Christianity* (Collegeville MN:
Liturgical Press, 1996) 54-64, 73-84.

[21]White, *Christian Worship*, 70.
[22]*Confessions* 10.33.
[23]Donald J. Grout, *A History of Western Music*, rev. ed. (New York: Norton,
1973) 11.
[24]Grout, *A History of Western Music*, 253.

polyphonic music adapted from the Latin mass to German strophic chorales. Demand exceeded supply, so many existing secular songs were adapted to accompany sacred words.[25] Lutherans kept choirs and sang a variety of hymns, a number of which have greatly enriched the worship of Western Christianity (for example, "A Mighty Fortress Is Our God"— words and music by Luther himself). On the other side of the Reformation, Zwingli, a skilled musician, rejected the use of music. Calvin tempered his radical position by permitting the singing of Psalms. The Psalter offered rhymed metrical translations of the Psalms with adapted popular melodies, newly composed melodies, or songs adapted from plainsong.[26]

Given the oral and visual context of church music, one would have expected the Radical Reformation to reject music in the same way they rejected visual representations. Quite the contrary.[27] The Free Church made music a major part of its church life.[28] Furthermore, despite the communitarian theology of unity, and therefore unison singing, the Free Church sang in harmony.

The development of polyphonic music, most notably in the Gregorian chants, necessitated the formation of groups who could read music and sing in harmony. The antiphonal singing of the early church eventually shifted to choral singing from which came the rich musical tradition of the medieval and Reformation churches (Anglican and Lutheran). The Counter Reformation, through the genius of Palestrina, brought polyphonic singing to its culmination, requiring competent and possibly professional musicians. From the late sixteenth century on, instrumental music in the church also began to increase. The use of organ, lute, and viols enhanced and sometimes even substituted for voices in churches not blessed with singers competent enough to sing the polyphonic music. In addition, organists of that period developed a huge repertory of music for worship services.

Again, given the congregational nature of the Free Churches, one would also assume the development of choirs would have been rejected. To the contrary, because of the rich tradition of post-Reformation choral

---

[25]Grout, *A History of Western Music*, 255.

[26]Grout, *A History of Western Music*, 258-59.

[27]Congregations of the Radical Reformation considered hymns parallel to the preaching of the Word, the Bible in verse form. See Hedwig Durnbaugh, *The German Hymnody of the Brethren 1720–1903,* Brethren Encyclopedia Monograph Series 1 (Warsaw IN: Light and Life Press, 1986) 1-9.

[28]White, *Christian Worship*, 136-38.

music, most Free Churches added choirs. Now it is nearly a requirement for a healthy congregation.

The issue of musical instruments is yet another matter. Fearful of the sensuality of non-Christian lutes and pipes, many early Fathers of the church had rejected instruments.[29] The Radical Reformation and Calvin did likewise. But like choral music, instruments eventually entered into the worship of most (not all by any means) Free Churches. The combination of choral music and the use of instruments can alter the nature and theology of congregational worship. When instruments are added, the use of the choir may result in a performance rather than an act of worship. If the preacher is an actor rather than one who reflects the meaning of the text for the congregation, then the entire service can shift to a performance. For some congregations, such performances attract new members. For most congregations, any performance, especially a mediocre one, means eventual death. Adding instruments does not automatically secularize music. It is the inclusion of virtuosity for virtuosity's sake, or dramatics for drama's sake that places the church's music into the mode of performance.

Fortunately, new forms will always appear. The influence of drumming, imported from Africa, has made many congregations of all types more vibrant and less dependent on skilled musicians. Because rhythm creates bonding, communal participation has returned![30] Often members of the congregation use drums, tympani, and shakers. Given this new direction, the congregation will participate more fully in the planning and direction of the worship service.

Music is intended to be an integral part of the worship experience. If the music distracts from spiritual focus or separates rather than unites, then it may be considered a performance. The distinction however is subjective and varies widely within the Free Church tradition. Music that is sung in

---

[29]Everett Ferguson, "Music," *Encyclopedia of Early Christianity*. Instruments also had national and ethnic attachments that had to be avoided. Apparently lutes and pipes recalled a Roman context not shared by the more acceptable kithra or lyre (Clement, *paed*. 2.4.43). Likewise a shofar would have signaled association with Judaism. See Joachim Braun, *Music in Ancient Israel: Archaeological, Written, and Comparative Sources* trans. Douglas W. Stott (Grand Rapids MI: Eerdmans, 2002) 316-18.

[30]V. Kofi Agawu, *African Rhythm: A Northern Ewe Perspective* (Cambridge: Cambridge University Press, 1995) 31-33. On drums and language see John F. Carrington, *Talking Drums of Africa* (New York: Negro Universities Press, repr. 1969; orig. 1949) 11-20.

one church may seem distracting to a visitor from another church, though both are of the same Free Church tradition. Taste in sacred music is likely one of the strongest differences among local congregations within the Free Church. One individual, leader, or musician cannot determine what moves the heart to give to and to commune with God, or causes someone to sense membership and ownership in a worshipping community. Again, the importance of communal decision making comes into play. The people will decide what music is holy.

Theology

1. *Jesus.* The single essential source of faith for the Free Church is the person of Jesus. While this could be a sophisticated statement, it is not. In fact, to the general public it may seem like an amusing oversimplification. The Free Church type may ask, "What would Jesus do?" or "Would Jesus drive an SUV?" Bumper stickers may ask the same question. Simple books on the life of Jesus, even Charles Sheldon's classic, *In His Steps*, will be popular. Unsophisticated art like Sallman's *Head of Christ* will adorn homes and church classrooms. For these churches, Jesus is a simple Palestinian Jew. Jesus has not been complicated by Pauline theology or patristic debates. It seldom occurs to Free Church constituents that our accounts of Jesus have been altered, reused or expanded by the first faith communities. It does not occur to them that the person presumably telling the Jesus story is a literary product of the real storyteller (like John Mark). It never occurs to them that the historical Jesus cannot be known with any exactitude. Jesus had a simple message of love, of forgiveness, of healing, of communal caring, of trust in God, and striving for a better way of life for all people.

In the early Jesus tradition there was little subservience to religious authorities, little acknowledgment of political power. Jesus sharply criticized Jewish rules regulating what was clean or unclean, or what was acceptable to eat (kosher) and what was not acceptable (nonkosher). Eliminating people from table fellowship was deemed sinful. And, in sharp contrast to those who considered dying for one's country the highest honor, Jesus considered love of enemy the most godlike quality. Jesus was Jesus. He was not called the Christ, not revered as Lord. Jesus was a child of God, not the Son of God.

The earliest traditions of the New Testament were Jesus-centered. The Gospel of Mark (written about 65 CE) contains primarily narratives about Jesus, especially healings, miraculous acts, and controversies. Only toward the end of Jesus' ministry, according to Mark, does the issue of Christology arise and even then Jesus appears to reject the messianic designation:

> Jesus went on with his disciples to the villages of Caesarea Philippi;
> and on the way he asked his disciples, "Who do people say that I am?"
> And they answered him, "John the Baptist; and others, Elijah; and still
> others, one of the prophets." He asked them, "But who do you say that I
> am?" Peter answered him, "You are the Messiah [Christ]." And he sternly
> ordered them not to tell anyone [not to say that] about him.
>
> (Mark 8:27-30)

The Gospel of Mark even lacks the postresurrection narratives that, in
Matthew and Luke, signal the beginnings of Christology.[31] The words of
Jesus initially were collected in an oral tradition about 40 CE. It expanded
and changed until about 55 CE. About 80 CE Matthew and Luke inserted
this sayings tradition into their Gospels. We have no separate written account of the sayings, except that we can see them when we compare what
is held in common between Matthew and Luke. We call that sayings source
Q (from the German *Quelle*, "source").[32] In the twentieth century a document, the *Gospel of Thomas*, was discovered, which looks much like what
we suppose Q must have been. These earliest Christian materials, Mark and
Q, portrayed Jesus as a human. It was Paul who first placed the man Jesus
in the Hebrew messianic nexus. In his first letter, Paul speaks of Jesus who
has become the Son of God:

> For the people of those regions report about us what kind of welcome we
> had among you, and how you turned to God from idols, to serve a living
> and true God, and to wait for his Son from heaven, whom he raised from
> the dead—Jesus, who rescues us from the wrath that is coming.
>
> (1 Thess. 1:9-10)

Even later on, in the letter to the Romans, Paul can speak of Jesus who
became the Messiah after his death and resurrection:

> Paul, a servant of Jesus Christ, called to be an apostle, set apart for the
> gospel of God, which he promised beforehand through his prophets in the

---

[31]See the issues in N. Clayton Croy, *The Mutilation of Mark's Gospel* (Nashville: Abingdon Press, 2003) 33-71.

[32]John S. Kloppenborg Verbin, *Excavating Q: The History and Setting of the
Sayings Gospel* (Edinburgh: T.&T. Clark, 2000) 80-87. For the text of Q and its
development see Burton L. Mack, *The Lost Gospel: The Book of Q and Christian
Origins* (New York: HarperSanFrancisco, 1993) 73-102, and Richard Valantasis,
*Reading Jesus: The Voice of Jesus and Early Christians in the Synoptic Sayings
Source, Q* (London: Routledge, 2004).

> holy scriptures, the gospel concerning his Son, who was descended from
> David according to the flesh and was declared to be Son of God with
> power according to the spirit of holiness by resurrection from the dead,
> Jesus Christ our Lord. . . .   (Rom. 1:1-4)

The earliest theology about Jesus must have been what we call
Adoptionism. Jesus was a human who was made divine by his quality of
life, his death, and his resurrection. Eventually the church rejected
Adoptionism because it led to the conviction one could *earn* the favor of
God. The rejection of Adoptionism did not make it go away. Just as most
British and Americans are Pelagians, who believe in the goodness of
humans,[33] at the same time, most are Adoptionists. This is true of most
English-speaking Christians, but is especially true of Free Church types.
Regardless of denominational allegiance, most American Christians will
assent to the theological language of their tradition, but they act as if God
will accept them by their doing good.

As noted above, the Apostle Paul identified Jesus as the awaited
messianic figure, or the Christ. Jesus was the agent promised by God to
reconcile all humans to one another and make all people children of God:

> Now before faith came, we were imprisoned and guarded under the
> law until faith would be revealed. Therefore the law was our disciplinarian
> until Christ came, so that we might be justified by faith. But now that faith
> has come, we are no longer subject to a disciplinarian, for in Christ Jesus
> you are all children of God through faith. As many of you as were baptized
> into Christ have clothed yourselves with Christ. There is no longer Jew or
> Greek, there is no longer slave or free, there is no longer male and female;
> for all of you are one in Christ Jesus. And if you belong to Christ, then you
> are Abraham's offspring, heirs according to the promise. (Gal. 3:23-29)

For Paul the identification of Jesus as the Messiah (the "anointed
[one]," expected king) carried with it implications of divinity: *Jesus is Lord*
("Lord" translates *Yahweh* in the Hebrew Scriptures). In the theological
world of Paul, Jesus Christ becomes the agent while God becomes the
source:

> [Y]et for us there is one God, the Father, from whom are all things and for
> whom we exist, and one Lord, Jesus Christ, through whom are all things
> and through whom we exist.   (1 Cor. 8:6)

---

[33]Graydon F. Snyder, *Irish Jesus, Roman Jesus: The Formation of Early Irish
Christianity* (Harrisburg: Trinity Press International, 2002) 235.

However, this Hebraic functional (task-oriented) definition of divinity became ontological (an aspect of ultimate reality) in the Hellenistic world. Consequently early Christian theologians engaged in considerable debate regarding the nature of Jesus as human and the nature of Jesus as divine. ("Very God of very God; very man of very man"—see the Nicene and Chalcedon creeds.) At the same time, the functional role of Jesus moved from dying on the cross and creating a new corporate life to appeasing the wrath of an angry God.[34]

The Radical Reformation brought a return to the Jesus orientation. The angry God was gone. To be sure, some few Anabaptists tried to keep the divinity of Jesus intact, but for the most part Jesus was a Master/Teacher/Lord who called for discipleship.[35] The very early *Martyrs' Mirror*, Anabaptist stories of sixteenth-century persecutions, described the life of Jesus as one who died on the cross as a martyr. Those who follow him may (did!) meet the same fate. There is nothing sacrificial in the crucifixion of Jesus. Jesus destroyed the authority of the powers (1 Cor. 2:8).

The Renaissance revolution brought with it, by means of historical research, a renewed interest in the Jesus of history. Many Free Church people accept this scholarly picture of a liberal Jesus who went about doing good. (Though many did not.) Significant leaders like Methodist Bishop Sprague, Mennonite theologian John Howard Yoder, or even Episcopalian Bishop Spong strongly proclaim "Jesus" only. Over the centuries that vibrant Jesus continues to reappear out of hierarchical structures and creedalism.

In terms of Free Church worship, Jesus theology occurs most clearly in those churches whose tradition does not originate from Europe. Specifically, native African churches and African-American Christians seldom refer to "Christ" or "Jesus Christ." In their hymns they use the names "Jesus," "Lord," and "Savior." Our survey of African-American traditional spirituals revealed no use of the name Christ.[36] For African-Americans the term Christ was associated with power, divinely authorized

---

[34]Gustaf Aulén, *Christus Victor: A Historical Study of the Three Main Types of the Idea of Atonement*, trans. A. G. Herbert (London: SPCK, repr. 1970; orig. 1931) 84-92.

[35]John Howard Yoder, *The Politics of Jesus* (Grand Rapids MI: Eerdmans, 1972) 58-63, 115-34.

[36]Those hymns marked "Traditional (Spirituals)" in the Methodist songbook, *Songs of Zion* (Nashville: Abingdon Press, 1981) nos. 74-171.

and enhanced, power that was used to suppress. For African-Americans and other oppressed groups Jesus was associated with God's intent to serve and to redeem.[37] Jesus, too, had been victim. In this split between Christology and soteriology the Free Church strongly tends to stress the function of Jesus rather than the ultimate being and power of the Christ.[38] While not every Free Church type would accept this description of Jesus, the point should be clear. For most, the source of faith is the man Jesus, his teaching and his own unwavering faith in God.

2. *Christology.* Congregationalists will use the terms "Christ" (for example, United Church of Christ, Disciples of Christ) and "Lord," but more to define their identity than to make a theological affirmation. Free Church types would find it hard to affirm that Jesus is the long-awaited Jewish king (except at Christmastime). They surely would hesitate to confess that Jesus had replaced the Roman emperor as Lord (*kurios*), especially an emperor turned divine (*filius dei*, Son of God). The continuing Jesus in our lives, the Christ, tends to be thought of as master, teacher, or example. So we think of ourselves as disciples (students) of Jesus (for example, Disciples of Christ). Not only are we students of the Teacher, but we are Followers of the Master. Discipleship has been a powerful theme for the Free Church type churches.

The first disciples followed Jesus. Despite the seeming affirmation of Mark 8:27-30 (par. Matt. 16:13-20; Luke 9:18-21), the disciples did not speak of Jesus as the Christ.[39] The first indication of messiahship came with the cynical (but accurate) accusation that Jesus was the "King of the Jews" (Mark 15:1ff. and parallels). The Roman centurion even recognized Jesus as the Roman emperor (*filius dei*, "Son of God," Mark 15:39 and parallels). Before any Gospel had been written, however, Paul had identified Jesus as "Jesus Christ our Lord." We have noted that appellation in the Adoptionist passage, Romans 1:1-6. More often Paul speaks of Jesus as an agent of God:

---

[37]Jacquelyn Grant, *White Women's Christ and Black Women's Jesus: Feminist Christology and Womanist Response* (Atlanta: Scholars Press, 1989) 212-18.

[38]Gerald O'Collins, *What Are They Saying about Jesus?* (New York: Paulist Press, 1977) 10.

[39]Wilhem Wrede, *The Messianic Secret*, trans. J. C. G. Greig (Greenwood SC: Attic Press, 1971) 129-33. Wrede considers the "messianic secret" (e.g., "don't tell") a later addition to Mark. That would explain why people around Jesus didn't know he was the Messiah. More likely the messianic secret keeps an early tradition that Jesus rejected for himself the power-loaded categorization Messiah.

> From now on, therefore, we regard no one from a human point of view; even though we once knew Christ from a human point of view, we know him no longer in that way. So if anyone is in Christ, there is a new creation: everything old has passed away; see, everything has become new! All this is from God, who reconciled us to himself *through Christ*, and has given us the ministry of reconciliation; that is, *in Christ* God was reconciling the world to himself, not counting their trespasses against them, and entrusting the message of reconciliation to us.
>
> (2 Cor. 5:16-19; italics added)

As a divinely appointed agent, Christ acts on behalf of God. Paul never identifies Jesus as God, nor does he speak of Jesus as God incarnate. Shortly after the death of Paul the two synoptic Gospels, Matthew and Luke, added to the Gospel of Mark birth narratives that implied the Incarnation. The Gospel of John explicitly stated that "the Word became flesh." Regardless of how we understand these New Testament narratives, by the end of the first century Jesus had become more than a divine agent. Jesus the Christ acted as God's promised sovereign, and by the second century Jesus Christ was in some sense a divine being. The Christological debates of the second to fifth centuries centered around the manner in which that divinity was present in the historical Jesus. Extreme leaders of the third and fourth centuries insisted either on total divinity (Athanasius or Apollinarius) or total humanity (Arius or Eusebius of Nicomedia). At the Council of Chalcedon (451 CE) the unity of both was affirmed. Because of Chalcedon, which only left the problems in limbo, many Christians could worship Christ as the divine emperor (Christological). Others could worship Jesus as the Savior (soteriological).

In terms of early Christian art neither Christology nor soteriology were dominant themes. One of the first portrayals of Jesus Christ as emperor can be seen in the apse of *Sta. Pudenziana* in Rome (ca. 400 CE).[40] Portrayals of Jesus on the cross do not occur until the fifth century, and even they show Jesus almost mocking those who would crucify him.[41] In early Christian art Jesus was neither the divine emperor nor a suffering savior.[42] Jesus

---

[40]Robin Jensen, *Understanding Early Christian Art*, 98-112.

[41]They are called the Triumphal Christ because Jesus was victorious over his executers. The earliest two are on the door of *Sta. Sabina* and on a casket in the British Museum. See Robin Jensen, *Understanding Early Christian Art*, 130-37, 150.

[42]Empty crosses appeared by the end of the fourth century, but crucifixes with a suffering Jesus are quite later (surely later than the great mosaics of *S. Apollinare*

heals the sick, raises the dead, and creates the food for the communal meal (the *Feeding of the 5,000* and the *Wedding at Cana*).

In the Reformation churches Christology shifted radically. Christ as divine ruler was dropped. Nor did Jesus appease the wrath of an angry God. Portrayals of Christ enthroned as the ruler of the universe disappeared. In the Radical Reformation the Jesus of the New Testament and early Christian art reappeared.

These theological changes are highly significant. Christ could no longer be used to buttress the power of the king or prince. Furthermore, Jesus, and therefore others, no longer suffered because of sin and the wrath of God. Nor do we. An interesting example would be the Hutterian doctors who treated patients as humans with a medical problem, not as sinners who suffered God's vengeance. One could well argue that modern medicine started with the Anabaptists who found healthy life in communal disciple-ship.[43]

The community of disciples finds in the words and deeds of Jesus a description of life together. They are family (for example, Church of the Brethren) and know each other as "brother" or "sister." Jesus himself spoke of his companions as brothers and sisters, his true family. No one spoke of Jesus as parent (Matt. 12:46-50). Speaking Christologically, Jesus was not the *head* of the family; the family *was* Jesus. And as with Paul, the resurrected body of Jesus was the same community of followers known now as the "body of Christ." The continuing presence of Jesus was known and made known by his Body. In Paul's eyes the Spirit created the Body with its necessary functions (1 Cor. 12:4-31). That Body continued the work of Jesus. Indeed, it was Jesus. When Jesus became the Head or the Lord, the community of believers became an organization with a Leader and that Leader could take on the parallel form of a human bishop or elder, or even ruler. At that point, then, Christology became a matter of defining the nature of Jesus rather than the continuing function of his disciples.

3. *The Spirit (inspiration)*. The Free Church has described itself more with following Jesus, and studying the Bible than with the presence of the Holy Spirit. For some, the Spirit may have little meaning (Anabaptist and other Baptist types). Discipleship is far more important. For others, the Spirit energizes and creates ecstasy for the congregation (Pentecostal and some African-American churches). Understanding Spirit, or the Holy Spirit,

---

Nuovo in Ravenna, early sixth century).

[43]Graydon F. Snyder, *Health and Medicine in the Anabaptist Tradition* (Valley Forge PA: Trinity Press International, 1995) 21.

is no simple matter. In the Bible the Spirit has multiple, though connected, meanings. Its most basic meaning refers to the wind (Gen. 1:2; Jer. 13:24) or the wind/breath that gives life (Ezek. 37:9-10). The Spirit (*ru'ach* in Hebrew) could create in a group an ecstatic state (1 Sam. 10:5-13), or bring the Word of the Lord through a prophet (Micah 3:8). The Spirit bestows leadership (2 Kings 2:15) and guides the people of Israel toward their end-time goal (Joel 2:28-29).

This rich Hebrew understanding of Spirit informs the New Testament.[44] There are two functions that especially relate to the Free Church. One function can be seen in Acts where each new expansion of the church is seen as the activity of the Spirit (Acts 13:4). Paul, on the other hand, speaks more often of the Spirit organizing the growing Jesus movement. Not only were leaders such as apostles, prophets, and teachers created by the Spirit, but so were others who dispensed wisdom or knowledge, spoke in tongues, or could heal. The church was the product of the power of the Spirit (1 Cor. 12).[45]

While the first Reformation churches may have held multifaceted interpretations of the power of the Spirit, for post-Tridentine (post-Council of Trent) Protestants the authority of the Word of God depended on inspiration. For the most part that meant the biblical author was inspired by the Spirit to write the biblical text. When scientific criticism was applied to this "inspired Word," it became necessary for some more conservative groups to defend the Bible with a doctrine of verbal inspiration. Inspiration was not simply a condition of the author. Verbal inspiration referred to the author as the conduit for the divine Word.

Such ideas are basically foreign to the Free Church type. Because the faith community selected the books of the New Testament, it is the inspiration of the congregation that determines the inspiration of the text. That is, no text of the Bible is inspired when presented to an uninspired congregation. Or even the reverse, the inspiration of the congregation can make an obscure text inspired. Verbal inspiration as such is not biblical. The New Testament text most often used to support divine inspiration is worth considering.

---

[44]James Dunn, *Jesus and the Spirit: A Study of the Religious and Charismatic Experience of Jesus and the First Christians* (London: SCM Press, 1975).

[45]Dunn writes that "the corporate dimension of religious experience is integral to Paul's whole understanding of the divine-human relationship" (*Jesus and the Spirit*, 260). Paul seldom, if ever, speaks of an individual experience of the Holy Spirit.

[10]You have observed my teaching, my conduct, my goal in life, my faith, my patience, my love, my steadfastness, [11]my persecution, my sufferings, the things that happened to me in Antioch, in Iconium, and Lystra, the persecutions I have endured. Yet the Lord rescued me from all of them. [12]Indeed, all who wish to live a godly life in Christ Jesus will be persecuted. [13]Evil people and impostors, deceiving and being deceived, will go from bad to worse. [14]But as for you, stay in what you have learned and believed, knowing from whom you have learned, [15]and that from childhood you knew the sacred writings, which are able through faith in Jesus Christ to make you wise about matters of salvation. [16]Every writing inspired by God [*theopneustos*] is also useful for teaching, for reproof, for correction and for education in righteousness, [17]so that everyone who belongs to God may be skilled, equipped for every good work.

(2 Tim. 3:10-17; authors' translation)

The Greek term *theopneustos* occurs only here in the Bible. Basically it means "God-breathed." Many translators and readers have assumed the term refers to the person writing the document. This has led to the present-day arguments over the nature of inspiration (verbal, infallible, ecstatic). The emphasis on the author has been overdone. The Spirit worked primarily in the life of the community. God working through the Spirit teaches the congregation (1 Thess. 4:8). According to the Gospel of John it is the Spirit that will lead the faith community into a deeper understanding of what Jesus has said (John 14:25-26). It is not so much a matter of the inspiration of the author as it is the presence of the Spirit in the congregation, or with the readers, as it (they) interprets what has been written. An inspired document then is one that has a proven track record in the faith community. It is not divisive or deceiving (2 Tim. 3:14), and can be trusted to instruct, correct and train for God's work (2 Tim. 3:16-17). So understood, these verses might be translated:

From childhood you have known the sacred writings, which are able through trust in the body of Jesus Christ to make you mature in the way of salvation. For every writing regarded as inspired by God is also useful for teaching.

The earliest faith community was formed by the presence of the Holy Spirit. According to the Gospel of John, at the first congregational meeting in the Upper Room, the despondent disciples were awakened by the presence of the risen Jesus. The Jesus community was formed when Jesus breathed on them the Spirit.

> When it was evening on that day, the first day of the week, and the doors of the house where the disciples had met were locked for fear of the Jews, Jesus came and stood among them and said, "Peace be with you." After he said this, he showed them his hands and his side. Then the disciples rejoiced when they saw the Lord. Jesus said to them again, "Peace be with you. As the Father has sent me, so I send you." When he had said this, *he breathed on them and said to them, "Receive the Holy Spirit.* If you forgive the sins of any, they are forgiven them; if you retain the sins of any, they are retained."
>
> But Thomas (who was called the Twin), one of the twelve, was not with them when Jesus came. So the other disciples told him, "We have seen the Lord." But he said to them, "Unless I see the mark of the nails in his hands, and put my finger in the mark of the nails and my hand in his side, I will not believe."
>
> A week later his disciples were again in the house, and Thomas was with them. Although the doors were shut, Jesus came and stood among them and said, "Peace be with you." Then he said to Thomas, "Put your finger here and see my hands. Reach out your hand and put it in my side. Do not doubt but believe." Thomas answered him, "My Lord and my God!" Jesus said to him, "Have you believed because you have seen me? Blessed are those who have not seen and yet have come to believe."
>
> Now Jesus did many other signs in the presence of his disciples, which are not written in this book. But these are written so that you may come to believe that Jesus is the Messiah, the Son of God, and that through believing you may have life in his name.
>
> (John 20:19-31; italics added)

Those present in the upper room constituted the new church. Unfortunately (?), Thomas the Twin was absent. When he appeared at the next meeting he wanted proof of the Resurrection, that is, he had failed to receive the Spirit. Jesus demonstrated for him the love of God, and, in response, he became a part of the new community. As the text indicates, most people will have to go through the Thomas experience. It is the role of the congregational leaders to help prepare the congregation for the reception of the Spirit.

4. *The Bible*. For the Free Church type the Bible is central. Preaching, worship, hymns, decision making, all have some basis in biblical material. This anchor in biblical material has served the Free Church well over the centuries because it has provided a consistent, available point of departure for the Christian life. As we continue, we shall see that worship, preaching, and teaching without a biblical point of departure would be unthinkable.

Jews, Christians, and Muslims are People of the Book. For all three religions there is an authoritative sacred writing. The Bible for the Jews consists of the first five books (Pentateuch) of the Hebrew Scriptures, the Torah. The Hebrew Scriptures contain two other sections: the Prophets (historical books and prophetic writings that expand the narrative and laws of the Torah) and the Writings (poetic and wisdom writings that reflect on the meaning of the Torah). The Torah is authoritative, but the Jews have constantly adapted and contextualized its meaning. This has resulted in massive tomes called the Mishnah and the Talmud. These writings consist primarily of rabbinical interpretations (commentary) based on the Torah.

We find in the New Testament that same practice of adaptation and contextualizing.[46] The writers of the New Testament books and letters, themselves Jews, altered the Greek text of the Hebrew Scriptures (the Septuagint) to fit the situation they were discussing. That fact is very important. The Hebrew Scriptures recorded the intent of God for the people of Israel and all humanity. The writers of the New Testament assumed the Hebrew Scriptures contained the promise of God now being fulfilled in their time. All crucial events and sayings had to be grounded in the promise of God. The New Testament formula for that grounding is *kata graphe* or "according to the scriptures" (1 Cor. 15:3-4; James 2:8). More often the phrase "that the scripture might be fulfilled" is used (for example, Mark 14:49; John 17:12, et al.). However, the most frequently used word is *gegraptai*, "it is written." The Gospel writers and Paul use it extensively. Luke 4:4-8 and Mark 11:17, for example, report that Jesus himself used the term. Even if the biblical quotes were contextualized or even inaccurate (from a textual point of view), nevertheless the direction of the Jesus movement had to be grounded in the Hebrew Scriptures. For example, *kata graphe* sanctioned the well-known, early confession in 1 Corinthians 15:3-4:

> For I handed on to you as of first importance what I in turn had received: that Christ died for our sins in accordance with the scriptures [*kata tas graphas*], and that he was buried, and that he was raised on the third day in accordance with the scriptures [*kata tas graphas*]. . . .
>
> (1 Cor. 15:3-4)

---

[46]E. Earle Ellis, *The Old Testament in Early Christianity: Canon and Interpretation in the Light of Modern Research* (Tübingen: J. C. B. Mohr, 1991) 77-124; idem, *Paul's Use of the Old Testament* (Edinburgh: Oliver and Boyd, 1957) 10-37; Richard Hays, *Echoes of Scripture in the Letters of Paul* (New Haven CT: Yale University Press, 1989). Hays argues that the original intent of the text in the Hebrew Scripture was not a primary concern for the interpreter (154-56).

The central affirmation of early Christianity had to be based on the Hebrew Scriptures, even though no specific Scripture indicates the Messiah would die for our sins. The closest would be Isaiah 53, the suffering-servant passage. Certainly there is no Scripture that suggests the Messiah would die, be buried, and rise in three days. The closest would be the Jonah story as radically interpreted by the Jesus words in Matthew 12:38-42:

> Then some of the scribes and Pharisees said to him, "Teacher, we wish to see a sign from you." But he answered them, "An evil and adulterous generation asks for a sign, but no sign will be given to it except the sign of the prophet Jonah. For just as Jonah was three days and three nights in the belly of the sea monster, so for three days and three nights the Son of Man will be in the heart of the earth. The people of Nineveh will rise up at the judgment with this generation and condemn it, because they repented at the proclamation of Jonah, and see, something greater than Jonah is here!"   (Matt. 12:38-41)

As with the Jonah story, most quotes of the Hebrew Scriptures alter the text or meaning in some form or another. For example, in Mark 1:2-3 the first part of the quote from Isaiah actually comes from Malachi. The second part, from Isaiah 40:3, has altered the original reading "A voice [of the prophet] cries, 'In the wilderness prepare the way of the Lord.' " In the Gospel of Mark it identifies the message of John the Baptist: "the voice of one crying out in the wilderness: 'Prepare the way of the Lord.' " A shift in punctuation changes the meaning.

Just as the Jews reinterpreted the Torah as needed, so the writers of the New Testament reinterpreted the Hebrew Scriptures written in Greek (Septuagint) as needed. Likewise the patristic writers reinterpreted both the Hebrew Scriptures and the New Testament as necessary.

As we have seen, the Reformation, especially Calvinists and the Radical Reformation, primarily rejected Tradition in favor of Scripture. The intent was to reject the theological evolution that had led to medieval Catholicism. The Word of God replaced Tradition. By rejecting Tradition, however, the Reformation lost the very interpretative system it needed. The Bible comes to us through a process of constant contextualization. Some parts of the Reformation church had to insist the Bible was written by God and was verbally infallible. That left the Christian with no way to contextualize the source of faith. Everything was true as written.

Within the Free Church type particularly there is also the temptation to become biblicists. That is, the centrality of Jesus might be replaced by the centrality of the Bible. The issue is serious. It has, in part, led to the demise of some Free Churches that have slipped over into Fundamentalism. When the Bible becomes more central than Jesus or the Body, then another kind of hierarchy is formed. The biblical interpreter becomes the authority. To be honest, though, the sense of biblical inerrancy, Fundamentalism, derives more from the post-Tridentine mainline churches, especially Calvinism, than from the Free Church type. A Fundamentalist Free Church would be a contradiction in terms.[47]

Inherent Marcionism is one reason why Free Church biblicism does not easily shift to Fundamentalism. Marcion was the early Christian who rejected the theology of an angry, or wrathful God. Because they hold so strongly to Jesus as the source of their faith, Free Church types often tend to place the New Testament above the Hebrew Scriptures. They may use the Hebrew Scriptures better to understand Jesus, or they may use select passages for edification (for example, Isa. 53, Psalm 23), but the failure to place the Hebrew Scriptures on the same level as the New Testament makes a doctrine of biblical inerrancy nearly impossible.

As we observe their praxis, it becomes clear the Bible does not function in the Free Church the same way as it does among Catholics or mainline Protestants. For congregational types it was the early faith community that created the Bible. The disciples of Jesus heard the teaching of Jesus and saved what was important to them. Following prophecies, logia, and select texts from the Hebrew Scriptures, the first community developed a Jesus tradition. Through the early decades the growing Jesus community decided which materials would guide them. After more than two centuries the church did choose, more or less, the books that make up our New Testament. Some books were chosen because they were believed to be an apostolic witness, others because they were favorites of certain powerful cities. Some books—*Shepherd of Hermas, Barnabas,* the *Didache*—eventually were left out.

For the most part the Roman Catholic Church also understood that the Bible was the product of the church. To the dismay of some, however, the Catholic Church considered its own church leadership as the final interpretative authority. A major point of the Reformation was to make the church again subservient to the Word. So we find in the Reformation churches a powerful doctrine of the Word (*sola scriptura*). In contrast to Catholicism, Reformed types believed the Word of God created the faith community,

---

[47]For a helpful reflection on this debate among Southern Baptists see Robert Benne, "Crisis of Identity," *Christian Century* (27 January 2004): 22-26.

even though it was actually the faith community that selected the canon. Following the Renaissance the world turned more scientific. The Bible itself was subjected to literary and historical criticism. Biblical scholars tried to separate out what was original (the Word?) and what was secondary accretion (community interpretation). In this world of critical analysis mainline pastors were taught to apply fairly severe criticism to the text in order to "rightly divide/explain the word of truth" (2 Tim. 2:15).

Strange as it may seem, at this critical juncture the Free Churches are closer to Catholicism than to classical Protestantism. The church produced the Bible, not vice versa. The text is rightly interpreted in the context of the faith community, not necessarily by scholarly exegesis.

Chapter 3

Styles of Congregational Bible Study

The Radical Reformation (congregational types) created a critical *re*formation of its own. While the church was the authority for the Catholic Church and the Word was the authority for the Reformation churches, for the Free Church type authority resided with the congregation as it read the Bible together. Put another way the church hierarchy did not authoritatively interpret the text, nor did a trained minister or educator. The laity had their own access to the Bible. Congregational Bible study may be a more universal mark of the Free Church than even adult baptism.

Even in the sixteenth century the transference of Bible study to the laity was remarkable. The Anabaptist annals, *The Martyrs' Mirror* and *The Hutterian Chronicle*, record conflicts between laity and their persecutors. Frequently, during the trials, the laity could quote appropriate biblical passages and, to the amazement of the learned interlocutors, these untrained believers often knew the biblical material better than they did. It may seem strange to modern readers that the laicization of the Bible was seen then as quite radical. Anyone can have a Bible today. But it did take the invention of the printing press and the growth of the Free Church type to make congregational Bible study possible.

Given the centrality of Bible study for the Left Wing of the Reformation, the lack of models and descriptions from the early church can be disconcerting. At early faith community gatherings someone read the Scripture (1 Corinthians 14:26-33). The text in 1 Corinthians does not describe a communal discussion of the text. Quite the contrary. Apparently only two or three persons could speak (vv. 29-30). The primary description of the faith community in Acts 2:43-47 speaks of praying together, eating together, and sharing with each other. No Bible study. Imprisoned in Philippi, Paul and Silas prayed and sang hymns (Acts 16:25). No Bible study.

One might suspect Paul was having a Bible study when the young man fell out of the window (Acts 20:7-12), but the text only mentions Paul "holding a discussion" and "speaking." At the request of the Ethiopian eunuch, Philip did explain the meaning of Isaiah 53 (Acts 8:26-35). No discussion of the text is mentioned. Otherwise we are left with the passage we have already mentioned (2 Timothy 3:14-17) where the scripture is read, discussed, and interpreted in the midst of a congregation inspired by the Spirit. Later descriptions of biblical studies occur very seldom. For example, in the *Shepherd of Hermas* the revelator Rhoda reads an instructional message to Hermas. It contains allusions to the Psalms (*Hermas* 3). Later the lady church instructed him to send a copy of the message to Clement (of Rome?) and one to the woman Grapte who would instruct widows and orphans. Hermas was to use the third copy with the elders of his city (*Hermas* 8).

Surely instruction in the Christian faith must have been required in all places. Hippolytus (*Apostolic Tradition* 16-20) speaks of a three-year catechesis. Our best example of a catechism appears in Augustine's *On Catechizing the Uninstructed*, though catechetical instruction and Bible study can hardly be equated. So we have no hint in the Patristic period of times when the first Christians came together to search the scriptures for daily guidance. For Free Church Christians this has been puzzling. The Free Church accepts the authority of the Scriptures and finds there, through group discussion, God's will for our time. If the early church did the same we have no record of it.

After Guttenberg, many could own a Bible. That did not mean the right of interpretation belonged to the laity. Among mainline churches especially, the pastor or educator had been taught the proper means of exegesis. The pastor knew the traditional meaning of the text. By means of preaching and teaching the pastor transferred the results of proper textual analysis to the congregation. It was not assumed that the layperson, trained in some other profession or trade, could appropriately determine the meaning of the text. But historically that is exactly what the congregational type believes. It is not strictly a heuristic problem, but also a deeply theological one. God's communication with us does not lie in the text itself, but in our openness to the text, the divine presence in the community of faith. In recent years a number of quite different movements continue to point in this direction.

Postmodern biblical interpretation

Isms come and go. It will surely be true of postmodernism. Nevertheless, the postmodernist concerns are both appropriate and useful.[1] There are three points to consider:(1) the time gap; (2) the nature of absolute truth; and (3) the meaning of words.

---

[1]A. K. M. Adam, *What Is Postmodern Biblical Criticism?* (Minneapolis: Fortress Press, 1995) 1-25.

Academic types assume that the period between the writing of the New Testament and today has created a chasm of understanding that cannot be overcome except by intense historical and literary study (they are called Modernists or Rationalists).[2] The current reader then must know the historical background of the text, the value system that determined the action of the people of that time frame, and the form in which materials were written. Otherwise, how can the current reader expect to understand the text, and know the meaning of the Word of God for today?

No doubt this assertion contains much truth. Any document should be read in its context. On the other hand, any strict application of this principle means that most, if not all, past literature would be totally obscure for the modern reader. Obviously that is not true. We can understand the conflict of power in Shakespeare's *Julius Caesar* without knowing the life of Shakespeare or the biography of Brutus. Surely we can understand loyalty to one's nation and one's father in *Aida* without knowing the form of a Verdi opera or the history of Egypt. The same is true of the Bible. We can assimilate Jesus' healing of a "leper" without knowing whether it was Hansen's disease or not. We can understand the surprise killing of Goliath without knowing who the Philistines were. Such information would be very helpful, but not always necessary. There is a time gap, but it does not prevent us from understanding the classical themes of antiquity. That is why we call them classical, and surely the Bible must be considered a classical book.

Secondly, many readers of the Bible assume there is an unassailable foundation of truth in the biblical material. On second thought, most readers will realize that unified truth does not exist. There are many perspectives in the New Testament. The Synoptic Gospels stress discipleship; the Gospel of John stresses truth; the Apostle Paul stresses faith. Through the centuries these varying perspectives have resulted in a variety of church communities. Nothing is absolutely correct; that is, no one person, institution, or document holds all the truth. So when the community of faith comes to the text it knows that multiple understandings are both possible and probable.

Third, the work of some linguistic philosophers (Deconstruction thinkers) like Derrida have raised serious doubts about the location of meaning for words.[3] Does meaning lie with the author? Does it lie with the first

[2]Adam, *What Is Postmodern Biblical Criticism?* 2-3.
[3]Adam, *What Is Postmodern Biblical Criticism?* 27-43.

audience? Or does it lie with anyone today who reads it? For example, when Paul used the Greek word *pistis* he might have meant a trusting personal relationship with others or he might have meant a set of convictions. His first Hellenistic audience probably thought he meant intellectual beliefs (faith). Reformation leaders thought *pistis* was the way we were set right with God. A modern reader might have any of these meanings, or even more, such as "accepting that which you cannot prove." What is the meaning of *pistis* in the letters of Paul? More or less, the postmodernist assumes the text means what the reader thinks it means.[4] In that sense postmodern biblical criticism parallels the Free Church approach to Bible study.[5] Furthermore, a postmodern approach to Bible study does not create a correct position that stands over against a wrong position.[6] Multiple interpretations will be considered as legitimate.

Postcolonial use of the Bible

The biblical text can have multiple meanings. In this postmodern world, several groups have sought to interpret the Bible in ways that would enhance their primary concern. Feminists[7] and minority groups[8] rightly suppose their presence and concerns have been slighted by the biblical writers themselves and certainly suppressed in the history of interpretation.

---

[4]Edgar McKnight, *Jesus Christ in History and Scripture: A Poetic and Sectarian Perspective* (Macon GA: Mercer University Press, 1999) 111-21.

[5]J. Denny Weaver, *Anabaptist Theology in the Face of Postmodernity: A Proposal for the Third Millennium* (Telford PA: Pandora Press, 2000) 21. Susan Biesecker-Mast, "Anabaptists and Postmodernity: A Risky/Risqué Proposition," in Gerald and Susan Biesecker-Mast, *Anabaptists and Postmodernity* (Telford PA: Pandora Press, 2000) 19-38.

[6]A series of postmodern approaches to the Bible has been collected by A. K. M. Adam, *Postmodern Interpretations of the Bible: A Reader* (St. Louis: Chalice Press, 2001). The scholarship is excellent. The conclusions are sometimes surprising.

[7]See Musa W. Dube, *Postcolonial Feminist Interpretation of the Bible* (St. Louis: Chalice Press, 2000) 12-52; also Elisabeth Schüssler-Fiorenza, *In Memory of Her: A Feminist Theological Reconstruction of Christian Origins* (New York: Crossroad, 1992) 3-40.

[8]James H. Cone, *God of the Oppressed* (Maryknoll NY: Orbis, 1997) ix-xviii, 49-56. For an Asian-American perspective see Benny Liew, "Whose Bible? Which (Asian) America?" *Semeia* 90/91 (2002): 1-20.

In recent years, representatives of these suppressed groups have sought to reconstruct our reading of the Bible.[9]

Postcolonial studies represent one such suppressed group. Unlike the others it is geopolitical in nature. In areas of the world where Christians have colonized an indigenous people (primarily Africa[10] and South America[11]), the dominant interpretation of the Bible most likely will be the one that benefits the colonizer, missionary, or dominant group.[12] To counteract such set interpretations, postcolonial academicians have developed hermeneutical procedures that recognize the culture of those colonized as well as the culture (Western) of those who were colonizers. For the most part these hermeneutical procedures are discursive in nature. That is, postcolonial writers dialogue sharply with those who represent colonizing (Western) interests.[13]

For the purposes of our study, however, the material nature of postcolonialism takes precedence over the discursive. The material types are concerned that people oppressed by colonizers can achieve a better life. Leaders working with those oppressed have developed a form of interactive Bible study. They see three levels of study. First the Bible is used as a basis for celebrative moments like Christmas, Easter, Pentecost, marriages, and funerals. The Bible buttresses the daily life of the people. Secondly, Bible

---

[9]Rasiah S. Sugirtharajah, "Biblical Studies after the Empire: From a Colonial to a Postcolonial Mode of Interpretation," in *The Postcolonial Bible*, ed. Rasiah S. Sugirtharajah (Sheffield UK: Sheffield Academic Press, 1998) 12-22; also Sugirtharajah, *Postcolonial Criticism and Biblical Interpretation* (Oxford: Oxford University Press, 2002) 25-26.

[10]J. N. K. Mugambi, *The African Heritage and Contemporary Christianity* (Nairobi, Kenya: Longman Kenya, 1989) 12-27. Michael Bourdillon, *Religion and Society: A Text for Africa* (Harare, Zimbabwe: Mambo Press, 1990) 265-71.

[11]Leonardo Boff, "Theological Characteristics of a Grassroots Church," in *The Challenge of Basic Christian Communities*, ed. Sergio Torres and John Eagleson (Maryknoll NY: Orbis Books, 1982) 124-44. For the complexity of Colonialism and Postcolonialism in South America see José Jotge Klor de Alva, "The Postcolonization of the (Latin) American Experience: A Reconsideration of 'Colonialism,' 'Postcolonialism,' " and "Mestizaje," in *After Colonialism: Imperial Histories and Postcolonial Displacements*, ed. Gyan Prakash (Princeton NJ: Princeton University Press, 1995) 242-70.

[12]Fernando F. Segovia, *Decolonizing Biblical Studies: A View from the Margins* (Maryknoll NY: Orbis Books, 2000) 133-42.

[13]José Jotge Klor de Alva, "The Postcolonization of the (Latin) American Experience," 242.

study can be a matter of historical discovery. The group may be curious about identifications and historic events. Who was Abraham, or what really did happen in front of Pilate? A third type of Bible study occurs when the people gather to talk about their problems in terms of the text. Who really owns the land? How does healing occur? How do we handle aging parents? What rights do we have?[14]

Those working with base communities feel there is a necessity for all three uses of the text. The people need to use the Bible as the basis for their life together, but they also need to find in Bible study answers to the constant issues in their life. The first use is rather automatic (for example, the Lukan story for Christmas), but the latter is much more complex. A combination of styles may look like this:

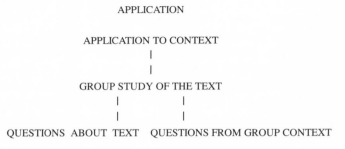

If the group only studies the text, then the text never reaches real life. If the group only talks about their lives, without any transcendent point of reference, they do nothing but wallow in self-pity or mutual introspection.[15] The system used in postcolonial study groups and by base communities closely parallels the style of biblical study used by the Free Church types. Speaking of the source of interpretation, Ernesto Cardenal wrote that the true author is the Holy Spirit working in the base community.[16]

---

[14]Carlos Mesters, "The Use of the Bible in Christian Communities of the Common People," in *The Challenge of Basic Christian Communities*, 197-210.

[15]Three examples of postcolonial Bible study can be found in Rasiah S. Sugirtharajah, ed. *Voices from the Margin: Interpreting the Bible in the Third World* (London: SPCK, 1991) 412-30. See also Ernesto Cardenal, *The Gospel in Solentiname*, trans. Donald Walsh (Maryknoll NY: Orbis, 1976–1982).

[16]Ernesto Cardenal, *The Gospel in Solentiname* 1:ix.

Transforming biblical study

Any open-ended Bible study still has problems with control. Even a well-meaning leader may have an agenda that is subtly forced on the group. Postcolonial leaders, for example, may seek improvement of the group's economic well-being. Is it possible for church groups to study the Bible without that leadership control? Can study groups draw their own conclusions about the meaning and intent of a text? Some teachers, like Walter Wink, a crypto-Free Church scholar, allow participants to find themselves in the light of biblical material.[17] The text is presented along with some basic background information. Then group members interact with each other and with the selected biblical passage. The leader does not use the leadership role as a means of directing the discussion. The leader, or expert, does not interject "correct" interpretations.

In fact there are no incorrect understandings of the text. Academic types will see this as exceptionally dangerous. And there is truth in their perception. No approach can be without dangers. While academic Bible study can be sterile, free-floating Bible study can lead to aberrations and serious misunderstandings, with dangerous consequences. A misunderstood God-directive can devastate the faith community. Still, experience has been that group study tends to correct itself. That is, someone gives an interpretation that may be idiosyncratic. Another person picks up the suggestion and makes of it something more useful for group discussion and community development. The whole group may then discover important information— triggered perhaps by an offhand, inappropriate remark. We call it the work of the Holy Spirit.

Wink's description of Bible study for small groups resembles the more academic discipline called Reader-Response criticism. Some scholars argue that the meaning of a biblical text does not lie with the intent of an author

[17]Walter Wink, *Transforming Bible Study* (Nashville: Abingdon Press, 1989). Sample group study questions can be found on pp. 128-51. Wink, *The Bible in Human Transformation: Toward a New Paradigm for Biblical Study* (Philadelphia: Fortress Press, 1973) 1-15. Wink sharply criticizes current biblical criticism. So also Norman K. Gottwald, ed., *The Bible and Liberation: Political and Social Hermeneutics* (Maryknoll NY: Orbis, 1983) see 2-9. Fernando Segovia makes the same criticism in his "Introduction: Pedagogical Discourse and Practice in Contemporary Biblical Criticism," in *Teaching the Bible: The Discourses and Politics of Biblical Pedagogy*, ed. Fernando Segovia and Mary Ann Tolbert (Maryknoll NY: Orbis, 1998) 1-28.

no longer known. Nor does it actually reside in the text itself, since a text offers no inherent interpretation. Instead, meaning comes from the community of readers or believers.[18] Because the meaning of the text evolves from listening to the text, it approximates the earliest use of the Jesus tradition and the epistles—oral presentation.[19]

These examples indicate current approaches to group Bible study that parallel the historic Free Church method. The present-day Bible study group opens with a prayer for the presence of the Spirit, reads the selected text, listens to or shares a contextual interpretation and then asks what it means for their time. There are no preconceived results. In congregational-type churches, Bible study often surpasses potlucks in popularity. In some Free Church groups Bible study draws more participants than Sunday morning worship!

[18]Edgar V. McKnight, *Postmodern Use of the Bible: The Emergence of Reader-oriented Criticism* (Nashville: Abingdon Press, 1988) 263-67.

[19]Robert M. Fowler, "Who Is the 'Reader' in Reader Response Criticism?" *Semeia* 31 (1985) 5-23.

Chapter 4

Elements of Community Formation

Membership

Becoming a Jew probably occurred less often than we suspect. Infants born in a Jewish family were Jewish. Circumcision marked the membership of a Jewish male baby. Later ceremonies (bar mitzvah and bat mitzvah) signified the moment of adult participation. An adult non-Jewish male could become a proselyte by receiving circumcision and immersing himself in water. While this appears to be true, the origin of the practice remains unknown (Acts 13:43). Practically speaking a woman could not become a Jew apart from the conversion (circumcision) of her husband (therefore the informal gathering of women at Philippi, Acts 16:13). Either sex could, however, become a "God-fearer" (Acts 13:16b). Membership in the Christian faith communities differed radically from Jewish antecedents. An initiatory rite for infants did not exist. Circumcision became irrelevant (Galatians 5:2-12). Circumcision (membership) had become a matter of the heart (Romans 2:29; 1 Corinthians 7:19).

Adults joined the new faith community through water baptism (1 Corinthians 1:14; Acts 2:38, 41; 8:38; 9:18). Some have assumed Christian water baptism derived from the adult immersion of Jewish proselytes. Such a connection cannot be determined with any certainty. Many others rather automatically assume baptism originated with John the Baptist (Mark 1:4-8).[1] John the Baptist immersed Jewish adults as an act of purification to prepare for the coming end-time. It had nothing to do with membership.

We don't really know the origin of Christian baptism. We do know the author of the Gospel of John reports that Jesus was baptizing more disciples than his predecessor, John the Baptist (John 3:22-26). Jesus himself equated baptism with his crucifixion (Mark 10:38). The identification of water baptism with the death and resurrection of Jesus became a central motif in adult membership:

---

[1]Everett Ferguson, "Baptism," *Encyclopedia of Early Christianity*, 160.

> What then are we to say? Should we continue in sin in order that grace may abound? By no means! How can we who died to sin go on living in it? Do you not know that all of us who have been baptized into Christ Jesus were baptized into his death? Therefore we have been buried with him by baptism into death, so that, just as Christ was raised from the dead by the glory of the Father, so we too might walk in newness of life.
>
> (Rom. 6:1-4)

Baptism marks adult conversion. It signifies death to the old life, and the beginning of a new life in the resurrected Body of Christ. Baptism has other meanings: purification by washing or becoming an adult in a fictive kinship. Through the centuries, however, baptism signifies in a public way death to the old way of life and resurrection to the new.

In the early church, conversion and baptism was an adult act.[2] The earliest known baptisteries in early Christianity were designed for adults.[3] Our first example, at Dura-Europos (which was covered over to protect it from opponents in 258 CE), was a rectangular step-in pool. Speaking architecturally, even after Constantine the baptisteries remained adult types, built like pools, or, portraying death and resurrection, even non-Christian burial sites.[4] It is not certain when the first Christians began to baptize infants. Tertullian (200 CE) opposed infant baptism (*De baptismo* 18). At about the same time the names of children found on catacomb *tituli* (tomb covers) still were not Christian. That is to say, children born in Christian families up through the third century were not automatically Christian.[5] By the middle of the third century, Origen stated that the apostles themselves had decreed infants should be baptized (*Comm. on Romans*, 5.9.11) and

---

[2]George Raymond Beasley-Murray, *Baptism in the New Testament* (London: Macmillan, 1962) 358.

[3]See J. G. Davies, *The Architectural Setting of Baptism* (London: Barrie and Rockliff, 1962). Though built for adults, most were too shallow for total body immersion (26).

[4]A. Khatchatrian. *Les baptistères paléochrétiens* (Paris: École pratique des hautes études, 1962). When baptisteries became a separate builtform, they were octagonal, circular, or square, much like the special Hellenistic tombs or heroon (xiii-xiv). (A "heroon" is a temple-shaped tomb, a temple to a hero.) Persons baptized in architectural tombs would have recognized the significance of death to the old life, J. G. Davies, *The Architectural Setting of Baptism*, 17.

[5]Peter Cramer, *Baptism and Change in the Early Middle Ages, ca. 200–ca. 1150* (Cambridge: Cambridge University Press, 1994) 132-36.

Cyprian of Carthage advocated infant baptism in his churches (*Ep.* 58).[6] By the middle of the fourth century, families identified their children as Christian. In the fifth century, the Augustinian doctrine of original sin made the baptism of infants almost necessary (*De pecatto originali* 44).[7]

Having noted the prevalence of adult baptism in the early church, it must be said that the New Testament witness is not so uniform.[8] The author of Acts speaks of corporate/household baptism:

> A certain woman named Lydia, a worshiper of God, was listening to us; she was from the city of Thyatira and a dealer in purple cloth. The Lord opened her heart to listen eagerly to what was said by Paul. When she and her household were baptized, she urged us, saying, "If you have judged me to be faithful to the Lord, come and stay at my home." And she prevailed upon us. (Acts 16:14-15)

And again in the case of the jailer:

> They answered, "Believe on the Lord Jesus, and you will be saved, you and your household." They spoke the word of the Lord to him and to all who were in his house. At the same hour of the night he took them and washed their wounds; then he and his entire family were baptized without delay. (Acts 16:31-33)

Jesus spoke of being like a child in order to enter the reign of God:

> At that time the disciples came to Jesus and asked, "Who is the greatest in the kingdom of heaven?" He called a child, whom he put among them, and said, "Truly I tell you, unless you change and become like children, you will never enter the kingdom of heaven. Whoever becomes humble like this child is the greatest in the kingdom of heaven. Whoever welcomes one such child in my name welcomes me. (Matt. 18:1-5)

According to the same Evangelist (Matthew) Jesus chastised the disciples for limiting the Jesus movement to adults:

---

[6]On the development of infant baptism see Beasley-Murray, *Baptism in the New Testament*, 306.

[7]Dale Moody, "Baptism in Theology and Practice," in *The People of God: Essays on the Believers' Church*, 41-50.

[8]So Oscar Cullmann, *Baptism in the New Testament*, trans. J. K. S. Reid (London: SCM Press, 1950) 23-46. Cullmann argues that baptism is not personal salvation, but reception into the Body of Christ. This corporate sense of belonging, a Free Church sine qua non, leads him though to suspect children were included.

Then little children were being brought to him in order that he might lay his hands on them and pray. The disciples spoke sternly to those who brought them; but Jesus said, "Let the little children come to me, and do not stop them; for it is to such as these that the kingdom of heaven belongs." (Matt 19:13-14)

The evidence seems conflictive. According to some parts of the literature the first Christians included the entire family in conversion actions. According to other parts of the literature individual adults were compelled by their new faith to leave the blood family in order to join the faith (called fictive) family:

And everyone who has left houses or brothers or sisters or father or mother or children or fields, for my name's sake, will receive a hundredfold, and will inherit eternal life. (Matt. 19:29)

or even more severely:

"Whoever comes to me and does not hate father and mother, wife and children, brothers and sisters, yes, and even life itself, cannot be my disciple."[9] (Luke 14:26)

The conflict cannot be resolved. There is no doubt that the first Christians wished for the conversion of the entire family, yet, assuming the validity of the archaeological evidence, there is no doubt that prior to Constantine conversion was primarily an adult decision. As early as the letters of Paul we can see the issue clearly:

To the married I give this command—not I but the Lord—that the wife should not separate from her husband (but if she does separate, let her remain unmarried or else be reconciled to her husband), and that the husband should not divorce his wife. To the rest I say—I and not the Lord—that if any believer has a wife who is an unbeliever, and she consents to live with him, he should not divorce her. And if any woman has a husband who is an unbeliever, and he consents to live with her, she should not divorce him. For the unbelieving husband is made holy through his wife, and the unbelieving wife is made holy through her husband. Otherwise, your children would be unclean, but as it is, they are holy. But if the unbelieving partner separates, let it be so; in such a case the brother

[9]In the social setting of Jesus the word "hate" would have meant the cessation of kinship and economic ties. See Wolfgang Stegemann, "The Contextual Ethics of Jesus," in *The Social Setting of Jesus and the Gospels*, ed. Wolfgang Stegemann, B. J. Malina, and Gerd Theissen (Minneapolis: Augsburg Press, 2002) 54-56.

or sister is not bound. It is to peace that God has called you. Wife, for all you know, you might save your husband. Husband, for all you know, you might save your wife. (1 Cor. 7:10-16)

The modern-day Free Church lives with the same conflict. Communitarian Free Churches value the family almost above all else. It is nearly inconceivable that an adult woman or man would abandon the blood family (their children) in order to participate in the faith family. So some Free Churches may indeed baptize infants (the United Church of Christ) or more likely offer services of dedication for infants whose blood family belongs to the faith community. Otherwise, most Free Churches practice adult baptism. Its importance cannot be overstated. Adult baptism signals that faith community and social matrix are not coextensive. An infant may be born into a church family, but does not join the faith community until an age when decisions can be made ("age of accountability").[10]

Normally such decision making occurs in a public situation. In some form or another, the leader will ask if anyone present wishes to join the faith community. Joining the faith community and making a confession of faith are almost identical. That is, confessing "Jesus is Lord" means participation in the Body of Christ. There is no meaning to a confession of faith other than declaring trust in the Jesus community. To be sure, many Christians suppose there is a moment when the individual is saved by faith and then only later does that faith take concrete form in the faith community (church). The Free Church generally denies there is such a moment of independent personal salvation. Salvation is the *process of belonging* to the Body of Christ.

When the leader asks if anyone wishes to join the church, normally that is the end moment of a much longer process. The prospective member has attended classes in membership and has consulted with significant church members. Consequently, the moment of decision will come as no surprise. On the other hand, there can be and will be persons present who make a decision at the moment of invitation. For them the procedure for membership will be the same. Someone transferring from another denomination will also receive instruction. A person becoming a Christian for the first time will be instructed before baptism. In any case they are joining the faith community, not simply being "saved."

The actual practice of baptism will differ from denomination to denomination. Sometimes forward, sometimes backwards; sometimes three times,

---

[10]Eller, *In Place of Sacraments*, 41-78.

sometimes once. There are always theological and historical reasons for these differences, often associated with the metaphor of dying and rising with Christ. We will not deal with those reasons here. In adult baptism there is always a confession of faith prior to the baptismal act. That includes an affirmation of faith in Jesus Christ and a rejection of evil (of this world).

Early Christian art showed both of these baptismal themes—life and death. A number of early Christian baptismal sites were decorated with a depiction of the *Good Shepherd*. It symbolized a welcome into the Christian community. There are no early portrayals of believers being baptized. There are a few examples of Jesus being baptized. He appears, perhaps with John the Baptist, as a small wonder worker, somewhat like Hermes or Hercules. The water does not cleanse Jesus; rather, Jesus the wonder worker cleanses the water. The sea or water tends to be a symbol of chaos—including society as a whole. The baptism of Jesus was a cleansing (rejection?) of that (Roman) society. The baptism of the believer was also a cleansing or rejection of the social matrix. Paul speaks of baptism as a death like that of Jesus (Romans 6:3-4).

Baptism and the Agape (Love Feast) were the primary rituals of the early church. For many mainline churches Baptism and the Eucharist are today the two sacraments. Sacraments, as enacted, mark the presence of God in the church. The Free Churches have no sacraments. They do believe in the presence of God in their worship, but do not assume any given ritual action in itself ushers in that presence. To the contrary, ritual practices assist in creating the divine-inspired community.

1. *Preparation for Membership*. a. *Membership class*. Anyone seeking membership in the faith community will attend several sessions prior to asking for baptism. The classes include:

(1) A study of those biblical texts relating to the meaning of baptism, including: the Baptism of Jesus (Matt. 3:13-17; Baptism by Water and the Holy Spirit (Matt. 3:11); Baptism and Rejection (Mark 10:38-40); Baptism and Death with Christ (Rom. 6:1-4); Baptism into the Life of the Faith Community (Acts 2:37-42); Baptism as an Affirmation of Good Conduct (1 Peter 3:13-22).

(2) A study of those biblical texts that describe membership in the faith community: Qualities of the New Life in Christ (Matt. 5:21-48; Rom. 12:9-21); Your Place in the Body of Christ (1 Cor. 12:14-26); Your Role in the Body of Christ as a Gift of the Spirit (Rom. 12:3-8); Equality of Membership (Gal. 3:27-28); the Goal of Spiritual Maturity (Eph. 4:11-13).

(3) A study of Christianity as seen from the Free Church perspective. Some resources: Donald Durnbaugh, *The Believers' Church: The History and Character of Radical Protestantism* (1970); Paul Sangster, *A History of the Free Churches* (British, 1983); John Skoglund, *Worship in the Free Churches* (1965).

(4) A study of this local congregation.

b. *Worship setting*. Since the act of baptism brings in a new member it occurs in the presence of the congregation. So-called *Winkeltaufe* (baptism in a corner, a private act) does not exist. At the appropriate moment the pastor leaves the congregation along with those about to be baptized. The congregation sings hymns until such a time that the pastor appears in the baptistery.

Unfortunately Revivalism and even Charles Wesley has made popular hymns of conversion that are "I" centered. So only a few "baptismal" hymns stress joining the faith community. Hymns like the following by John B. Geyer (1967), based on Romans 6 are most appropriate:[11]

We know that Christ is raised and dies no more.
Embraced by death, he broke its fearful hold,
and our despair he turned to blazing joy.
    Hallelujah!

We share by water in his saving death.
Reborn, we share with him an Easter life
as living members of our Savior Christ.
    Hallelujah!

The God of splendor clothes the Son with life.
The Spirit's fission shakes the church of God.
Baptized, we live with God the Three-in-One.
    Hallelujah!

---

[11]Hymn poems (and other worship resources) quoted herein are as they appear in two current Free Church hymnals. The hymnal titles are abbreviated; the hymns and other resources are cited by number (#). CH = *Chalice Hymnal* (St. Louis MO: Chalice Press, 1995). CH was "authorized" in 1987 by the General Assembly of the Christian Church (Disciples of Christ) at the instigation of the Association of Disciple Musicians. CH is of course also used in other Free Churches. HWB = *Hymnal. A Worship Book* (Elgin IL: Brethren Press; Newton KS: Faith and Life Press; Scottdale PA: Mennonite Publishing House, 1992). HWB is in use in churches of the Church of the Brethren, the General Conference Mennonite Church, the Mennonite Church in North America, and of other "Anabaptists and Pietists." HWB is our "control" text for this quoted material.

A new creation comes to life and grows
as Christ's new body takes on flesh and blood.
The universe, restored and whole will sing:
    Hallelujah!   (CH #376; HWB #443)[12]

Before baptizing, the pastor reads one of the above-mentioned biblical texts and then prays for the initiate. After the prayer the pastor asks at least three types of questions:

(a) Do you accept Jesus as Lord?
(b) Do you reject the evil of this world?
(c) Do you give your life to God's will
    as a part of this faith community?

Following an affirmative answer to these questions the candidate for baptism is immersed under water. The pastor lays hands on the head of the newly baptized member and prays for the presence of the Spirit. A deacon then covers the new member who is led to a room for changing clothes. Following all the baptisms the pastor asks the congregation members if they will support the new members as they develop in Christian life and faith. Following the affirmative answer the new members stand somewhere in the sanctuary and are greeted warmly by their new faith family. Sometimes members of the family and the congregation again lay on hands and pray for the presence of the Spirit. For many these moments of baptism are vividly remembered and their importance cannot be overestimated.

Ordinarily the new members are incorporated into the faith community by some form of the Agape—a reception or even a meal.

Communion

Frequency of communion differs considerably among the Free Churches, as does the praxis—though one cannot greatly vary the taking of the bread and cup. The praxis will reflect the theology of each denomination, but let us start first with a general Free Church understanding of communion.

In some mainline churches (for example, Missouri Synod Lutheran) the "real presence" may be described as Christ's presence in the elements, made possible by words of consecration spoken by a "rightly" ordained religious leader. In the Free Church tradition, the "real presence" of Christ, like the word of God, is located in the gathered community. Mutual sharing of the bread and the cup makes Christ's presence possible. The community

---

[12]CH lacks stanza 3; HWB has "Hallelujah!" where CH has "Alleluia!"

then, not the bread and the cup, is the location of the Body of Christ. Indeed the community is the Body of Christ rather than the bread.[13]

This critical difference between Free Church and mainline church occurred as a misunderstanding of the institution of the communion in the New Testament. There are two communion meals in the New Testament.[14] Both are found in Paul's letter to the Corinthians and both stress the formation of the early Christian faith community. The first is a meal that follows the pattern of a Jewish fellowship meal or *kiddush*: the cup first as an aperitif and the bread second as the food.[15] In 1 Corinthians 10:16-17 Paul writes:

> The cup of blessing that we bless, is it not a sharing (formation of community) in the blood of Christ? The bread that we break, is it not a sharing (formation of community) in the body of Christ? Because there is one bread, we who are many are one body, for we all partake of the one bread. (1 Cor. 10:16-17)

As in all societies, so in the Christian community, sharing in the breaking of bread creates community or fellowship.[16] The cup of wine acts as the liquid appetizer or aperitif, the Spirit, which assembles the community before the meal proper.

In 1 Corinthians 11, the second account, we find a communion in which the death of Jesus is remembered.[17] The body (bread) is broken first so that the Spirit (the cup): may be released. We would translate the passage as follows:

---

[13]Eller, *In Place of Sacraments*, 79-128.

[14]Hans Lietzmann, *Mass and Lord's Supper: A Study in the History of the Liturgy*, trans. Dorothea H. G. Reeve (Leiden: Brill, 1979; orig. 1926) 209-12. Lietzmann refers to the fellowship meal as the Jerusalem type and the *anamnesis* as the Pauline type.

[15]John E. Skoglund, *Worship of the Free Churches*, 24-25. H. J. Klauck, *Herrenmahl und hellenistischer Kult* (Münster: NTAbh N.F. 15, 1982) 330-31, 369-70.

[16]Horton Davies, *Bread of Life and Cup of Joy: Newer Ecumenical Perspectives on the Eucharist* (Grand Rapids MI: Eerdmans, 1993) 122-29. Francis J. Moloney translates *koinonia* in a similar communal way: "common union." See his *A Body Broken for a Broken People: Eucharist in the New Testament* (Melbourne: Collins Dove, 1990) 107.

[17]Davies, *Bread of Life*, 1-16.

> For I received from the Lord what I also handed on to you, that the Lord Jesus on the night when he was betrayed took a loaf of bread, and when he had given thanks, he broke it and said, "This [act of breaking the bread] is my body for you. Do this in remembrance of me." In the same way he took the cup also, after supper, saying, "This [act of drinking the] cup [together] is the new covenant in my blood. Do this, as often as you drink it, in remembrance of me." For as often as you eat this bread and drink the cup, you proclaim the Lord's death until he comes.
>
> (1 Cor. 11:23-26)

In both types of Eucharist the emphasis is on action or doing. We have mistakenly supposed the bread was the body of Christ and the wine was the blood of Christ. The translated text should read that the body of Christ is created by the breaking of the bread and the Spirit is released by the sharing of the cup. Both of these texts refer back to the Last Supper of Jesus with the disciples:

> While they were eating, he took a loaf of bread, and after blessing it he broke it, gave it to them, and said, "Take; this is my body." Then he took a cup, and after giving thanks he gave it to them, and all of them drank from it. He said to them, "This is my blood of the covenant, which is poured out for many. Truly I tell you, I will never again drink of the fruit of the vine until that day when I drink it new in the kingdom of God."
>
> (Mark 14:22-25)

The Synoptic tradition has cautiously melded together an account of the Jewish-style Last Supper (Passover) with the emerging Communion (already adapted in the Pauline tradition). The words of Jesus are both historic and symbolic. The ancient Passover celebrates annually God's deliverance of the Jewish people from the hands of the Egyptians (Exodus 12:43–13:10) and the formation of the new people of Israel. Jesus took that ancient celebration as a moment to prophesy the formation of a new deliverance and a new people.[18] As in the Passover, Jesus broke bread, but, referencing the coming deliverance on the cross, he spoke of his broken body as it formed the new people of God. Likewise, as the wine created a new spirit at the Passover, so Jesus spoke of the wine as the new Spirit that poured out of his broken body.

Eating a common meal together (Agape; potluck), sharing the breaking of bread and drinking the cup, these are the foundation actions of the

---

[18]For a definitive analysis see Geoffrey Wainwright, *Eucharist and Eschatology* (New York: Oxford University Press, 1981) 60-61.

church from its very beginning. They are the formation of the faith community in the name of Jesus.[19]

1. *Agape*. In the early church the Agape meal (Love Feast) consisted primarily of bread, fish, and wine. It would be difficult to deny that this meal somehow relates to the Feeding of the 5,000 (Multiplication of the Loaves and Fishes) and the Wedding at Cana. In the Feeding of the 5,000 Jesus takes five loaves and two fish, offered by a boy, and feeds 5,000 men as well as women and children:

> When it was evening, the disciples came to him and said, "This is a deserted place, and the hour is now late; send the crowds away so that they may go into the villages and buy food for themselves." Jesus said to them, "They need not go away; you give them something to eat." They replied, "We have nothing here but five loaves and two fish." And he said, "Bring them here to me." Then he ordered the crowds to sit down on the grass. Taking the five loaves and the two fish, he looked up to heaven, and blessed and broke the loaves, and gave them to the disciples, and the disciples gave them to the crowds. And all ate and were filled; and they took up what was left over of the broken pieces, twelve baskets full. And those who ate were about five thousand men, besides women and children.
>
> (Matt. 14:15-21)

The basic narrative for the presence of wine comes from the Wedding at Cana in the Gospel of John:

> Now standing there were six stone water jars for the Jewish rites of purification, each holding twenty or thirty gallons. Jesus said to them, "Fill the jars with water." And they filled them up to the brim. He said to them, "Now draw some out, and take it to the chief steward." So they took it. When the steward tasted the water that had become wine, and did not know where it came from (though the servants who had drawn the water knew), the steward called the bridegroom.   (John 2:6-9)

Also in the Gospel of John the resurrected Jesus has a final meal of bread and fish with his disciples:

> Jesus said to them, "Come and have breakfast." Now none of the disciples dared to ask him, "Who are you?" because they knew it was the Lord. Jesus came and took the bread and gave it to them, and did the same with the fish.   (John 21:12-13)

---

[19]Dale Stoffer, *The Lord's Supper* (Scottdale PA: Herald Press, 1997). Frank Ramirez, *The Love Feast* (Elgin: Brethren Press, 2000) 4-6.

In even later sources the Agape is mentioned, though not described (2 Peter 2:13; Jude 12). The author of the *Didache* describes the liturgy of the Fellowship meal with the cup first, but refers to it as a "Eucharist." Apparently he does not know the liturgy of bread and the cup as the remembrance of the crucifixion:

> [1]And concerning the Eucharist, hold Eucharist thus: [2]First concerning the Cup, "We give thanks to thee, our Father, for the Holy Vine of David thy child, which, thou didst make known to us through Jesus thy child; to thee be glory for ever." [3]And concerning the broken Bread: "We give thee thanks, our Father, for the life and knowledge which thou didst make known to us through Jesus thy Child. To thee be glory for ever. [4]As this broken bread was scattered upon the mountains, but was brought together and became one, so let thy Church be gathered together from the ends of the earth into thy Kingdom, for thine is the glory and the power through Jesus Christ for ever."   (*Didache* 9:1-4)

In early church art the Agape meal, the Feeding of the 5,000, and the Wedding at Cana occur far more often than any other New Testament scenes. Obviously the meal theme was central to the early Christians. The connection with the New Testament narratives can be easily observed. An Agape scene shows seven people eating at a crescent shaped table surrounded by seven baskets of bread, two fish on the table and a cup of wine. Of course, this scene is a stylized symbol of the Agape. There are occasional hints of a real Agape where many people are seated at the tables (for example, in the hypogeum of *S. Sebastian*).

The New Testament practice of the Agape shifted into the popular Hellenistic meal for the dead, a time when family and friends met to eat with the deceased. A meal was shared either on top of the tomb or through a tube. Many early Christians, especially in Rome, assimilated that meal by eating the Agape with their own dead. This was particularly true for special dead like the martyrs. Eventually the practice of a meal with the dead was forbidden (fifth century) and remnants of the practice became a part of what we now call the Roman Mass.

The Agape disappeared into a medieval synthesis between the Eucharist and the Agape. It first reappeared in the Left Wing of the Reformation, where among some groups common meals were assumed (for example, the Hutterites).[20] We know the Agape today as the potluck meal

---

[20]For example, Methodists first learned of the post-Reformation Agape in an encounter with the Moravians and Count Zinzendorf (1727) Frank Baker,

so common in congregational types (and assimilated in North America by many mainline groups). Some Free Church denominations have a formal Agape, called the Love Feast (for example, the Church of the Brethren) attached to the Eucharist.

2. *Eucharist/Communion.* While the fellowship meal may seem more prominent than the Eucharist in the early church, we should not be misled. The primary celebration of the church was indeed the remembrance (*anamnesis*) Eucharist that reenacted the death of Jesus.[21] While not explicit, in an early apologist, Justin Martyr, the Eucharistic ritual starts with the breaking of bread as in 1 Corinthians 11:

> Then we all rise together and pray, and, as we before said, when our prayer is ended, bread and wine and water are brought, and the president in like manner offers prayers and thanksgivings, according to his ability, and the people assent, saying Amen; and there is a distribution to each, and a participation of that over which thanks have been given, and to those who are absent a portion is sent by the deacons. And they who are well to do, and willing, give what each thinks fit; and what is collected is deposited with the president, who succors the orphans and widows and those who, through sickness or any other cause, are in want, and those who are in bonds and the strangers sojourning among us, and in a word takes care of all who are in need.
>
> (*Apologia* 67)

Strangely, the Eucharist never appears in early Christian art. One can only conclude that the Agape was the popular celebration while the *anamnesis* Eucharist was the official or traditional celebration. In the early medieval synthesis the death of Jesus was associated with the death of the martyr in such a way that the Eucharist picked up both the meal for the dead and the *anamnesis*.

The Reformation broke the unity of Agape and Eucharist. For Calvin it was a return to biblical authority. For Luther it was a rejection of anything not biblical. In either case the synthesis would not stand. The use of relics as the basis for the Agape (meal for the dead) was rejected. Still, especially among Anglicans and Lutherans, the remembrance Eucharist remained sacramental.

Methodism and the Love-Feast (London: Epworth Press, 1957).

[21]Nils A. Dahl, "*Anamnesis*: Memory and Commemoration in Early Christianity," in *Jesus in the Memory of the Early Church* (Minneapolis: Augsburg, 1976) 11-29.

While theological heirs of the Radical Reformation universally claim the separation of church and state created the needed ethos for the rise of the Free Church, perhaps the semiotic alteration of the Mass produced the same result. It took a priest, divinely ordained, to change the bread and wine into the body and blood of Christ. In those areas that became Protestant, priests could no longer administer the sacrament to people waiting to receive divine grace and power. The usefulness and power of priests disappeared. With it went the power of the ecclesiastical and political hierarchies. This opened the door for the Left Wing nonsacramental Agape and Eucharist.[22]

It did take the Free Churches to break completely with the medieval synthesis. Architecturally the communion table was so placed (away from the front wall) that it served more as a triclinium, a table for food, than a place where sacrifice was made. (Reformed churches made the same alteration.) The longitudinal nave gave way to a meeting room where the pulpit was central, and chairs, or pews, could be arranged to maximize the community. The term "real presence" was never mentioned. The bread was treated with respect, but not with liturgical care. The wine referenced more the Spirit than blood.

The breaking of the bread may be mentioned in terms of the crucifixion, but symbolically it was either breaking the bread with another person to establish the Body, or it was taking a piece from a whole loaf to signify participation in the community of faith. The wine (or grape juice) referenced the gift of the Spirit that accompanied the formation of the Jesus community.

3. *Worship setting.* Only the bread and the wine remain constant, though one may assume the New Testament words of institution will be said or repeated. Otherwise the variations for the taking of communion multiply in proportion to the number of congregations that exist. A few things can be observed.[23]

Music will introduce the communion time. Some examples of Free Church communion faith would be:

---

[22]See Christopher Elwood, *The Body Broken: The Calvinist Doctrine of the Eucharist and the Symbolization of Power in Sixteenth-Century France* (New York: Oxford University Press, 1999) 172.

[23]For other examples of the worship setting see Eller, *In Place of Sacraments*, 132-44.

For the bread which you have broken,
for the wine which you have poured,
for the words which you have spoken,
   now we give you thanks, O Lord.

By this promise that you love us,
By your gift of peace restored,
By your call to heav'n above us,
   hallow all [CH: consecrate] our lives, O Lord.

In your service, Lord, defend us,
In our hearts keep watch and ward,
In the world to which you send us,
   let your kingdom come [CH: will be done], O Lord
      (Louis Benson, *Methodist Hymnal*, 1964; CH #411; HWB #477)

Become to us the living Bread
by which the Christian life is fed,
renewed, and greatly comforted.
   Alleluia!

Become the never-failing wine,
the spring of joy that shall incline
our hearts to bear the cov'nant sign.
   Alleluia!
      (Miriam Drury, *The Worshipbook*, 1972; CH #423; HWB #475)

I come with joy to meet my Lord,
forgiven, loved, and free,
in awe and wonder to recall
his life laid down for me,
his life laid down for me.

I come with Christians far and near
to find, as all are fed,
the new community of love
in Christ's communion bread,
in Christ's communion bread.

As Christ breaks bread and bids us share,
each proud division ends.
The Love that made us, makes us one,

and strangers now are friends,
and strangers now are friends.
                    (Brian Wren, *The Hymnbook*, 1971; CH #420; HWB #459)

Following the musical preparation the communion begins with a text or series of texts related to the sharing of the bread and cup. An appropriate text would be the synoptic account of the Last Supper:

> While they were eating, he took a loaf of bread, and after blessing it he broke it, gave it to them, and said, "Take; this is my body." Then he took a cup, and after giving thanks he gave it to them, and all of them drank from it. He said to them, "This is my blood of the covenant, which is poured out for many. Truly I tell you, I will never again drink of the fruit of the vine until that day when I drink it new in the kingdom of God."
> (Mark 14:22-25)

> I therefore, the prisoner in the Lord, beg you to lead a life worthy of the calling to which you have been called, with all humility and gentleness, with patience, bearing with one another in love, making every effort to maintain the unity of the Spirit in the bond of peace. There is one body and one Spirit, just as you were called to the one hope of your calling, one Lord, one faith, one baptism, one God and Father of all, who is above all and through all and in all.   (Eph. 4:1-6)

Following the reading of texts, the congregation may join in the reading of a faith statement such as:

O God,
    your steadfast love has been ours for generations.
Through Christ, you brought us out of the abyss of death
    and into the light of eternal love.
With joy and thanksgiving, we proclaim our salvation,
    remembering Christ's death and resurrection,
        until he comes again.
As we break bread and share the cup together,
    may Christ be present with us,
    and may the Spirit bind us together
        as Christ's body in the world.

The pastor then prays that Christ will be present as the bread and wine are shared.

At this point the variations make a single description impossible. We will describe several possible formats:

a. *Communicants remain in the pew*. In a larger congregation it may be impractical to gather around the table. In that case the bread is passed on a plate. The bread will be either a piece of bread large enough to share or a piece of bread especially baked for breaking at communion. Obviously a communion wafer would be theologically inappropriate and functionally difficult to administer. Following the theological logic used for the breaking of bread, then the wine should be passed in a common cup so that all members share in the same Spirit. We do not know of any Free Church congregation that uses the common cup. Health concerns and the Prohibition era have overcome a long ritual tradition. So the wine is passed in a holder containing small glasses.

The leader or a deacon reads the traditional communion text:

> For I received from the Lord what I also handed on to you, that the Lord Jesus on the night when he was betrayed took a loaf of bread, and when he had given thanks, he broke it and said, "This is my body that is for you. Do this in remembrance of me." In the same way he took the cup also, after supper, saying, "This cup is the new covenant in my blood. Do this, as often as you drink it, in remembrance of me." For as often as you eat this bread and drink the cup, you proclaim the Lord's death until he comes. (1 Cor. 11:23-26)

The bread is passed on the plate. Every other person takes a piece. When all have been served, two persons break the piece of bread as they say in unison (using the Agape formula of 1 Cor. 10:16b): "The bread that we break, is it not a sharing in the body of Christ?"

Then the glasses of wine are passed. When all have been served, together they drink the cup as they repeat in unison (using the Agape formula of 1 Cor. 10:16a): "The cup of blessing that we bless, is it not a sharing in the blood of Christ?"

The leader ends with a prayer of thanksgiving, and the congregation sings a final hymn of joy.

b. *Communicants come to the table.* Instead of remaining in the pews, after the reading of the eucharist text, the congregation comes forward by twos. There is a plate with either a piece of bread or a loaf of bread. One of the two communicants takes the bread. Together, facing each other, the pair makes the declaration: "The bread that we break, is it not a sharing in the body of Christ?"

Instead of returning to the pews, everyone forms a circle. The deacons serve the glasses of wine. When all have been served they drink the cup as they repeat in unison: "The cup of blessing that we bless, is it not a sharing in the blood of Christ?"

As they remain standing the leader offers a prayer of thanksgiving and joy. While the glasses are collected the members sing a final hymn.

c. *Communicants break from a loaf.* Following the reading of the eucharistic text the members come forward one at a time. A loaf of bread is held by the leader. The communicant breaks a piece from the whole loaf and says: "We who are many are one body, for we all partake of the one bread."

Each member returns to the pew until all have taken a piece from the loaf. Then each one returns to the table and takes a drink of the wine. (The one cup would be preferable, of course.) Each says: "We who are many are one body, for we drink the cup of the Lord."

When all have partaken, the leader offers a prayer of thanksgiving and a hymn of joy is sung.

4. *Issues.* a. *Family.* The issue of child membership confounds not only the practice of baptism, but also communion. Unbaptized children are often present in the meeting room while communion is celebrated. The elements of communion, the bread and the cup, are not sacred in Free Church theology. They only take on special significance as the communicants break the bread together and share in the cup. After the service they are simply bread and juice. Still, many Free Church congregations are reluctant to allow children to share in the communion. They are also reluctant to make the children nonparticipants in the church family. There are three solutions.

(1) Prepare a parallel service for the children in another space. That solves the problem except the children really are excluded from the church family and they will never have observed a communion service until they are baptized.

(2) Treat the communion for adults as an Agape for the children. They are served food, like grapes and cookies, but not the bread and wine.

(3) Encourage the children to stay in the meeting room with friends and family, but do not offer them the bread and wine. They may feel left out, but they do gain a sense of this primary act of worship.

b. *Shut-ins.* Another problematic situation occurs with members of the community who are too ill to attend communion, members who are permanently isolated in their homes or in a nursing facility, or members who are incarcerated. Just as *Winkeltaufe* destroys the sense of a faith community so "taking communion" to those isolated denies the corporate meaning of the Eucharist. At the same time, the congregation cannot withhold from any member the opportunity to break the bread and share in the cup. There is only one possibility. Church members must be present to participate with the shut-in in the breaking of bread.

c. *Institutional Communion*. It is difficult to determine when the congregational type communion also can be a part of institutional worship. The communion, of course, is a celebration of community formation and community maintenance. There is no reason for communion where those actions are not needed. Communion belongs in the faith community. When it shifts to an institution then it has become a sacrament—an action to celebrate the presence of God among those persons present. Communion services in colleges, in hospitals, in denominational headquarters, and ecumenical meetings are now nearly universal. The only solution may not be acceptable, but it should be stated. Communion services should be held as the function of a local church where members of that church are invited. It would be preferable for the celebration to occur in the meetinghouse, but, since no place is holy, that would not be necessary.

5. *Foot washing*. In the account of the Last Supper (not the Passover) found in the Gospel of John, Jesus washes the feet of the disciples:

> Now before the festival of the Passover, Jesus knew that his hour had come to depart from this world and go to the Father. Having loved his own who were in the world, he loved them to the end. The devil had already put it into the heart of Judas son of Simon Iscariot to betray him. And during supper Jesus, knowing that the Father had given all things into his hands, and that he had come from God and was going to God, got up from the table, took off his outer robe, and tied a towel around himself. Then he poured water into a basin and began to wash the disciples' feet and to wipe them with the towel that was tied around him. He came to Simon Peter, who said to him, "Lord, are you going to wash my feet?" Jesus answered, "You do not know now what I am doing, but later you will understand." Peter said to him, "You will never wash my feet." Jesus answered, "Unless I wash you, you have no share with me." Simon Peter said to him, "Lord, not my feet only but also my hands and my head!"
>
> (John 13:1-9)

Although, at the time of Jesus, the host often had a servant wash the feet of a guest, a description of the custom occurs only here in the New Testament.[24] In the story of the woman who bathed the feet of Jesus with her tears, Jesus notes that the host Simon ought to have washed his feet with water (Luke 7:36-50). In the John story Jesus urged the disciples to

---

[24]J. C. Thomas, *Foot Washing in John 13 and the Johannine Community* (Sheffield UK: JSOT, 1991). He traces the practice through the sixth century (126-85).

continue to wash each other's feet (John 13:14-15). Despite this request by Jesus, apparently not all Jesus' followers continued to wash each other's feet as a part of worship. In 1 Timothy 5:9-10 we do learn that qualified widows were those who washed the feet of the saints. In the early Fathers an occasional mention of foot washing occurs as an act of humility, hospitality, or even sacrifice (that is, penance). For the most part the meaning of the John passage became an analogy for baptism. About the seventh century we can note the practice of foot washing as a part of the Maundy Thursday service.[25]

While we cannot fully discern the history of the foot washing practice, we do know that currently foot washing occurs on Maundy Thursday with most denominations. A few denominations make it a part of their worship at other times (for example, Seventh Day Adventists, and the Brethren churches).

Praxis. The participants will arrange themselves in whatever manner seems most convenient: around a table, in a circle, or in a separate room. Unless planned well in advance the women and men will meet in separate groups.

Opening prayer:

Come now, tender Spirit of our God,
    wash us and make us one body in Christ;
    that, as we are bound together
        in this gesture of love,
    we may no longer be in bondage
        to the principalities and powers
            that enslave creation,
    but may know your liberating peace
        such as the world cannot give. Amen.

Text: John 13:1-15

Washing feet: The designated starter puts on an apron/towel. The first one kneels and, in a washpan provided, washes the feet of the next person. The one washing dries the feet with the apron/towel. They both stand, hug each other (the Holy Kiss described in chapter 5), and say a blessing such as "Peace be with you!" Person number two does the same to person number three until all have been washed. Gradually another washpan is

[25]Everett Ferguson, "Foot Washing," *Encyclopedia of Early Christianity*, 433-35. Eller, *In Place of Sacraments*, 110-14.

passed with a bar of soap so that all can wash their hands. Then, at a signal from the leader, all return to their original place.

Singing: There are hymns that celebrate the washing of feet, such as Waddell's "Jesus took a towel":

> Jesus took a towel and he girded himself,
> then he washed my feet, yes, he washed my feet
>
> Jesus took a basin and he knelt himself down,
> and he washed, yes, he washed my feet.   (HWB #449)

For the most, however, the service calls more for familiar hymns that do not require printed words and music. Some such are: "Lord, I want to be a Christian," or "Guide my feet (while I run this race)."

Closing Prayer:

> Lord Jesus,
>   we have knelt before each other
>   as you once knelt before your disciples,
>   washing another's feet.
> We have done what words stammer to express.
> Accept this gesture of love as a pledge
>   of how we mean to live our lives,
> Bless us, as you promised,
>   with joy and perseverance in the way of the cross. Amen.

Weddings

Oddly enough, given the importance of family, there is almost nothing about weddings in the Bible. Jewish weddings at the time must have been fairly formal, elaborate, and frequent, but nothing, not even art, gives us a hint about the format of a wedding. The Wedding at Cana in John 2:1-11 mentions only the presence of guests, the function of a hired, non-Jewish caterer who didn't know the servants (v. 9), who chided the groom (v.10), and did not recognize the changing of water into wine:

> Jesus said to them, "Fill the jars with water." And they filled them up to the brim. He said to them, "Now draw some out, and take it to the chief steward [*caterer*]." So they took it. When the steward tasted the water that had become wine, and did not know where it came from (though the servants who had drawn the water knew), the steward called the bride-groom and said to him, "Everyone serves the good wine first, and then the inferior wine after the guests have become drunk. But you have kept the good wine until now."   (John 2:7-10)

Certainly the presence of the chief steward or Gentile caterer indicates a wedding of some magnitude. Yet among the guests invited the gospel writer mentions only the wife of a local carpenter, his son, and a ragtag group of the son's friends. The thirsty friends may well have caused the shortage of wine. The chief steward made his remarks about the wine to the bridegroom—a hint that the bride and the bride's family were subordinate to the planning of the groom. The wedding guests had already consumed considerable wine—they needed yet another 120 gallons (v. 6)! Such Jewish wedding parties must have been happy events. The caterer, who would have had considerable experience, was amazed that the groom saved the best wine for last—a time when the guests would have been too inebriated to know the difference. Early Christian art scenes of the Wedding at Cana show only Jesus with his wand, changing jars of water into wine.

Matthew has two parabolic accounts of a wedding. When the king threw a wedding party for his son, the invited guests failed to arrive. Preparations for the banquet had been lavish: oxen and fat calves were slaughtered for the wedding feast (Matthew 22:4). So the king sent his servants to bring in those not heretofore invited. For one man the unexpected invitation resulted in disaster:

> "But when the king came in to see the guests, he noticed a man there who was not wearing a wedding robe, and he said to him, 'Friend, how did you get in here without a wedding robe?' And he was speechless. Then the king said to the attendants, 'Bind him hand and foot, and throw him into the outer darkness, where there will be weeping and gnashing of teeth.' For many are called, but few are chosen."   (Matt. 22:11-14)

Even though he was man of the street, his failure to wear a wedding garment (a tuxedo!) caused him to be cast out!

Matthew's Parable of the Bridesmaids informs us that several young women would serve as attendants for a wedding.

> "Then the kingdom of heaven will be like this. Ten bridesmaids took their lamps and went to meet the bridegroom. Five of them were foolish, and five were wise. When the foolish took their lamps, they took no oil with them; but the wise took flasks of oil with their lamps. As the bridegroom was delayed, all of them became drowsy and slept. But at midnight there was a shout, 'Look! Here is the bridegroom! Come out to meet him.' Then all those bridesmaids got up and trimmed their lamps. The foolish said to the wise, 'Give us some of your oil, for our lamps are going out.' But the wise replied, 'No! there will not be enough for you and for us; you had better go to the dealers and buy some for yourselves.' And

while they went to buy it, the bridegroom came, and those who were ready
went with him into the wedding banquet; and the door was shut. Later the
other bridesmaids came also, saying, 'Lord, lord, open to us.' But he
replied, 'Truly I tell you, I do not know you.' "   (Matt.25:1-12)

Again, the size of the wedding party, ten young bridesmaids, indicates
a substantial celebration. Apparently the wedding was set for daylight
hours, so five of the young ladies (inappropriately called "foolish") took
enough oil for the scheduled evening hours. The five so-called "wise"
young ladies (cautious and uptight) took more oil than would be needed.
Without prior warning the bridegroom, in charge of the party, shifted the
hours.

Though we lack other details, we can see that a Jewish wedding at the
time of Jesus involved many guests of different class strata, celebrated with
a banquet consisting of rich meat and considerable wine, utilized many
young women in the wedding entourage, and was controlled by the bridegroom. Of course, these references are meant theologically, but presumably
they reflect a reasonable portrait of some Jewish weddings. We can assume
from these New Testament references that the first Christians entered the
Hellenistic world with a wedding tradition. At some point in time that
Jewish-based tradition was altered. Eventually the Christian wedding
became more Hellenistic than Jewish. The purpose of the Hellenistic-type
marriage involved more of a concern for reproduction and family lineage
than did the Hebraic covenant between man and woman.[26]

Actually the early Fathers said little about weddings.[27] Tertullian was
likely the first to mention the elements of a wedding ceremony (*Pud.* 4.4;
Coron. 13.14-14.2). The liturgy used came primarily from the Greco-
Roman world. It included a betrothal before the wedding itself. The
betrothal ceremony consisted of a kiss, the joining of hands, and the giving
of a ring. As for the wedding itself, Tertullian insisted that a Christian man
and woman be married in the presence of the faith community. He rejected
the wearing of a garland as pagan, and proposed a veil instead. Following
a blessing there may have been communion. Later Fathers advocated a
crown of flowers and then even a metal crown. Following the ceremony,

---

[26]Sarah M. Treggiari, *Roman Marriage: Justi Coniuges from the Time of
Cicero to the Time of Ulpian* (Oxford: Clarendon, 1991) 227-28.

[27]Kenneth Stevenson, *Nuptial Blessing: A Study of Christian Marriage Rites*
(New York: Oxford University Press, 1983) 13-32. Willy Rordorf, "Marriage in the
New Testament and in the Early Church," *Journal of Ecclesiastical History* 20
(1969): 193-210, esp. 209-10.

the wedding bed was decorated with flowers and blessed (a non-Christian fertility rite).[28]

1. *The meaning of marriage.* Apart from the wedding, with its many cultural intrusions, the impact of the Jewish/covenantal perception of marriage cannot be overestimated. Though no marriage ceremonies appear in the Hebrew Scriptures the marriage contract (Tobit 7:12-13) and the subsequent prayer of Tobias and Sarah (Tobit 8:4-8) reflect the covenant meaning of a Jewish marriage:

> Then Raguel summoned his daughter Sarah. When she came to him he took her by the hand and gave her to Tobias, saying, "Take her to be your wife in accordance with the law and decree written in the book of Moses. Take her and bring her safely to your father. And may the God of heaven prosper your journey with his peace." Then he called her mother and told her to bring writing material; and he wrote out a copy of a marriage contract, to the effect that he gave her to him as wife according to the decree of the law of Moses.   (Tob. 7:12-13)

> When the parents had gone out and shut the door of the room, Tobias got out of bed and said to Sarah, "Sister, get up, and let us pray and implore our Lord that he grant us mercy and safety." So she got up, and they began to pray and implore that they might be kept safe. Tobias began by saying,
> "Blessed are you, O God of our ancestors,
>   and blessed is your name in all generations forever.
> Let the heavens and the whole creation bless you forever.
> You made Adam, and for him you made his wife Eve
>   as a helper and support.
> From the two of them the human race has sprung.
> You said, 'It is not good that the man should be alone;
>   let us make a helper for him like himself.'
> I now am taking this kinswoman of mine,
>   not because of lust,
>   but with sincerity.
> Grant that she and I may find mercy
>   and that we may grow old together."
> And they both said, "Amen, Amen."   (Tob. 8:4-8)

The covenant (Judeo-Christian) union of a man and a woman results in two key elements.

---

[28]Paul F. Bradshaw, "Wedding," *Encyclopedia of Early Christianity*, 1176-77.

a. *The sexual union is ontological in nature.* It is not the companionship of two people but the formation of a single unit of identity. Matthew's Jesus quotes the Genesis passage as the reason there cannot be a divorce:

> Some Pharisees came to him, and to test him they asked, "Is it lawful for a man to divorce his wife for any cause?" He answered, "Have you not read that the one who made them at the beginning 'made them male and female,' and said, 'For this reason a man shall leave his father and mother and be joined to his wife, and the two shall become one flesh'? So they are no longer two, but one flesh. Therefore what God has joined together, let no one separate."　　　　　　　　　　　　　　　　　　(Matt. 19:3-6)

That is, the sexual union of a man and a woman has so created a mutual identity that separation is no more possible than saying a child doesn't have a parent. Paul says much the same thing in 1 Corinthians 7:

> For the wife does not have authority over her own body [identity], but the husband does; likewise the husband does not have authority over his own body [identity], but the wife does.　　　　　　　　　(1 Cor. 7:4)

b. *The marriage relationship is covenantal.* The characteristics of an ontological unity will be covenantal, not individualistic friendship (romance). The unity depends on mandatory involvement in life together: mutual care; financial support; family obligations; sexual relationship. Qualities of friendship, based on personal choice, rather than covenant, fail to encourage these values. Though the author of 1 Timothy refers to a church leader, his description reflects the covenantal quality of marriage relationship:

> Now a bishop must be above reproach, married only [at least?][29] once, temperate, sensible, respectable, hospitable, an apt teacher, not a drunkard, not violent but gentle, not quarrelsome, and not a lover of money. He must manage his own household well, keeping his children submissive and respectful in every way—for if someone does not know how to manage his own household, how can he take care of God's church?
>
> 　　　　　　　　　　　　　　　　　　(1 Tim. 3:2-5)

While two people in a marriage relationship may be (should be) good friends, friendship does not imply lifelong loyalty and unfailing support of each other. If only friendship defines a relationship between persons, society as we know it could not exist. Mutual obligation stands at the center of a society and the sense of mutual obligation starts with sexual or

---

[29]Note the attack on celibacy in 1 Tim. 4:3.

marriage unity. As seen, for example in 1 Timothy, the family sense of covenant marks the faith community. A major function of the faith community is to share that same sense of covenant with all of society.

Little wonder then that almost all denominations strongly protect the core family. It is not simply that the family is the anchor of the congregation and the community, but also because the ontological nature of the covenant relationships derives from the sexual union—the two becoming one flesh. From that relationship children are brought into the new faith family (1 Cor. 7:14). Others can be incorporated in the same way.

2. *Wedding planning*. Like communion, weddings in the Free Church take many forms. As we have seen, Christian wedding ceremonies borrowed heavily from the social matrix. That is still true today. So it would be foolhardy to describe a nonexistent pattern. Nevertheless some things are held in common.

a. *Marriage counseling*. A wedding would be unthinkable without prior discussion between the couple and the pastor. Such counseling would consist of several sessions in which the following would be considered: the meaning of the marriage covenant, plans for the ceremony, the role of the couple in congregational life, dealing with conflict, knowing compatibilities and incompatibilities, and recognizing their resource basis. This follows the covenantal assumption that marriage is more than romance. The couple must have the skills and resources to form a social unit. So premarital counseling could include personality testing (for example, Meyers-Briggs), as well as exercises in communication and reconciliation. Obviously one person cannot direct all of these sessions. A congregation will have contacts with persons who can.

Normally the pastor will help plan the wedding itself, but some larger churches will offer a committee to help the couple and to make arrangements. In the congregational-type church some issues can become complex. Hardly anyone would care to suppress the joy of a couple on their wedding day. Yet some traditions can violate the theology of a Free Church.

b. *Invitations*. However complex this issue may be for the bride and groom, the theological issue is straightforward. Like baptism and communion, the wedding is an event in the life of the community of faith. It should never be celebrated privately. While the families involved may invite whomever they wish, a blanket invitation must be offered to the congregation involved.

3. *Worship setting*. a. *The Procession*. The issue does not concern so much the number of participants (ten bridesmaids in the Jesus parable!), but a procession that moves the wedding party from the back to the front. The

woman and man should together approach the table, the pastor and witnesses. The Free Churches may not have an exemplary attitude toward
women, but they were among the first ecclesiastical groups to ordain
women and encourage their participation in church life. The medieval practice of transferring the woman from the father to the husband seems
demeaning to many. Furthermore, the practice bypasses the fact that a new
family is being incorporated into the faith family—not the transfer of a
woman from one family to another.[30] Consequently both bride and groom
should process together. Both sets of parents (or blood-family representatives) should stand and "give" the bride and groom to each other and the
assembled faith family.[31]

The congregation should be seated in such a way as to participate (by
gesture and approbation) in this approach to the table and in the reception
of the new family into the church.

b. *The vows*. If the pastor has a license from the state to join the two in
matrimony, the service need have no set format. At some time, however,
the two persons will make a vow to each other. Following that vow the
pastor will ask the congregation to pledge support and express love for this
new family.

c. *The service*. The community is seated in such a way that the
centrality of the table signals the new unity that is about to occur. Instrumental music begins the mood of worship. The congregation may sing an
appropriate hymn, such as Brian Wren's "When love is found" (1978):

> When love is found and hope comes home,
> > sing and be glad that two are one.
> When love explodes and fills the sky,
> > praise God and share our Maker's joy.   (CH #499; HWB #623)

---

[30]Even in the patriarchal Hebrew Scriptures there is no indication that a
daughter was given by her father to her husband. The problem of Leah being forced
on Jacob may be the closest example. It is clear though that the wife joined the
family of the husband. That is true in most cultures and often a dowry is required.
In the rather fascinating 1 Cor. 7:36-38 Paul tells a father that he should not pass his
daughter on to a husband, as was the custom, unless she so wished.

[31]There is no Free Church solution to the vexing problem of family name.
Logically the bride would not take on the family name of the groom. Though an
acceptable procedure, it creates social and legal problems that could obviate the
values gained.

Following the music the couple enters the meeting room, perhaps from different directions. There is no tradition regarding the number and relationship of those accompanying the two. As they stand before the pastor and the table, the pastor asks: "Do the families bless this marriage?" Both sets of parents respond: "We, the parents of N_____ and N_____ bless this marriage and deliver them into the hands of their new family at N_____ Church."

The pastor announces the purpose of this moment and then reads the text or texts chosen by the bride and groom. Some favorites are Song of Solomon 8:6-7 and/or 1 Corinthians 13.

Following a prayer of commitment, the pastor helps the couple make vows to each other. There is no standard form in the Free Church, but after the vows the pastor will lead the congregation in the following communal vow.

Pastor: As the community of faith for this couple, will you now pledge
          to support them with your prayers and actions?
Congregation:
          N_____ and N_____, we are thankful for God's love and
          grace that brings you together. We are witnesses to the vows you
          have made to each other, and we commit ourselves to help you
          fulfill your vows. We pledge to you our prayers, our counsel, and
          our continued care. May God also grant us strength as we strive
          to be faithful to each other and to Christ, our Lord.

The couple is presented to the congregation and, as a final hymn is sung, leave as husband and wife. The couple will be congratulated and received as a new family unit at the reception/meal. Since a meal in itself creates the community, no special format for the wedding Agape will be necessary.

d. *The wedding Agape*. The Agape meal maintains the sense of congregational community and serves to form and renew it. New members are welcomed through the Agape. So are new families. The newly married couple will have an Agape. It is so traditional one can hardly imagine a wedding without a reception/meal. At this point, decisions are difficult. Obviously the faith community should offer an Agape meal/reception for the new couple, their family, and their friends. The couple was married in the faith community and that community should incorporate them into its faith family. The planning committee or the deacons would orchestrate that occasion. Yet, many couples would not want it that way. Many would prefer to plan their own reception/meal at a local restaurant or hall.

While this decision may seem inconsequential, it is not. The decision to have the meal/reception outside the church context makes the faith family subordinate to the blood family. It follows the medieval, feudal perception that a marriage unites two families in a new blood relationship. And while political marriages may be a thing of the past, beneficial marriages or friendship marriages are not. Or, put another way, a new covenant can best be formed where covenant relationships are the basis for a faith family.

Needless to say there may be compromises. The faith family may participate in the outside meal/reception or the two families, now joined, may participate in the church Agape.

4. *Postscript.* Most people, including members of Free Churches, will have never participated in a wedding as just described. Some of us have, but not enough to claim we have described a developing tradition. It would be better to say we have described a theological desideratum. The wedding procedure is simply too rooted in tradition and too loaded with cultural complexities to make the Free Church ideal a reality. We will try to work with some of those complexities.

a. *Man and woman.* The material here assumes the ontological necessity of the union between woman and man. Some Christians would not accept that. Some would say that celibacy is a higher calling and a more godlike reality. They would refer to Jesus and Paul[32] as examples. The Free Church would deny that. Many of us are certain that Paul was married and even suspect also Jesus was.[33] We could argue they must have been married. Otherwise their sense of reality would be skewed. Such a theological assumption wreaks havoc on the single people in our society. Despite the assumption of marriage as normative, in no way does the Free Church discourage singles from participation in congregational life. Indeed, most denominations have special fellowship programs for older single adults. If the sense of reality depends on a covenant relationship, then the single person must not be excluded from such covenants. A group of

---

[32]Graydon F. Snyder, "The Tobspruch in the New Testament," *New Testament Studies* 23 (1976): 117-20; idem, *First Corinthians: A Faith Community Commentary* (Macon GA: Mercer University Press, 1992) 95, 132.

[33]William E. Phipps, *Was Jesus Married? The Distortion of Sexuality in the Christian Tradition* (New York: Harper & Row, 1970) 61-70. On the apocryphal relationship of Mary Magdalene with Jesus see Karen King, *The Gospel of Mary of Magdala: Jesus and the First Woman Apostle* (Santa Rosa CA: Polebridge Press, 2003) and Ann Brock, *Mary Magdalene, the First Apostle* (Cambridge MA: Harvard University Press, 2003) 89-104.

persons composed solely of single people cannot completely fill that void. The church family, based as it is on the covenant relationship, will offer to the single persons covenant relationships (not simply friendship). The single person can experience wider family loyalties, raising children, male and female dynamics, borrowing and lending—everything that goes with covenant except the sexual bond itself.

While, in regard to female participation, the Free Churches were likely in front of the mainline churches, this has not always been the case with homosexuality. The homosexual population probably spreads equally among American denominations. But given their congregational nature, the Free Churches likely include more publicly "open and affirming" churches than the mainline churches. In such faith communities the role of the celibate homosexual who is not in a covenant relationship would be same as any other celibate single person. A formal homosexual union creates another issue. Free Churches are family oriented. A homosexual bond would seem to undermine the traditional expectation of a nuclear family, so some Free Church congregations may be more negative toward such unions than are more liturgically oriented denominations.

The Left Wing of the Reformation shifted authority from hierarchy or liturgy to the Bible. So most Free Church opponents of homosexual unions use the Bible as the authoritative basis for their position. The argument from the Bible doesn't convince everyone. For those who believe sexuality was created only for the purpose of reproduction, a case can be made against homosexual unions but, of course, homosexual men and women can adopt and lesbians can conceive by artificial insemination. For those who believe that sexuality was created to form covenant relationships, as the Free Church does, then homosexual bonding seems less of a problem. Since the Free Churches do stress covenant bonding, it should be no surprise that homosexual bonding will, in some cases, be acceptable. The double nature of sexuality, that is, reproduction and covenant, has caused considerable consternation in many Free Church congregations.

b. *Blood families*. Theologically the key moment of the wedding is the transfer of the bride and groom from their respective blood families to their new faith family. While not directly connected with a wedding, the shift from birth family to faith community lies at the heart of the Jesus movement. When asked about his mother, brothers, and sisters, Jesus gestured to his disciples and said that these were now his brothers and sister (Mark 3:31-35). The identity of the blood family with the faith family did not occur until the latter part of the third century. The Anabaptist movement reinstated the original perception. Baptism made the young adult independent of the birth family. The wedding brings the new family, independent of blood families, into a faith company of brothers and sisters, perhaps even mothers and fathers.

While this may be theologically appropriate, in many instances it cannot happen as we have described it. In modern America a young couple would be fortunate if each had two parents at their wedding. Of course, if at least one birth or adoptive parent is present the transfer can occur. But if, because of separation, divorce, death, lack of living parents, there is no one to "give away" the bride and groom, then careful thought must be given to the procedure. A church member acting in loco parentis will not do. Some relative or childhood friend, representing the blood family, must act as a surrogate.

Healing

Healing is deeply imbedded in the Jesus tradition. The narrative found in Mark 1:21–3:6 recounts Jesus healing a woman with a fever, a paralytic, a leper, and a man with a withered hand, and casting out an unclean spirit. In later chapters he makes a blind man to see and a deaf man to hear and cures an epileptic boy. The early church was a healing community. Some claim that this ministry of healing, and of caring, made the church grow as rapidly as it did.[34] In any case, early Christian art often shows Jesus, with wand in hand, healing the paralytic, the deaf, the blind, and the leprous, and even raising from the dead.[35] After Constantine, the Christian church amplified its ministry of healing by the construction of hospitals in major cities throughout Europe. It remains true today.

Healing is not unique to Free Church. There is no Christian denomination that doesn't practice a healing ministry in some form or another. However, because of the congregational nature of the Free Churches there is a significant theology of healing and therefore a particular practice.

First, some terms should be defined. For the most part the Christian community engages in healing *illnesses*. *Diseases* (organic abnormalities) and accidents are medical matters that fall outside the pale of spiritual healing. For the most part what we call *illnesses* lie in the eye of the beholder.[36]

---

[34]For example, Rodney Stark, *The Rise of Christianity* (San Francisco: HarperSanFrancisco,1997) 73-94.

[35]Jensen, *Early Christian Art*, 32-34, 122-23.

[36]Dominic Crossan, *The Historical Jesus: The Life of a Mediterranean Jewish Peasant* (New York: HarperSanFrancisco, 1991) 336-37. Allan Young, "The Anthropologies of Illness and Sickness," *Annual Review of Anthropology* 11 (1982):

Since the social matrix, the beholders, normally determines illness and
health, the definition of an illness differs from culture to culture. For
example, we consider epilepsy a serious mental problem, while in the
Roman culture it could be considered a divine gift (for example, Nero). So
healing may be as much a social redefinition as it is some change in the ill
person.

In religious societies illness often is associated with sin. In such a case
sin is defined as disobedience. Patients do often want to know what they
did to deserve their medical problem. Unfortunately (from our perspective)
the Hebrew Scriptures consistently identify illness with sin, though good
health is a gift of God, not a reward for good behavior.[37] In the Jesus tradition that identification of illness with sin occurs only once (Mark 2:1-12).[38]

> Then some people came, bringing to him a paralyzed man, carried by four
> of them. And when they could not bring him to Jesus because of the
> crowd, they removed the roof above him; and after having dug through it,
> they let down the mat on which the paralytic lay. When Jesus saw their
> faith, he said to the paralytic, "Son, your sins are forgiven." Now some of
> the scribes were sitting there, questioning in their hearts, "Why does this
> fellow speak in this way? It is blasphemy! Who can forgive sins but God
> alone?" At once Jesus perceived in his spirit that they were discussing
> these questions among themselves; and he said to them, "Why do you raise
> such questions in your hearts? Which is easier, to say to the paralytic,
> 'Your sins are forgiven,' or to say, 'Stand up and take your mat and walk'?
> But so that you may know that the Son of Man has authority on earth to
> forgive sins"—he said to the paralytic—"I say to you, stand up, take your
> mat and go to your home." And he stood up, and immediately took the mat
> and went out before all of them; so that they were all amazed and glorified
> God, saying, "We have never seen anything like this!"
>
>   (Mark 2:3-12)

257-85.

[37]Graydon F. Snyder, *Inculturation of the Jesus Tradition: The Impact of Jesus
on Jewish and Roman Cultures* (Harrisburg PA: Trinity Press International, 1999)
189-201. Hector Avalos, *Illness and Health Care in the Ancient Near East* (Atlanta:
Scholars Press, 1995) 409.

[38]Biblical scholars recognize that Mark often inserts one story into another. In
the case of the paralytic, the forgiveness narrative (vv. 5b-10) has been inserted into
the healing narrative. In that case there is no healing narrative in the Jesus tradition
connected with forgiveness of sin.

For the most part the Jesus tradition connects healing with community functions like preaching, teaching, or serving.[39] Healing opened the boundaries of community to include persons as spirit-gifted who were otherwise rejected.[40] For Paul healing itself is one such gift of the Spirit in the life of the faith community:

> Now you are the body of Christ and individually members of it. And God has appointed in the church first apostles, second prophets, third teachers; then deeds of power, then *gifts of healing*, forms of assistance, forms of leadership, various kinds of tongues.   (1 Cor. 12:27-28; italics added)

According to the apocryphal Acts healing was a major element in evangelism (though often on a competitive note), and likewise early Christian art through the fourth century witnesses to the importance of healing.[41] The victory of Augustinian views of sin over the Pelagian sense of goodness eventually reattached illness directly to sin. So in the medieval synthesis confession and penance brought about healing. The sixteenth-century Hutterites broke the sin connection by insisting that illness was contagious, and caused by poor diet and carelessness.[42]

After the Reformation forgiveness rather than penance began to play a key role in healing. Rather than do penance it would be appropriate for the ill person to pray for divine forgiveness. It would be also appropriate for the church to pray for God to have mercy and make the ill person whole once more.

Actually, that is not the Free Church understanding of forgiveness and healing. God's forgiveness comes through the community of faith. The person who is ill will want to find acceptance by the community that acts as the instrument of God's grace. It is not strictly a matter of forgiveness of

---

[39]Helge Kjaer Nielsen, *Heilung und Verkündigung: Das Verständnis der Heilung und ihres Verhältnisses zur Verkündigung bei Jesus und in der ältesten Kirche* (Leiden: Brill, 1987) 120-24.

[40]Donald Senior "Understanding the Gospel Healing Stories," audio tape (Cincinnati: St. Anthony Messenger Press, 2001); Donald Senior and Carroll Stuhlmueller, *Biblical Foundations for Mission*, 149-51.

[41]Ramsey MacMullen, *Christianizing the Roman Empire (A.D. 100–400)* (New Haven CT: Yale University Press, 1984) 25-30.

[42]The Catholic hierarchy severely persecuted the so-called heretical Hutterites, but secretly visited very successful Hutterian physicians. See *The Chronicle of the Hutterian Brethren*, vol. 1 (Rifton NY: Plough Publishing House, 1987) 487-88.

sin as we traditionally speak of it. The ill person will be made whole when
he or she becomes one with the community. The ill person seeks to adjust
to a medical situation and the community seeks to adjust to her or his new
health condition. The result may mean personal restoration to health or it
may mean corporate adjustment. For example, a person going blind may
ask for the service of healing. The service of healing may indeed improve
confidence in eyesight. More likely it will mean the faith community will
accept the new situation and find ways to encourage and assist an impaired
friend. The disease of blindness may remain, but the illness has been
healed. The person going blind will feel God's grace through the adjustment made by the community of faith. Nevertheless, forgiveness for sin can
play an important role in personal healing, as we shall see in our discussion
of the James text.

Exorcism presents another problem. Many of the healings found in the
New Testament actually culminated in the casting out of unclean or evil
spirits:

> Jesus departed with his disciples to the sea, and a great multitude from
> Galilee followed him; hearing all that he was doing, they came to him in
> great numbers from Judea, Jerusalem, Idumea, beyond the Jordan, and the
> region around Tyre and Sidon. He told his disciples to have a boat ready
> for him because of the crowd, so that they would not crush him; for he had
> cured many, so that all who had diseases pressed upon him to touch him.
> Whenever the unclean spirits saw him, they fell down before him and
> shouted, "You are the Son of God!" But he sternly ordered them not to
> make him known.   (Mark 3:7-12)

The liturgy of demon exorcism continued through the medieval period.
Assuming demon possession reflected personality disorders, exorcism
became unnecessary for the Reformers. After the Renaissance such
phenomena had rational explanations, which eventually spawned psycho-
logical cures. Western rationalism has made it very difficult for us to
understand the casting out of demons. Recently, modern studies in the
social setting of the Gospels have made it possible, though difficult, for us
to approach New Testament healings and exorcisms without the prejudice
of a Western mind.[43] Despite the general loss of healing liturgies that deal

---

[43]Stevan L. Davies, *Jesus the Healer: Possession, Trance, and the Origins of
Christianity* (New York: Continuum, 1995) 22-42; John Pilch, *Healing in the New
Testament: Insights from Medical and Mediterranean Anthroplogy* (Minneapolis:
Fortress Press, 2000) 13-16.

with demon possession, the Free Church healing service deals with the total person and the whole community. The prayer for healing and the laying on of hands transform illnesses into something useful and functional. That transformation includes making unclean spirits clean.

There are two forms of the healing service: public and private.

1. *Worship setting for public healing.* The simplest service of healing is a congregational prayer. During prayer time the ill person may ask for prayer. In the pastoral prayer the pastor includes the one who asked. Other members of the congregation may be invited to offer additional prayers.

If the member requests a healing service, then a more formal arrangement can be made. Public healing can and should be a part of the regular worship. At the designated moment the person requesting the healing will come before the table. As this occurs the congregation will sing a hymn.

a. *Congregational singing.* A favorite is the African-American spiritual, "(There is a) balm in Gilead":

> There is a balm in Gilead
> to make the wounded whole,
> There is a balm in Gilead
> to heal the sinsick soul.   (CH #501; HWB #627)

Another hymn would be "At evening, when the sun had set":

> At evening when the sun had set,
> the sick, O Lord, around you lay.
> In what distress and pain they met,
> but in what joy they went away!
>
> Once more the Healer comes, and we,
> oppressed with various ills, draw near.
> And though your form we cannot see,
> we know and feel that you are here.
>
> Your touch has still its ancient pow'r;
> no word from you can fruitless fall.
> Meet with us in this sacred hour
> and in your mercy heal us all.   (HWB #628)

b. *Scripture.* This may be read by the leader or read in unison. If oil is used, then Psalm 23 could be read:

> Even though I walk through the darkest valley,
> I fear no evil;
> for you are with me;

> your rod and your staff—
>   they comfort me.
> You prepare a table before me
>   in the presence of my enemies;
> you anoint my head with oil;
>   my cup overflows.

And from the New Testament Mark 6:6b-13:

> Then he went about among the villages teaching. He called the twelve
> and began to send them out two by two, and gave them authority over the
> unclean spirits. He ordered them to take nothing for their journey except
> a staff; no bread, no bag, no money in their belts; but to wear sandals and
> not to put on two tunics. He said to them, "Wherever you enter a house,
> stay there until you leave the place. If any place will not welcome you and
> they refuse to hear you, as you leave, shake off the dust that is on your feet
> as a testimony against them." So they went out and proclaimed that all
> should repent. They cast out many demons, and anointed with oil many
> who were sick and cured them.   (Mark 6:6b-13)

If oil is not used, the two healing stories would be appropriate, but
others, like Mark 3:7-10, cited above, might be read, or Acts 3:1-10:

> One day Peter and John were going up to the temple at the hour of
> prayer, at three o'clock in the afternoon. And a man lame from birth was
> being carried in. People would lay him daily at the gate of the temple
> called the Beautiful Gate so that he could ask for alms from those entering
> the temple. When he saw Peter and John about to go into the temple, he
> asked them for alms. Peter looked intently at him, as did John, and said,
> "Look at us." And he fixed his attention on them, expecting to receive
> something from them. But Peter said, "I have no silver or gold, but what
> I have I give you; in the name of Jesus Christ of Nazareth, stand up and
> walk." And he took him by the right hand and raised him up; and immedi-
> ately his feet and ankles were made strong. Jumping up, he stood and
> began to walk, and he entered the temple with them, walking and leaping
> and praising God. All the people saw him walking and praising God, and
> they recognized him as the one who used to sit and ask for alms at the
> Beautiful Gate of the temple; and they were filled with wonder and amaze-
> ment at what had happened to him.   (Acts 3:1-10)

c. *Laying on of hands*. The pastor places a few drops of oil in his right
palm and places it, along with the other hand, on the head of the person to
be healed. Or the pastor simply places both hands on the person's head. At
that point deacons, and/or people significantly concerned, come forward

and place hands on the ill person (obviously that means hands on the shoulders of persons who have direct contact).

The pastor and others then pray for healing:

N_____, you are anointed for repentance, recognizing that all of us have known and contributed to brokenness.

N_____, you are anointed for faith, that your trust in God's love and power may be confirmed and strengthened.

N_____, you are anointed for healing, that you may be restored to the wholeness of being that God wills for all of us.

or

O God,
We come to you at this moment because you love us.
You know us more deeply than we know ourselves.
You desire wholeness for each of your children,
    broken though we are in body, mind, and spirit.
As we come before you,
    we pray for healing in each of our lives.
Restore N_____ according to your will
    through the One who suffered and conquered for us,
        even Jesus Christ. Amen.

After the prayer for healing all return to their seats.

2. *Worship setting for private healing.* At times the act of healing does involve sin, alienation from the community of faith and even from the world at large. General confession in a public situation is not enough to deal with the guilt and pain. Though reconciliation sometimes may be a public matter (Matthew 18:15-20), confession of sin usually ought not be. Confession of sin normally occurs with a pastor or trusted leader. The pastor cannot forgive sin, neither privately nor publicly. The pastor cannot say, "I absolve you of your sins." Actually the pastor cannot say, "Your sins are absolved." The pastor does not speak for God. So in the Free Church, absolution is impossible except as it comes from God through the congregation. When there is an illness that may have been caused by rather severe alienation, then a private healing will be necessary. Some Free Churches follow a rather informal service while some follow rather closely the description of healing in James:

Are any among you suffering? They should pray. Are any cheerful? They should sing songs of praise. Are any among you sick? They should call for the elders of the church and have them pray over them, anointing them with oil in the name of the Lord. The prayer of faith will save the sick, and the Lord will raise them up; and anyone who has committed sins will be forgiven. Therefore confess your sins to one another, and pray for one another, so that you may be healed. The prayer of the righteous is powerful and effective.   (James 5:13-16)

The pastor meets with the ill person in some private place, such as home, hospital room or the church study. The reason for the anointing can vary: illness, preparation for surgery, family crisis, or even serious conflict. Impending death is not a cause for anointing. Some member or members of the faith community (deacons) will accompany the pastor.

a. *Explanation.* The pastor explains that this service will be an opportunity for the ill person to make a confession regarding sin, alienation, severe tension, or conflict. The confession will be kept private.[44]

Scripture:

Out of the depths I cry to you, O LORD.
    Lord, hear my voice!
Let your ears be attentive
    to the voice of my supplications!
If you, O LORD, should mark iniquities,
    Lord, who could stand?
But there is forgiveness with you,
    so that you may be revered.
I wait for the LORD, my soul waits,
    and in his word I hope;
my soul waits for the Lord
    more than those who watch for the morning,
more than those who watch for the morning.   (Psalm 130:1-6)

The thought of my affliction and my homelessness
    is wormwood and gall!
My soul continually thinks of it
    and is bowed down within me.
But this I call to mind,
    and therefore I have hope:
The steadfast love of the LORD never ceases,
    his mercies never come to an end;
they are new every morning;
    great is your faithfulness.

------

[44]If absolute privacy is needed, the person to be anointed might write a confession on a piece of paper. The pastor then shreds the paper and notes the confession has been made.

"The LORD is my portion," says my soul,
    "therefore I will hope in him."   (Lamentations 3:19-24)

Truly I tell you, whatever you bind on earth will be bound in heaven, and whatever you loose on earth will be loosed in heaven. Again, truly I tell you, if two of you agree on earth about anything you ask, it will be done for you by my Father in heaven. For where two or three are gathered in my name, I am there among them.   (Matthew 18:18-20)

Are any among you suffering? They should pray. Are any cheerful? They should sing songs of praise. Are any among you sick? They should call for the elders of the church and have them pray over them, anointing them with oil in the name of the Lord. The prayer of faith will save the sick, and the Lord will raise them up; and anyone who has committed sins will be forgiven. Therefore confess your sins to one another, and pray for one another, so that you may be healed. The prayer of the righteous is powerful and effective.   (James 5:13-16)

b. *Anointing*. The leader places a few drops of oil in the right palm and places that on the head of the supplicant. The accompanying persons then likewise place hands on the ill person.

c. *Prayer*. Led by the pastor they all pray for forgiveness and healing. An example would be as follows.

N_____, you are anointed as an act of simple obedience, as we come together before God and one another, claiming the promise that wherever two or three gather in Christ's name, Christ is there in their midst with health-giving power.

N_____, you are anointed as an act of penitence, as we confess before God and one another that we all together need the forgiveness and the wholeness made possible by Christ's forgiving spirit.

N_____, you are anointed as an act of petition, as we ask before God and one another that we be renewed in that hope which holds firm even in the midst of suffering and pain, and in that love that binds us to each other with cords of compassion.

d. *Closing*. The pastor and accompanying persons leave after appropriate handshakes, hugs, or the kiss of peace.

Gifts of the Spirit

The gift of the Spirit has many implications in biblical and religious history. In Hebrew Scriptures the Spirit could create charismatic groups seized with prophetic frenzy who possessed special insight (1 Samuel 10:9-13). The Spirit can be the source of the prophetic word (Micah 3:8).

Without the Spirit the words of seers, diviners, priests, and false prophets are futile (Micah 3:5-12). In the New Testament there are also several functions of Spirit. For John the Spirit will lead us into all truth (John 16:13). For the author of Acts, the Spirit guides the nascent faith community in its worldwide mission (Acts 1:8). For Paul again and again the Spirit creates a functional community:

> Now there are varieties of gifts, but the same Spirit; and there are varieties of services, but the same Lord; and there are varieties of activities, but it is the same God who activates all of them in everyone. To each is given the manifestation of the Spirit for the common good.
>
> (1 Cor. 12:4-7)

According to Paul, at least, the function of the Spirit is to guide the members of the body into those roles necessary for the faith community to function. Given his list of functions and his use of the human body analogy, we can assume the majority of these gifts relate to the interior administration of the nascent faith community. Some assume the appointment of apostles, prophets, and teachers signals the gift of translocal functions as well as local.[45] Translocal persons are not directly responsible to any local community (1 Corinthians 9:1-2; *Didache* 11:3). Local administrators like overseers and helpers occur in all the Pauline churches, chosen from the congregation (Phil. 1:1), but there is no head of the body (Christ) until the later or secondary Pauline letters (Eph. 1:22-23).

The early church certainly had a variety of offices, and there were designated leaders. Administrative leadership reflected both the Jewish and the Hellenistic background. Elders were natural Jewish leaders who made corporate decisions because of their age, wisdom, and family position (Ruth 4:4, 7-12). According to the Synoptics the elders often oppose Jesus (Mark 14:53), and Luke is aware that the Jews at the time of Jesus were led by an "assembly/council of elders" (Greek *presbyterion*, "presbytery," that is, the Sanhedrin; Luke 22:66). On the other hand, bishops or overseers must have derived more from the city administration of the Hellenistic world. The developing power of such a bishop first appears about 112 CE in the writings of an exceptional leader, Ignatius of Antioch. Ignatius notwithstanding, congregations chose their own bishops in the first centuries (*1 Clement* 44). Eventually the elders or presbyters elected the bishop from their own ranks (Cyprian, *Ep.* 55.8). One ought not read this development

---

[45] Adolf von Harnack, *The Mission and Expansion of Christianity*, trans. James Moffatt (New York: Harper, 1962) 319-68.

as simply the intrusion of Hellenistic administrative practices.[46] Any organization the size of the fourth-century church would need authoritative leaders.

Given the need for recognized leaders, the gift of the Spirit eventually became an ordination procedure. The ceremony still consisted of prayer and laying on of hands, but the blessing of the hands conveyed a Spirit that created a sacramental change in the individual. It made the priest different from the common people (Gregory of Nyssa, *Bapt. Chr.*). For Augustine the ordination ceremony impressed an indelible character on the candidate's soul (*De bapt: c. Donat.* 1.1.2). Once so ordained, a minister or priest could move from congregation to congregation. Ordination, along with baptism and the eucharist, had become a sacrament.

While we know about the gifts of the Spirit from biblical literature, very little reference to church roles appears in the archaeological remains. While one can discern class levels in tomb inscriptions (by names or types of burials), neither social level (slave, freedperson, free, noble) nor leadership function occurs. We can discern martyrs by the third century, but not until 231 CE do bishops of Rome receive mention in burial vaults. Otherwise there is no designation for prophet, teacher, deacon, healer, or other functions. Architecturally speaking, the first church buildings show no place for a leader to preside.

So the early church was quite democratic: no names of leaders, no special place for leaders to sit or stand, no art that reflects the formation of leadership. (Of course apostles and eventually martyrs appear.) As we have seen, there were people with special functions, such as teachers, healers, and deacons. Local leadership must have consisted of overseers, servants, and elders (1 Timothy).[47] There is no description of ordination in the New Testament.[48] Addressing the younger Timothy, the author of 1 Timothy says the gift of ministry came to him through prophecy (Spirit?) and was confirmed by the laying on of hands (by the elders: 1 Tim. 4:14).[49] The

---

[46] As does Edwin Hatch, *The Organization of the Early Christian Churches* (London: Longmans, Green, and Co., 1892) 20-23.

[47] Richard Hanson, *Christian Priesthood Examined* (Guildford and London: Lutterworth Press, 1979) 34-35.

[48] Fisher Humphreys, "Ordination in the Church," in *The People of God*, 288-98.

[49] R. Alastair Campbell, *The Elder: Seniority within Earliest Christianity* (Edinburgh: T.&T. Clark, 1994). Elders were not themselves ordained (140), but, as in Jewish practice, were heads of households (246).

laying on of hands occurs several times in the New Testament. For the most part it refers to blessing (Mark 10:13-16) or to healing (Mark 6:5). Persons commissioned for tasks also received the laying on of hands from the faith community (Acts 6:6; 9:17; 13:3). There is no indication of special divine authority.

While the Left Wing of the Reformation took a return to biblical community quite seriously, the real issue in the sixteenth century was political. Forerunners of the Free Church broke radically with the idea of a state church. For the first time since 300 CE the Christian church rejected any relationship with the state and rejected state control of the church. As a result the practice of infant baptism, and the payment of a church tax ceased. A second political upheaval occurred with the rejection of the ecclesiastical offices—the power of the hierarchy (bishops and cardinals) and the creedal/intellectual authority of the magisterium (priests, ministers, and teachers). The effect of this rejection was enormous and impacts us even until today. The resulting formula for authority was the well-known phrase "priesthood of all believers." To implement the leadership of the laity, the Bible was translated and published in the vernacular. Laity then became biblically literate. As the laity read or heard the Bible in the context of the faith community, they could interpret the text as it applied to them. That break with the hierarchy and magisterium (ordained leaders and learned teachers) exists to this time and must be considered a major contribution of the Free Church to Christianity around the world.

The rejection of church authority created another critical situation—not often mentioned as such. The lack of ordained leaders left the church without designated persons who had the right to speak for God. Consequently the sacraments in the medieval sense were no longer available. No Free Church minister could lay hands on a child/person and assure salvation. No Free Church minister could bless the bread and wine to transform it into the body and blood of Christ. No Free Church minister could conclude the prayer of confession with a proclamation of absolution. No Free Church minister could lift his or her hands and bless the congregation. No Free Church minister could offer assurance of eternal life to a dying person. No Free Church bishop could permanently change a person through ordination. Free Church ministers were chosen by the congregation, not ordained by God. Ordination/installation were no longer sacraments. The Free Church today celebrates only two primary rituals: baptism and communion.[50]

---

[50]The Catholic church has seven sacraments: baptism, confirmation, eucharist,

So beginning with the Radical Reformation the faith community recognized leadership roles as gifts of the Spirit. There was no ordination of special leaders who in any way became professional, lifelong administrators and teachers. Various members of the congregation assumed the tasks of administration and what we call pastoral care. They exercised their spiritual gifts of teaching, healing, calling on the sick, evangelizing, and interpreting the biblical text. For Free Church faith communities, the pastor was one among many called by the Spirit. The theology here is clear and the application of that theology should be congruent. No ordination of special persons, and no creation of persons ontologically different from the people of the congregation. Everyone has a calling. To be a follower of Jesus is a vocation in itself. In fact, baptism is ordination because by baptism one enters into the priesthood of all believers (1 Peter 2:9).[51]

Worship setting for installation. Celebrating the Gifts of the Spirit will normally occur at some time prior to the beginning of a new educational year. Volunteers will be asked to come forward. That would include teachers, board members, commission members, ushers, greeters, and administrators—all volunteers with a specific role to fulfill. As they come forward, the congregation will sing a commission hymn like "There are many gifts":

> Now one has the gift of wisdom,
> another the calling to speak,
> one the ability to comfort,
> another the calling to teach.

> A body has many members,
> yet all work in unity.
> The church is the body of Christ,
> his arms, ears and eyes, hands and feet.

> Not all are called to be prophets,
> and not all are called to preach,
> but all should aim for the best gifts
> and love is the greatest of these.

---

penance, marriage, ordination, and extreme unction; Protestants, only two: baptism and communion. See, e.g., the discussion by Rob L. Staples, *Outward Sign and Inward Grace: The Place of Sacraments in Wesleyan Spirituality* (Kansas City MO: Beacon Hill Press, 1991) 85-97.

[51]Dale Brown, "Brethren" in Baptism and Church: A Believers' Church Vision, ed. Merle Strege (Grand Rapids MI: Sagamore, 1986) 29-37.

Chorus: There are many gifts, but the same Spirit.
There are many works, but the same God,
And the Spirit gives as it chooses.
Praise the Lord. Praise God.
(Patricia Shelly [1976]; HWB #304)

After the volunteers have assembled, the congregation will commit them with the blessing of the Spirit. Appropriate members will come forward and lay hands on the volunteers in a way commensurate with the numbers involved. Laying on of hands, as in baptism, passes on the divine blessing for a specific calling in the faith community. The congregation will then call on the Spirit to bless them:

In company with your faithful people in every age,
We have called out those with gifts for your service, O God.
Fill them with the love of Christ
and the power of the Spirit
as they carry out the church's ministry.

Following the blessing the pastor or leader will close with a prayer of affirmation. Insofar as possible the congregation then greets those just commissioned.

Ordination. According to the theology of spiritual gifts, the local pastor should be one of those commissioned at the gifts ceremony. In the history of the Free Church that has been true from time to time, but for the most part commissioning the pastor has now become impossible. Almost all Free Churches call a pastor already ordained.[52] That pastor was trained apart from the congregation and was ordained by an extracongregational ordaining body. For the most part that ordination transfers from congregation to congregation. There is a fair likelihood that the local congregation, about which we are writing, will never see an ordination service. Even if it does, while the person ordained might be a member of that congregation, the ordained would serve a congregation elsewhere. There are exceptions. Some independent churches may call a pastor and ordain her or him. It would be rare, however.

Some crises do threaten the Free Church: the encroachment of Fundamentalism; the desire to have the state make religious decisions; the

---

[52]Marjorie Warkentin, *Ordination: A Biblical-Historical View* (Grand Rapids: Eerdmans, 1982) 62-63. In the early church, officers were commissioned leaders who guided the church for the end-time (29-37). After Constantine leaders were ordained for the church as directors of a permanent institution (51).

personal salvation movement; and many others. Perhaps none seems more critical than ordination. Moveable ordination may take away the possibility for the congregation to follow the lead of the Holy Spirit. Having an ordained pastor independent of the congregation potentially sets up once more a leader who can correctly interpret the Bible, can make critical decisions, indeed, can act as the very magistrates who were overthrown by the Radical Reformation.

While ordaining or installing a pastor for each local church may be the ideal, but unlikely, situation for the Free Church, the current practice of choosing from a pool of nationally or state ordained "qualified" clergy, still leaves room for the movement of the Spirit. A search committee that truly represents the local church family, and is willing to work and pray together for as long as it takes, can allow for the Spirit to move in its midst as it seeks out and choose a person called to be the pastor.

Death and dying

In most cultures of the world there is no more important community function than the funeral. Needless to say, that is equally true for Free Church types. There is, of course, grief for the person no longer present. More importantly, though, the reconstruction of the family and community takes place at that time. If a church mother has died, the faith community will need to restructure itself, for example, in such a way that another person visits the sick or presides at church dinners. If the father of a family has died, one offspring will need to carry out the will of the father, help to keep the family members in contact with each other, and organize family reunions. These things often happen at the funeral itself, so everyone involved normally attends.

Theology of death and resurrection. Other than the death of Jesus, there are no descriptions of a burial in the New Testament. In the Hebrew Scriptures there are several, though none more elaborate than the death of Jacob (Israel) in Genesis 48–50:

> When Joseph saw that his father laid his right hand on the head of Ephraim, it displeased him; so he took his father's hand, to remove it from Ephraim's head to Manasseh's head. Joseph said to his father, "Not so, my father! Since this one is the firstborn, put your right hand on his head." But his father refused, and said, "I know, my son, I know; he also shall become a people, and he also shall be great. Nevertheless his younger brother shall be greater than he, and his offspring shall become a multitude of nations." So he blessed them that day, saying,
> "By you Israel will invoke blessings, saying,

'God make you like Ephraim and like Manasseh.' "
So he put Ephraim ahead of Manasseh. . . .

So Joseph went up to bury his father. With him went up all the servants of Pharaoh, the elders of his household, and all the elders of the land
of Egypt, as well as all the household of Joseph, his brothers, and his
father's household. Only their children, their flocks, and their herds were
left in the land of Goshen. Both chariots and charioteers went up with him.
It was a very great company. When they came to the threshing floor of
Atad, which is beyond the Jordan, they held there a very great and sorrow-
ful lamentation; and he observed a time of mourning for his father seven
days.   (Gen. 48:17-20; 50:7-10)

The family gathers at the deathbed; a final testament is made; blessings
are given; a new leader is indicated. The burial itself lasted several days
with public mourning, grief, and a massive entourage to the gravesite. Of
course, Jacob's burial was exceptional, but the narrative indicates generally
what would normally occur. Most burials of the ancient world would differ
only as a matter of length of time and number of participants.

The Jews considered death the end of life. No afterlife was anticipated.
In a deep sense the high moral nature of Judaism resulted from that
perception—this life is all there is. The satisfactory nature of that life lived
depends on a high quality of covenant relationship with God and the Jewish
community. Consequently Jews describe life in terms of obedience to the
will of God as expressed in the laws of the covenant. Without such
covenant satisfaction death would be understood cynically: "Eat, drink, and
be merry, for tomorrow we die."

Despite the limitation of life to present time, the Jews did not believe
a person ceased to exist at death. This is a critical philosophical problem.
Hellenistic thinkers could think of nonbeing (see 1 Cor. 1:28); Jews could
not. Hellenistic thinkers thought in terms of individuals; Jews did not.
Individuals could cease to exist; collectivities could not. So communal
persons could not leave their corporate existence even though they were no
longer historically present. Jews spoke of such a continued existence in
Sheol.

If I ascend to heaven, you are there;
    if I make my bed in Sheol, you are there.   (Psa. 139:8)

It is surprising then that Judaism did not embrace a theology of resurrection. Only the apocalyptic Daniel indicates what would eventually come to
be the Christian teaching:

"At that time Michael, the great prince, the protector of your people, shall arise. There shall be a time of anguish, such as has never occurred since nations first came into existence. But at that time your people shall be delivered, everyone who is found written in the book. Many of those who sleep in the dust of the earth shall awake, some to everlasting life, and some to shame and everlasting contempt. Those who are wise shall shine like the brightness of the sky, and those who lead many to righteousness, like the stars forever and ever. . . . "   (Dan. 12:1-3)

In Christian teaching deceased persons are restored to their prior corporate existence. It was called "resurrection from among the dead ones" (for example, 1 Cor. 15:12-13 *anastasis nekron*). The resurrection of Jesus formed the primary Christian community, the (resurrected) Body of Christ (Romans 12:5). Resurrection of the person occurs when the community of faith brings back the deceased to the Body.

Significant changes occurred when Christian belief in resurrection as restoration of the community entered the Greco-Roman world. Different anthropologies saw the resurrection in different ways. More Platonic types did not understand persons as collectives. Indeed they did not see the essence of humanity in the body (either individual or corporate) but in the psyche. In the biblical world psyche referred to the life of a person:

He called the crowd with his disciples, and said to them, "If any want to become my followers, let them deny themselves and take up their cross and follow me. For those who want to save their life [*psuchēn*] will lose it, and those who lose their life [*psuchēn*] for my sake, and for the sake of the gospel, will save it. For what will it profit them to gain the whole world and forfeit their life [*psuchēn*]? Indeed, what can they give in return for their life [*psuchēs*]?"   (Mark 8:34-37)

Platonists, as in Orphic and Pythagorean circles, thought of the psyche as the spiritual essence of what it is to be human (see Plato's *Phaedo* 107D-114). It has been translated in English as "soul" or even "self." That eternal psyche or essence could not die. Under the influence of Platonists, then, Christian belief in the resurrection was shifted to immortality.[53] After death the soul would go to heaven (ultimate reality) or hell (final nonreality).

---

[53]Rightly Oscar Cullmann, *Immortality of the Soul or Resurrection of the Dead?* (New York: Macmillan, 1964) 60. However, for Cullmann there is an interim wait until the end-time (48-57). "Body" does not mean for him a return to corporate existence (38-39).

On the other hand, Aristotelian types, like the Epicureans, did not believe in a human essence. Death was the end. Even the Stoics, so influential in early Christianity, rejected the Platonic view of the soul. While not many early Christians would have rejected the resurrection, the more materially minded Aristotelian position probably forced a more literal view. Consequently the bodily resurrection was seen as an end-time resurrection of the flesh instead of a resurrection from among the dead ones.

Influenced by these powerful voices, the early Fathers were not of one mind. Because of these conflicting perspectives we are at a loss to define an early Christian doctrine of resurrection. Even to this day the resurrection will often be understood inappropriately either as immortality of the soul or the restoration of a physical body.

Burial traditions. Despite the Hellenistic impact on the doctrine of the resurrection, another powerful force was at work. Perhaps more than any other aspect of church life, death and burial customs adapt to cultural expectations. That was true of the early church. While early writers wrestled with immortality and physical resurrection, the faith community went in quite a different direction. In Greco-Roman culture, as well as many others, it was assumed the deceased was in some way still present. Romans not only buried their dead but also later met with them on the anniversary of their death. Consequently most graves were constructed in such a way that family and friends could eat with the deceased—even feed them. By the end of the second century Christians were doing the same thing. In the *Martyrdom of Polycarp* we find the first mention of such a celebration (155 CE). By the beginning of the third century we find in the catacombs of Rome both art and inscriptions that refer to the meal with the dead. Underneath the present floor of St. Sebastian's in Rome can be found a large number of graffiti that indicate, as they ate the meal, how the family felt about the deceased and for what and to whom they prayed (Peter and Paul).[54]

Despite Plato and Aristotle, a Christian burial consisted of the entombment, a marker with inscriptions, a final salutation ("Live!"), a meal with the departed, and a prayer for peace ("Rest in peace"). It was assumed the family would return in a year for a remembrance meal. Generally speaking the Christian funeral has followed that line rather than immortality or end-time resurrection of the flesh.

---

[54]Snyder, *Ante Pacem*, 180-88, 251-58.

1. *Worship setting.* Trying to categorize and describe Free Church funerals would be a lost cause. Because they are Free Churches, and because funerals are highly cultural in nature, each congregation has its own practice. Denominational books of worship describe several appropriate funerals, but none will prescribe procedures. There are no rules. Still some important observations can be made.

Given the customs and laws of North America, it would be difficult to avoid the use of an undertaker and the process of embalming. It is generally assumed that the body can be seen at a funeral home during the time of the wake or visitation. Whether at a funeral home or a church, the viewing of the body has been critically important. Friends and relatives need to acknowledge that the deceased no longer lives, yet still is a presence among them. The casket will be open at the funeral home and often will be open at the church service. Lack of a body as in prior cremation, or an ocean accident, makes the reconstruction of the community much more difficult. It leaves the perception that the person is somewhere else.[55]

2. *The funeral.* Funeral services are not normally lengthy or complex. The community meets to express grief and hope. Following an opening prayer the leader will often recite a number of biblical texts reflecting the mood of the moment: for example, Psalm 23; Psalm 121; John 11:17-44; John 14; 1 Corinthians 15. The congregation then will sing a number of well-known hymns, perhaps including the favorite of the deceased. Some oft-used hymns would be "For all the saints"; "If death my friend and me divide"; "Precious Lord (take my hand)."

Statements about the loved one need to be articulated. In the Free Church that is a puzzle. Sometimes a family member makes a statement. Sometimes anyone can speak. Especially in some African-American churches, a designated spokesperson reads greetings from family and friends. The pastor might deliver a eulogy along with a short meditation. There is no set pattern. The leader does need to be aware that, given freedom of expression, a maze of emotions can break forth: words of guilt, anger, grief, love, despair, humor. During the sharing the "resurrection" begins to occur. Few, if any, negative statements are made. Statements of appreciation, even humorous stories, invade the grieving situation. With that shift in the tenor of the service, the congregation joins in hymns of hope: "Lift every voice and sing," "Guide me, O thou Great Jehovah,"

---

[55]Since the resurrection is a communal experience, after the funeral, cremation, or donation of the body to science would be quite acceptable.

"Easter people, raise your voices," or "Love divine, all loves excelling" would be good examples.

Following a prayer of thanksgiving for the deceased, directors close the casket and designated pallbearers carry it to the waiting hearse. Family and friends go to the cemetery for a short burial service.

3. *The repast (Agape)*. During the burial period a group of church members prepare for the repast. As indicated above, the church of the first century ate together a meal called the Agape (Love Feast) or the Lord's Supper. Often this meal in common was connected with the communion (bread and cup), but not always. By the end of the second century the Agape had folded into the Hellenistic meal for the dead. About the fifth century the Agape and the meal with the dead were dissociated (Augustine, *Faustum* 20.20). It is impossible to say when church meals returned. The Anabaptists had rather formal meals together. Later the Baptists became famous for potlucks.

In any case, today the funeral will be followed by a potluck or repast. It must be. While few would consider these repasts "meals for the dead" they do have many characteristics of that ancient celebration. The deceased has a presence at the meal. The meal consists of food furnished by the faith community as a gift to the deceased and a sacrifice to God. Stories are told that recall the joy and happy memories of the one who has died. There is laughter and happiness. Resurrection occurs. Sins are forgotten or disappear. Enemies forgive and are forgiven. There is a new life in the community. Bread is broken together. There is enough food for everyone and for others who might be in need or cannot be present. As they sit at tables together the family reorganizes itself. Perhaps even the faith community will do the same. We call it resurrection.

In the earliest church the repast was repeated in the presence of the deceased. Most Christians in America tend to set aside one day for such a memorial. The annual memorial should be an Agape meal where the deceased are mentioned and their resurrection acknowledged.

Chapter 5

Order of Worship in the Free Church Tradition

The time of worship creates the congregation and celebrates the divine presence among the people. The style of worship differs from Sunday to Sunday. Of course, there are prayers, hymns, music, the reading of biblical texts, a sermon, greetings, intercessions, and offering. While all of these elements can be found in the Free Church worship, there is no set order. Free Church-type denominations do not use a book of worship or worship manual. In fact, we know of no congregational-type denomination that furnishes a "worship book" for congregants. Most do offer worship aids for the pastor. Prayers and readings can be found in the back of most hymnals.[1]

The entire service of worship is designed, of course, to bring people from their individualism into a transcendent community of faith. Certain elements in particular, however, create community. People are greeted as they enter the place of worship. Sometimes the congregants greet each other. Preferably they would all greet each other, but failing that they would greet those closest to them. Most congregational-type churches do what is often called "sharing of joys and concerns." Whatever direction that might take, and it varies considerably, it enables the members to share with church family what is important to them. Prayers call on the divine presence in the life of the congregation and the world in which the congregation participates.

Preaching cannot be done in an emotional vacuum. To hear the "Word of truth rightly divided" (classical mainline church) the congregation needs to be in a sober, reasonable mood. To interact with the text (Free Church) the congregation must be inspired, even joyful. During the service the worship leader may use the order, the announcements, and the directions in such a way that the congregation senses a mood of excitement and anticipa-

---

[1]The subtitle of *Hymnal. A Worship Book* (HWB), of the Church of the Brethren, the General Conference Mennonite Church, the Mennonite Church in North America, and other "Anabaptists and Pietists," would seem to belie our contention regarding "no worship book" in Free Churches. However, HWB is not a worship *manual*, but—as the main title says—a *hymnal* to which have been added certain worship resources—prayers and readings. The UCC has a Book of Worship but its use is optional and it is a leadership resource.

tion. This is not usually difficult, however, because the people generally arrive with the expectation that good things will happen and that they will find themselves in some way in the divine presence and the bosom of the faith community.

The faith progression of public worship

There are two key words in Greek for "worship." They are *diakonia* which would translate more as "ministry" and *leitourgia* which can be indeed translated as "worship." Both have a root meaning of *service* in the "helping" sense of the word. The term "liturgy" means simply a work or a service. So we call the Sunday morning event a *Dienst* or a Service. The rubric is very appropriate for the Free Church. The presentation of the text to an inspired congregation will result in action.

When the pastor chooses a theme, a text, and a worship service, it is assumed there will be a resultant action. It may be simply that some parishioners decide to make a donation for Church World Service, or that a number of the congregation will protest violent toys. An action is assumed. It is a *Dienst*. The ultimate goal of worship is service to God and God's reign.

The order of service has altered through the ages. In the Hebrew Scriptures, Isaiah 6 has often been cited as a model for the proper order of worship:

> In the year that King Uzziah died, I saw the Lord sitting on a throne, high and lofty; and the hem of his robe filled the temple. Seraphs were in attendance above him; each had six wings: with two they covered their faces, and with two they covered their feet, and with two they flew. And one called to another and said:
> "Holy, holy, holy is the LORD of hosts;
>   the whole earth is full of his glory."
> The pivots on the thresholds shook at the voices of those who called, and the house filled with smoke. And I said: "Woe is me! I am lost, for I am a man of unclean lips, and I live among a people of unclean lips; yet my eyes have seen the King, the LORD of hosts!"
> Then one of the seraphs flew to me, holding a live coal that had been taken from the altar with a pair of tongs. The seraph touched my mouth with it and said: "Now that this has touched your lips, your guilt has departed and your sin is blotted out." Then I heard the voice of the Lord saying, "Whom shall I send, and who will go for us?" And I said, "Here am I; send me!"   (Isa. 6:1-8)

The components of Isaiah's experience are indeed classic: Vision, Praise, Confession, Forgiveness, and Sending.

Vision. The community of worshippers gathers in the presence of God. That presence might be found in a temple (as in Isaiah 6), in a tent (as in the Tabernacle or Tent of Meeting, Exodus 26; 33:7-11), or in open spaces (Exodus 19:16-17). In the Hebrew Scriptures that place normally would be a known "sacred place," though not necessarily (Joshua 3:1-6). The first Christians came into the presence of God in homes (Colossians 4:15), though edifices were not really necessary:

> The God who made the world and everything in it, he who is Lord of heaven and earth, does not live in shrines made by human hands, nor is he served by human hands, as though he needed anything, since he himself gives to all mortals life and breath and all things.
>
> (Acts 17:24-25)

Vision—that is, awareness of the presence of God—is absolutely essential for life. Without a sense of transcendence, there can be no sense of being human. Vision may derive from either oral interpretation or visual perception. Revelation of the vision comes through those who speak for God. Without vision we grope in darkness:

> Therefore it shall be night to you, without vision,
>   and darkness to you, without revelation.
> The sun shall go down upon the prophets,
>   and the day shall be black over them.   (Micah 3:6)

Worship starts with Vision. Free Church buildings offer little in the way of mystery and inspiration. The front of the meeting place offers no image of a king or a president, no mosaic or statue of Jesus, and certainly no symbol of the Virgin Mary. Awareness of the presence of God comes more from greeting the gathering congregation, and in knowing others are gathering who wish to "see Jesus." As members of the congregation enter the meeting room, they greet each other with a handshake, a hug, or even a kiss. They become aware of the kind of peace and happiness that would occur if the reign of God were to be realized. For a period of time they experience that end-time—what is often called "the now and the not yet"— a moment of Vision.

Praise. In response to the Vision the people offer praises to God. It could hardly be otherwise. The song of the Seraphim and those congregated (Isaiah 6:3) called out the total otherness of the Vision. *Qodesh, qodesh, qodesh*, translated into Greek, *Hagios, hagios, hagios*, does not refer to any divine quality, as the words "Holy, holy, holy" might appear to the English reader. To be *holy* is to be separate, as Yahweh says in Hosea 11:9:

I am God and no mortal,
the Holy One in your midst.

One perception of Jesus is that he is the "Holy One" in the presence of the people (Mark 1:24). When the first Christians spent time in praise they were recognizing the otherness of God as seen in Jesus (Acts 2:47). Praise of God often followed a healing (Acts 3:8-9), though more often it occurred in worship (1 Peter 1:7), even as singing (James 5:13).

Given the liturgy and architecture of Free Churches, praise does not occur so much as awe or mystery, as it does thanksgiving. The congregation expresses thanks that the Lord (God?) has brought them together once more. Praise comes as congregational awareness. Or some may praise God for waking them up and bringing them to church (this is a standard formula). Members offer praise to God both by words and music. In recent years many Free Church types (especially independent churches) start their worship with praise teams that lead the congregation in songs of adulation.

Confession. Isaiah confessed he was a man of unclean lips. Having seen the Vision and having acknowledged the presence of God (Praise), the worshipper(s) must feel inadequate and unworthy. Isaiah confessed he and his people possessed unclean lips, that is, their lives were not congruent with their words. In the New Testament the vision of divine action could also engender confession of inadequacy. Peter's shock at the miraculous catch of fish would be a good example (Luke 5:1-11). More often confession accompanied repentance or conversion. The authors of Mark and Matthew were aware that repentance (Mark 1:15) began with confession that led to forgiveness (Mark 1:4-5; Matthew 3:2-6). The strange Ephesians, who had believed in magic, confessed, burned their books, and were converted (Acts 19:18-19). Even more than conversion, confession marks the restoration of a relationship lost. The classic Parable of the Prodigal Son depends on a change of heart and a confession of the son to his father (Luke 15:18-21; see also James 5:16). Acknowledging Christ as the one who restores comes after a confession like that of the prodigal son ("I have sinned against heaven and before you"), so confession of faith in Jesus as Lord or Christ became a central part of worship. As for confession of inadequacy or sin, as a part of the worship it was in place by the time of Tertullian (*Paenit.* 9). Often confession was public because, following apostasy, it involved reinstatement into the congregation. By the fifth century confession became a private matter.

The Reformation dropped the requirement of private confession. There are several reasons. A major antagonism between Luther and the Roman

Catholic church was the practice of penance. A confessor-priest assigned penance privately. The Reformation rejected the entire process. More to the point, in the Radical Reformation, as we have seen, original sin was rejected. Sin first developed as the child became an adult. Even then sin referred more to alienation or inadequacy than peccadillos or "naughty deeds."

The diminution of sin had a profound affect on Western Christianity. What had been theological/sin-causation shifted to natural/sociological-causation. Sin no longer played the role in human existence that it did in medieval Catholicism. Though the Left Wing might not have known it, it became, and remained, Pelagian rather than Augustinian.[2] Consequently, confession as a liturgical element lapsed. That is not to say that Free Church members are "less sinful." Nevertheless, sin is not handled by private, or public, or liturgical confession. That fact presents a nearly insoluble faith problem. Free Church types have only a minimal opportunity for confession in a communal setting. Leaders responsible for worship apparently understand this. Consequently many of the hymns in this tradition reference confession.

The very popular "Amazing grace" speaks of wretchedness, being lost and blind. "Just as I am, without one plea" confesses chaos, conflicts, and struggles and then speaks of the forgiveness God offers through grace. Even Whittier's sweet hymn poem, "Dear Lord and Father of mankind," confesses striving, strain, stress, and heat of desire. Most of the confession hymns are "I"-oriented though there are occasional community confessionals such as the Whittier hymn just mentioned. Some very popular hymns do stress the first-person plural. Charles Wesley's "Love divine, all loves excelling," refers to our "troubled breast" and "love of sinning." Given the lack of liturgical confession in the Free Church, such hymns may be a necessary component for meaningful worship.

Corporate confession is yet another matter. The Free Church does lack the liturgical moments for even the most obvious sins:

We have not loved our neighbors as ourselves.
We have not done justly,
    nor loved mercy,
        nor walked humbly with our God.

---

[2]Snyder, *Irish Jesus, Roman Jesus*, 216-27.

All Christians should join in such corporate confessions. At this point the Free Church fear of repeatable liturgy does harm to the faith life of the congregation.

Confession for institutional sins raises yet another problem. Can the Free Church confess the sins of the state, or the church at large? The Radical Reformation rejected responsibility for the state as well as state church. While Free Church Christians certainly differ regarding institutional responsibility, nevertheless separation of church and state still plays a powerful role in American life. Surely every congregation recognizes national complicity in wars, in colonialization, in economic abuse of other countries. Yet it is difficult for Free Church congregations to confess:

> "*We* did that,"
> "*We* caused the war in Iraq,"
> "*We* caused the demise of South American coffee growers."

The first-person plural tends to shift to a third-person plural. Likewise, when a mainline church makes an unpopular decision such as the closing of schools or hospitals, the Free Church types find it difficult to confess to corporate ecclesiastical sin: "We caused the closing of that inner-city Catholic school."

On the other hand, nonalignment has theological advantages. Congregationalists could pray for both the Vietnamese and the Americans. Congregationalists can pray for both the Catholic church and the children who lost their parents' chosen way of education. In that sense the Free Church types don't belong to either side, but can confess the sin of both.

Forgiveness. In the Isaiah passage one of the Seraphim touches the lips of Isaiah with a coal and takes away his guilt. Communion with God lies at the heart of the Judeo-Christian faith. Communion could not be possible without a sense of divine forgiveness and acceptance. So reflections on the mercy (*chesed*) of God abound in the Hebrew Bible, often with very moving poetic expression:

> Seek the LORD while he may be found,
>   call upon him while he is near;
> let the wicked forsake their way,
> and the unrighteous their thoughts;
> let them return to the LORD,
>   that he may have mercy on them,
> and to our God,
>   for he will abundantly pardon.   (Isa. 55:6-7)

or

> Have mercy on me, O God,
>> according to your steadfast love;
> according to your abundant mercy
>> blot out my transgressions.
> Wash me thoroughly from my iniquity,
>> and cleanse me from my sin. (Psa. 51:1-2)

The New Testament reflections on forgiveness may not be as moving as those in the Hebrew Scriptures, but the centrality cannot be overstated. Paul could proclaim to all that God through Christ had forgiven them:

> Let it be known to you therefore, my brothers, that through this man for-giveness of sins is proclaimed to you; by this Jesus everyone who believes is set free from all those sins from which you could not be freed by the law of Moses. (Acts 13:38-39)

Forgiving or reconciling was the primary function of the Christ event:

> So if anyone is in Christ, there is a new creation: everything old has passed away; see, everything has become new! All this is from God, who recon-ciled us to himself through Christ, and has given us the ministry of recon-ciliation; that is, in Christ God was reconciling the world to himself, not counting their trespasses against them, and entrusting the message of reconciliation to us. So we are ambassadors for Christ, since God is making his appeal through us; we entreat you on behalf of Christ, be reconciled to God. (2 Cor. 5:17-20)

As in the 2 Corinthians passage, often we can forgive each other because we have been forgiven:

> Put away from you all bitterness and wrath and anger and wrangling and slander, together with all malice, and be kind to one another, tender-hearted, forgiving one another, as God in Christ has forgiven you. (Eph. 4:31-32)

There is a strong quid pro quo in the New Testament, especially in the Jesus tradition. Despite the strong Lutheran sense of *sola gratia* (Romans 1:16-17), the best-known statements on forgiveness tie divine forgiveness to human forgiveness. For example the Lord's prayer:

> And forgive us our debts,
>> as we also have forgiven our debtors. (Matt. 6:12)

In fact, according to the Parable of the Unforgiving Servant, if we do not forgive others we will receive divine punishment:

> And in anger his lord handed him over to be tortured until he would pay his entire debt. So my heavenly Father will also do to every one of you, if you do not forgive your brother or sister from your heart.
>
> (Matt. 18:34-35)

Very few, if any, would disconnect divine forgiveness from human/community forgiveness. The issue is one of primacy. Do we only know the grace of God as, or after, we have known forgiveness toward others? Or did God in Christ on the cross grant forgiveness to us all regardless of our response? Later discussions of forgiveness and grace do not particularly elucidate the primacy issue. Most of the church Fathers dealt more with grace and human nature than mutual forgiveness. Again, the debate between Pelagius and Augustine sets the stage for the Reformation. Pelagius believed the grace of God created in us the possibility of living according to God's will. Augustine believed the Fall made us sinful from birth, so only through grace could we become free.

As we have indicated, the Free Church has no choice. It must embrace Pelagianism. There is no meaning to adult baptism unless it is a free-will choice. The young adult, raised with a God-given free will, chooses to follow Jesus and to join with those who have made the same decision. Repentance, confession, baptism, and community acceptance are all one indivisible act. One would expect and will find in the Free Churches a deep sense of the quid pro quo found in the words of Jesus: "Forgive us our sins as we have forgiven those who sin against us." While personal repentance and thanks for divine forgiveness run deep in Free Church worship, so does the sense of mutual forgiveness. In the words attributed to St. Francis of Assisi:

> Lord, make me an instrument of your peace. . . .
> For it is in giving that we receive;
>   it is in pardoning that we are pardoned;
>   it is in dying that we are born to eternal life.

When one believes it is necessary to make peace with your brother or sister before you come before God (Matthew 5:21-24), then human forgiveness has almost become a precondition for divine forgiveness. There is more, however. The person coming to the altar performs a prior action. A sacrifice has been made.

Sacrifice is inherent (?) in the human psyche. In order to restore relationships something must be done, something must be given. Of course,
especially in the later New Testament writings, the death of Jesus was considered the primary sacrifice (Ephesians 5:2; Hebrews 9:11-14; 1 John 2:2).
However, there are many other types of sacrifice: worship itself (Hebrews
13:15); financial support (Philippians 4:18); and above all self- (corporate)
sacrifice (Romans 12:1-3).

Among the early Fathers the sacrificial death of Jesus remained central,
so that eventually his sacrifice was reenacted in the Eucharist. Many other
forms of sacrifice were practiced: worship, giving, sharing with the poor,
personal purity, and self-sacrifice. The most radical self-sacrifice was that
of the martyrs. Their days of martyrdom eventually composed a calendar
of celebrations associated with the place of their martyrdom or their personal remains. After Constantine these celebrations coalesced with the celebration of Christ's death. The Roman mass then was reenacted over the
relics of the martyrs.

There was yet another form of self-sacrifice—penance. Instead of
sacrificing to God, the religious actor may take on a discipline to compen-
sate for sin. Such a discipline might occur as a part of repentance and conversion, but more likely as a means of restoring fellowship with the faith
community. Members who sinned after baptism were considered outcasts,
even in the New Testament material (1 Cor. 5:3-6; Matt. 18:15-20). For
some there was no way to return (Heb. 6:4-6). For others forgiveness was
possible (James 5:15-16; Matt. 18:21-22). Official opportunity to be reinstated or accepted has often been found in *Hermas* 32 (second century), but
Hermas probably only refers to the expectation that sin should not occur
after conversion—yet, in fact, it indeed does.[3] Following *Hermas*, the early
Fathers (third century) generally approved of some form of repentance.
Tertullian spoke of *paenitentiam* as a form of satisfaction (*Paenit.* 5-6). By
the time of Gregory the Great (d. 604), the Christian who sinned could do
exercises of contrition, at first somewhat public, but later a private matter
between member and priest.

These issues are critical. The Reformation broke with the medieval
sense of sacrifice and the medieval practice of penance. Luther, with his
insistence on *sola gratia* could not possibly have tolerated a system that
allowed mercy and forgiveness to be earned. Penance disappeared. Equally

---

[3]Carolyn Osiek, *Shepherd of Hermas* (Minneapolis: Fortress Press, 1999) 28-
30, 114-15; Graydon F. Snyder, *Shepherd of Hermas* (Camden NJ: Nelson, 1969)
69-71.

unacceptable was to reenact the death of Christ in the Eucharist in conjunction with the death of the martyrs (over the relics). The sacrifice of the mass also disappeared. Yet no church could exist without some method of restoration for those who had broken faith in some form or another. The Free Church has handled the issue primarily with disciplines derived from conflict resolution.

Sending. As a result of his experience with the call of God, Isaiah offered to be sent. Every narrative of a call results in sending, of course. Abram was called to leave his country and his father's house in order to form the nation of Israel (Gen. 12:1-2). The word of the Lord came to Jeremiah in order to make him a prophet to the nations (Jer. 1:1-5). After the terrifying vision of the wheel and the creatures, Ezekiel was called to be a prophet to the people of Israel (Ezek. 2:3). The Vision of the divine results in a sending. When Jesus encountered Peter, Andrew, James, and John, they were called to "fish for people" (Mark 1:17). Likewise Saul (Paul) responded to the vision of Jesus by becoming the apostle to the Gentiles (Acts 9:15). To be sure, not everyone who saw Jesus responded, though the author of the Gospel of John could not quite understand why (John 14:9). According to early descriptions of worship (Col. 3:16-17 and Eph. 5:19-20) there is a standard admonition for behavior appropriate to a Christian. Worship will climax in action.

A key mark of the Free Church is that it makes decisions on the basis of the text. To be "Free" means that there is no state or religious authority that determines what action will be taken. There is no assigned minister, no required lectionary, no required order of worship, no required congregational organization, and no required actions to take. To be sure many of these elements may be standard, but none are required. Decisions are made by the congregation at a church council or, perhaps, a church board.

A composite order of worship

While the Christian order of worship follows the standard outline seen in Isaiah 6, over time additions and alterations occurred. As we have seen, Luther kept the medieval heritage except that he rejected the sacrificial mass. According to Lutheran liturgical books, the order of worship in the sixteenth century appeared thus:

Singing
Prayer
Sermon
Admonition
Communion

Singing
Postcommunion prayer
Benediction

As we have noted, Calvinists tended to reject the medieval heritage and return to what they perceived to be the practice of the early church. The exposition of the Word became central. The Reformed order tended to look like this:

Prayer
Confession
Singing (Psalms)
Prayer for enlightenment of the Spirit in the preaching
Sermon
Collection
General prayer
Communion (at appointed times) while a psalm is sung
Benediction

These orders have shifted through the years. The Free Church generally has moved more toward corporate involvement. A typical order of worship might proceed as follows:

Opening hymn or several hymns
Call to worship
Introductions
Joys and concerns
Opening prayer (unison)
Choir music (This may fit in any number of places in the service.)
A time for children
Pastoral prayer and prayers of the people
Hymn
Scripture
Sermon
Offering
Hymn
Blessing and sending

The order of worship in a Free Church situation is so fluid, that any prescribed order can only approximate what happens. The above order shows congregational participation in singing and prayers. Music by a choir has become nearly a requirement in many Free Churches. Without prescribing any specific order of worship, in order to indicate what could and should happen, we will add to the Isaianic format described above most of the elements of a Free Church worship service.

Bible study prior to the sermon. Unless the churches of the Radical Reformation are willing to return to the church leader as magister or learned expert, it is essential that the preacher speak contextually. Before the sermon the speaker needs to know what the biblical text means to the congregation.[4] Otherwise the sermon may be only a combination of academic analysis of the text and rhetorical skill.[5] Admittedly, many churches do not offer opportunities for the people to engage in dialogue with the one who will preach. They should. Bible study prior to the sermon, referred to as "collaborative preaching," differs from what was described in chapter 3 since it aims to inform the pastor, rather than elucidate the study group. In collaborative preaching, the faith community would choose or appoint a representative group to discuss the text with the person who will speak. This representative group should meet once a week with the preacher. In any case, there are useful procedures for placing the passage in context:[6]

1. The text itself. There is a reason for studying the Bible. It possesses authority for most Christians. As the text is presented, the nature of that authority needs to be acknowledged in some way: by a statement, by gesture, by vocal presentation. The authority differs from group to group and even within a group. For some it is the Word of God; for others it comes from a spokesperson of God; and for yet others it may be a classical text from antiquity that offers ethical and practical advice for living.
2. Formation community. The Bible is the product of the people of God. Every text had a meaning and purpose in the life of the community for which it was written. While precise definition of the various communities might take considerable effort, some recognition would be imperative. For example, Jeremiah comes from a Jerusalem under threat of destruction. Amos and Hosea speak to a Northern kingdom split off from primary Judaism. The Gospels came from nascent faith communities in places like Antioch, Ephesus, or Rome. The letters of Paul addressed certain problems facing churches in cities like Corinth or Thessalonica. Someone, preferably not the pastor, should present briefly what can be known about the original community of the text.

---

[4]See, e.g., John S. McClure, *The Roundtable Pulpit: Where Leadership and Preaching Meet* (Nashville: Abingdon, 1995) 52-58.

[5]For an informative history see James F. Kay, "Reorientation: Homiletics as Theologically Authorized Rhetoric," *The Princeton Seminary Bulletin* 24 (2003): 16-35.

[6]See Paulsell, ed., *Listening to the Spirit*, 20-21.

This enables the faith community of this century to understand its own context in light of the biblical text.

3.   Literary form. For the most part the collaboration group will recognize different forms in the Bible: psalms, hymns, parables, stories, commandments, sayings, proverbs, letters, and the like. What function do these forms have? Should a parable be taken as historically accurate narrative? Or does a proverb have the same authority as a commandment? Again someone might note the importance of the form of the text being considered.

4.   Context. While a study of literary, social, and political contexts can indeed involve complex research, the negative rule is simple: Do not take the passage out of context. For example, don't make the sovereignty of God a heavenly entity when it has political implications for the Roman Empire. Even more important, the study group needs to attempt to discern the social context of the text so that the passage can be appropriately applied to the modern day.[7] For example, the story of the Good Samaritan may directly apply to our problems of prejudice, but the Parable of the Sower has little or nothing to do with modern agriculture.

5.   Congregational meaning. The function of the group is to discern the meaning or application of the text. All persons should describe what the text means in their lives today. Leadership here is important. The speaker or pastor listens. If the pastor directs the discussion then the result will be antithetical to the Free Church tradition as well as the postmodern styles of Bible study described in chapter 3.[8]

Greeting before worship. While the timing of the greeting in the early church may be uncertain, the fact of it is not. Because the new faith community was a new family, it was essential that the first Christians greet each other as brother and sister (note the incredibly long list of greetings in Romans 16). Logically the greetings would occur first, as those of Paul to the community in Ptolemais (Acts 21:7) and the church in Jerusalem (Acts 21:19). It may be that greetings were given elsewhere. The community greeting mentioned in the greeting section of the epistles indicates it would occur at least after the reading of the letter (1 Thessalonians 5:26; 1 Corinthians 16:20; 2 Corinthians 13:12; Philippians 4:21; 1 Peter 5:14;

---

[7]Edgar V. McKnight, *Jesus Christ in History and Scripture: A Poetic and Sectarian Perspective* (Macon GA: Mercer University Press, 1999) 266.

[8]John S. McClure, *Other-wise Preaching: A Postmodern Ethic for Homiletics* (St. Louis: Chalice Press, 2001) 4-7.

Hebrews 13:24). One wonders if the earliest Jesus followers placed the greeting after some type of introduction, including the reading of letters.

Many of the New Testament requests to greet one another included what is described as the "kiss of peace."[9] The kiss of peace signaled the formation of the faith family by creating fictive kinship across otherwise clearly defined boundaries (Jew/Gentile, slave/free, male/female). By the time of Justin Martyr the kiss greeting had become a formal part of the worship (*1 Apology* 65:2): "After the prayers have been completed we greet each other with the holy kiss." Tertullian (*Or.* 18) also connected the kiss of peace with prayers, but other Fathers complained about abuses (Clement of Alexandria, *Paed.* 3.11.81). In the Western church it eventually was limited to special celebrations or else dropped altogether.

Free Church types may or may not share the holy kiss on special occasions like baptism and weddings. Perhaps because of twentieth-century sexual freedom, for members to be greeted at the door of the church by a hug or even a kiss would not seem uncommon. In any case, anyone entering the meeting place will be welcomed, perhaps even by assigned volunteers. The gathering congregation will give a special welcome to newcomers. After a warm welcome they will be given some kind of bulletin or "worship prompter"—a brief introduction to and outline of the order of service.

Theologically the greeting starts the worship process. Greetings begin the sense of vision. Church members enter the door as individuals. Met at the door, they become members of a faith family. The shift to family of God has begun. That change brings satisfaction and joy—a prelude to the inspiring presence of the Holy Spirit. Still there is a deeper sense of worship involved. Each person has sacrificed individualism. Each person is sacrificing time and energy that could have been spent elsewhere—a day off from work to relax, a picnic with family, a trip to the lakeshore. Entering the church begins the process of a sacrifice on which all communities depend.

In any case the people of God were strictly admonished to be certain every person who came to worship had been welcomed. In an extraordinary passage Isaiah says:

Do not let the foreigner joined to the LORD say,

---

[9]William Klassen, "The Sacred Kiss in the New Testament: An Example of Social Boundary Lines," *New Testament Studies* 39 (1993): 122-35. E. Kreider, "Let the Faithful Greet Each Other: The Kiss of Peace," *Conrad Grebel Review* 5 (1987): 29-49.

"The LORD will surely separate me from his people";
and do not let the eunuch say,
     "I am just a dry tree."
For thus says the LORD:
To the eunuchs who keep my sabbaths,
     who choose the things that please me
     and hold fast my covenant,
I will give, in my house and within my walls,
     a monument and a name
     better than sons and daughters;
I will give them an everlasting name
     that shall not be cut off.
And the foreigners who join themselves to the LORD,
     to minister to him, to love the name of the LORD,
     and to be his servants,
all who keep the sabbath, and do not profane it,
     and hold fast my covenant—
these I will bring to my holy mountain,
     and make them joyful in my house of prayer;
their burnt offerings and their sacrifices
     will be accepted on my altar;
for my house shall be called a house of prayer
     for all peoples.
Thus says the Lord GOD,
     who gathers the outcasts of Israel,
I will gather others to them
     besides those already gathered.   (Isa. 56:3-8)

Opening songs. As we discussed above (see the Isaiah 6 passage), the opening moments of worship engender and celebrate the presence of God in the faith community. Just as music was an essential part of Jewish tradition,[10] we can be certain that singing was a part of worship in the early church (Ephesians 5:19; Colossians 3:16).[11] Through the centuries music has been integral to that process.[12] For any church, but especially for the Free Church, the following considerations are crucial.

---

[10]Joachim Braun, *Music in Ancient Israel/Palestine: Archaeological, Written, and Comparative Sources*, 1-5.

[11]See Snyder, *Ante Pacem*, 291-93. Stephen G. Wilson, "Early Christian Music," in *Common Life in the Early Church*, ed. Julian Hills (Harrisburg PA: Trinity Press International, 1998) 390-401.

[12]Andrew Wilson-Dickson, *The Story of Christian Music* (Minneapolis: Fortress Press, 2003) 24-28.

1. *Lyrics*. The words of the opening hymn center on the anticipated presence of God, Jesus, or the Holy Spirit. The words are sung by the congregation as it gathers, therefore the corporate formulation is essential ("we"-words). Fortunately, in contrast to other parts of the worship, there is a plethora of suitable hymns. Robert Collyer's "Unto thy temple, Lord, we come" calls for divine presence, and stresses the meeting place as "the common home of rich and poor, of bond and free, and great and small." Marty Haugen's "Here in this place" describes perfectly the Free Church sense of gathering. This hymn calls God to enter the meeting place as a "new light is streaming" amidst a congregation made up of young and old who will share dreams; lost and forsaken, blind and lame who will be raised up at the sound of the divine name; rich and haughty, proud and strong who will become meek and lowly as they sing the song. All this will be celebrated by taking the bread of new birth and the wine of compassion. Perhaps the hymn most congruent with Free Church theology and practice was written by the Dutch writer Huub Oosterhuis, "What is this place?" (1967/1968; translation by David Smith, 1970).

> What is this place where we are meeting?
> Only a house, the earth its floor,
> walls and a roof sheltering people,
> windows for light, an open door.
> Yet it becomes a body that lives
> when we are gathered here,
> and know our God is near.
>
> Words from afar, stars that are falling,
> sparks that are sown in us like seed.
> Names for our God, dreams, signs, and wonders
> sent from the past are what we need.
> We in this place remember and speak
> again what we have heard:
> God's free redeeming Word.
>
> And we accept bread at his table,
> broken and shared, a living sign.
> Here in this world, dying and living,
> we are each other's bread and wine.
> This is the place where we can receive
> what we need to increase:
> God's justice and God's peace.   (CH #289; HWB #1)

2. *Rhythm*. Rhythm creates community. The nature of the community doesn't matter: politics, sports, entertainment, or whatever. Granted, not all

rhythmic events create community, but community can hardly exist without rhythm. Around the world group meetings assemble to the sound of drums. As we have already noted in chapter 2, there seems to be an internal mechanism in the human system that responds to drum beats, and that internal response corresponds to the response of others. As we saw in chapter 3, rhythm creates bonding.[13]

Before a faith community can pray and interpret the Scripture it forms a rhythmic community. That sense of rhythm automatically occurs with the beat of the music. Perhaps due to the influence of recent music styles, clapping has returned in many cases to the Christian worship service.[14] A pianist may direct the beat, but more and more that has become the role of a drummer or even a guitarist. In some churches, the choir, congregants, or the children will accompany opening hymns with a variety of small rhythm instruments.

Because dance has not been a part of the tradition of Free Church worship, it is not readily integrated into many congregations. Dance can, however, add an exciting and new dimension to worship. It's visual beauty emanates from the discipline of those who have learned the steps and movements and from the sense of freedom it offers to worship with one's whole being. Just like the choir, dance enhances the worship experience both for those performing the dance and the congregation who sees it and participates in the corporate rhythm. The simple worship space comes alive in new ways with the movement of the dancers. Many African-American churches have begun to include dance in worship and have established dance teams.

The call to worship. The goal of the call to worship is to invoke the presence of God in the congregation. Though excellent calls to worship can be found in books of worship, ideally, they should be composed for each specific occasion. The call to worship may be read by the leader but in Free Church worship it is often recited in unison by all, or spoken or sung by leader and congregation antiphonally. In a variation of this format, the

---

[13]Vitor Kofi Agawu, *African Rhythm: A Northern Ewe Perspective*, 31-33. Walter Freeman, "A Neurobiological Role of Music in Social Bonding," in *The Origins of Music*, 411-24. Adam Kendon shows the function of group motion to create what he calls "interactional synchrony." See his "Movement Coordination in Social Interaction," in *Nonverbal Communication*, compiled by Shirley Weitz (New York: Oxford University Press, 1974) 150-68.

[14]H. F. Stander, "The Clapping of Hands in the Early Church," *Studia Patristica* 26 (1993): 75-80.

voices of only men, only women, or only children and youth can be heard alternately. When appropriately done, the call to worship summons the congregation into *kairos* time; that is, it will be the point at which they will begin to sense the divine presence in this particular time and place. In addition the call to worship will produce the feeling that the people, having arrived in all their diversity, are now gathered in unity for a shared purpose.

Although varying from week to week, the call to worship will always speak of the power and presence of God, aspects of God, and of God's working in and with the community. The pastor or leader could articulate the call of God to the people, while the congregation responds ready to receive that call. In the Free Church the call to worship may be preceded by chimes or bells. It might even be accompanied by soft music to set the mood for the reception of the Spirit of God.

Introductions. Introduction of guests simply extends the original greeting. When there is a new face or one not recently seen, someone will introduce the visitor to the congregation. If no one knows the newcomer, a person seated close by might acquire the information and make the introduction. Visitors ought not need to introduce themselves. In large congregations it may not be possible to introduce all newcomers, so a general greeting will need to suffice. The worship leader will warmly welcome them, and the congregation will greet them after the service.

Congregational blessing. The faith community comes together in several ways. Welcoming each other starts the process—everyone in a small congregation or those sitting nearby in a large congregation. In addition to the welcome, congregants offer to each other some type of blessing, such as "May the peace of God be with you." Since, unlike pastors of mainline churches, the Free Church pastor does not grant the blessing, this blessing of each other acts as the primary way for the congregants to bless and be blessed. If personal greetings are not possible the entire congregation might bless each other or even sing a blessing:

> May God grant you a blessing,
> may God grant you a blessing,
> may God grant you a blessing evermore.
> Revere the Lord.
> May God grant you a blessing.
> (*Bwana awabariki*, a Swahili folk hymn, HWB #422)

The act of blessing and being blessed has powerful and mysterious implications. The people of God, themselves blessed, were chosen by God to be a blessing to all nations:

> Now the LORD said to Abram, "Go from your country and your kindred and your father's house to the land that I will show you. I will make of you a great nation, and I will bless you, and make your name great, so that you will be a blessing. I will bless those who bless you, and the one who curses you I will curse; and in you all the families of the earth shall be blessed."   (Gen. 12:1-3)

We all who are Jews and Christians see ourselves as having been formed to bless the world! Can we define that blessing? We cannot be certain, for we ourselves have been chosen to bless. We do know the blessing carries well-being and life satisfaction:

> So he came near and kissed him; and he smelled the smell of his garments, and blessed him, and said,
>> "Ah, the smell of my son
>>> is like the smell of a field
>>>> that the LORD has blessed.
>> May God give you of the dew of heaven,
>>> and of the fatness of the earth,
>>> and plenty of grain and wine.
>> Let peoples serve you,
>>> and nations bow down to you.
>> Be lord over your brothers,
>>> and may your mother's sons bow down to you.
>> Cursed be everyone who curses you,
>>> and blessed be everyone who blesses you!"   (Gen. 27:27-29)

We do know the blessing comes from God, and expresses God's power in our lives. While we know power as energy, the blessing takes on material form. The blessing physically passes on from generation to generation. Most obviously the *pater familias* gives the blessing to his eldest son, or all the sons, a tangible irreversible event. He does it by the laying on of hands, and pronouncing the words of blessing. As a physical action the blessing can be stolen. Incredibly, using deceit, Jacob and Rachel stole the blessing from the elder son, Isaac (Gen. 27:1–28:5). Jacob, the father of the Jewish tribes, came to that position by trickery. Physically the blessing passes to others by words, by touch (as in the case of Jacob) or the breaking of the common bread (Mark 6:41) and drinking the common cup (1 Cor. 10:16).

Incredible, yes, also very mysterious. What does the blessing do? Put in present-day terms, the blessing creates a positive attitude. It creates the expectation that all will be well. Given such a God-driven attitude, all things indeed will be well. The person blessed belongs to the people of God, the community of the blessed. Regardless of the existential situation of the blessed community, all will go well. Each member can expect that. Nevertheless, we are speaking of an attitude, not a fact, an attitude shared by a community. In the Beatitudes people are poor, meek, hungry, thirsty, and reviled, yet blessed (Matt. 5:3-11). The author of 1 Peter says those who suffer or are reproached as Christ-followers are blessed (3:14; 4:14). The most radical comes from Paul who encourages the Roman readers to bless (not curse) those who persecute them (Rom. 12:14). Even blessed enemies will have a change of attitude and community! Yes, mysterious!

Joys and concerns of the congregation. In preparation for the time of prayer the gathered people share joys and concerns. Individual prayer concerns can be made in writing before the service and delivered to the pastor, or they can be voiced by individuals prior to or in the context of prayer. The faith community shares its times of special happiness, not simply times of illness and troubles. When a congregation becomes large, it may be necessary to entertain only written petitions. The pastor can also make the prayers more general, while a list of names of those in need appears in the bulletin. Concerns may be political as well as personal or congregational. Separation of church and state does not exempt the Free Church from concern for world peace, for people caught in economic disasters, for a desire for good government, or for concern over nations enduring oppression.

Petitions present other problems. To pray to God for a specific request introduces nearly insoluble theological problems. Such a petition assumes God has control of all things. To be sure, many religious actors do automatically assume their god is in control. So many around the world can pray for material success, for cures, even for vengeance on enemies. To ensure answers to such prayers, groups that promise God's intervention have evolved. Of course, in such groups certain rituals must be followed. We refer to these rituals as magic. Magic can involve certain incantations, sacrifices, superstitious actions, or financial gifts. By the second century such magical practices had even appeared in Christianity.[15]

Specific petitions seldom occur in the Bible itself. We know best the prayer of Jesus in Gethsemane:

> And going a little farther, he threw himself on the ground and prayed, "My Father, if it is possible, let this cup pass from me; yet not what I want but what you want."   (Matt. 26:39)

---

[15]See a short history and examples in *The Greek Magical Papyri in Translation*, ed. Hans Dieter Betz (Chicago: University of Chicago Press, 1986) xliv-lii.

It serves as a model for petitionary prayer. It does ask for a specific result (avoiding death on the cross), yet places both the petition and the results in the hands of God ("Thy will be done"). Jesus also taught us to pray for daily bread, or bread for tomorrow. Again it is set in a context that anticipates the coming reign of God.

A second theological disaster comes with unanswered prayer. Few things in life can be more devastating than to pray to an all-powerful, all-knowing God without results. Unanswered prayer leaves the believer with a deceased loved one, for example, and a demolished faith. One thinks of the anguish expressed by Martha and Mary (John 11:21, 32) at the death of Lazarus: "Lord, if you had been here, my brother would not have died."

Free Church worshippers find themselves in a difficult position. There is no standard liturgy. Church worship has few limitations. Ecclesiastical or academic leaders cannot dictate faith in God. Consequently, prayer petitions can be quite specific: cures for terminal illnesses, safety in travel, better employment. To make matters worse, the electronic church or even the revival movement deliberately has shifted toward magic.[16] If not magic then at least an unbending quid pro quo: do this for God and us and God will answer your prayer. There are no known statistics, but one suspects a major cause of disaffection from church and Christianity comes from such a faulty understanding of God and from the pain of unanswered petitionary prayer.

In order to avoid this problem the local church must continually educate its members about the God function. Given the Free Church sense of covenant, the relationship with God will be considered an open mutuality. God works together with the believers to realize the Reign. While it may not solve the problem, the community, inspired by God's presence, could agree on what may be petitioned:

> "Truly I tell you, whatever you bind on earth will be bound in heaven, and whatever you loose on earth will be loosed in heaven. Again, truly I tell you, if two of you agree on earth about anything you ask, it will be done

---

[16]For a helpful analysis see Tex Sample, *The Spectacle of Worship in a Wired World: Electronic Culture and the Gathered People of God* (Nashville: Abingdon, 1998) esp. 92-93. On adapting traditional forms to contemporary worship see Thomas G. Long, *Beyond the Worship Wars: Building Vital and Faithful Worship* (Bethesda MD: Alban Institute, 2001); and Earle Fike, "The Shape of Our Worship," *Brethren Life and Thought* 49 (2004): 59-64.

for you by my Father in heaven. For where two or three are gathered in my
name, I am there among them." (Matt. 18:18-20)

When two or three are gathered in the name of Jesus they act out of the
covenant relationship. They would not pray for something alien to their
relationship to God (as seen in Jesus). So, inappropriate petitions will be
kindly rephrased: "Thy will be done."

Opening prayer. From the beginning public prayer played an essential
role in the faith community. When the Jesus people met they prayed.
According to Acts they met (in the upper room) for the breaking of bread
and praying (Acts 1:14; 2:42).[17] Paul mentions prayer as a constant part of
the new Hellenistic churches (1 Corinthians 14:13-15, and later Ephesians
6:18). The long prayer in *1 Clement* 59-61 could be an example of a public
prayer as used in the early Roman church. By the end of the second century, times of prayer, often daily, had become set.[18] Theologically the
prayers were usually directed to the divine parent (as "Father" in the Lord's
Prayer [*Didache* 8:2], though "Lord and Master" in others such as Clement)
in order to indicate the familial relationship of the gathered congregation
(for example, Rom. 8:14-17). The public (opening?) prayer normally included thanksgivings, both in terms of past actions as well as present
blessings. The Free Church opening prayer will stress the presence of God
the Parent with the gathered children of God.

Anthem. A choir is almost a necessity in today's churches. The choir
fulfills multiple functions. It offers appropriate choral music to enhance the
worship experience, especially for those congregations that may find music
to be more spirit-inducing than words alone. As previously mentioned, in
addition to the meaning of the words, the rhythm of the music also helps
create community—both among the members of the choir as well as the
larger body of worshippers. A choir provides the opportunity for those who
are musically gifted and also those musically interested to participate in
leading parts of the worship. The Book of Ezra indicates the importance of
the singers for those who returned to Jerusalem in order to rebuild the
temple. Their numbers appeared separate from the rest of the people. "They
had two hundred male and female singers" (Ezra 2:65b). In Nehemiah there
are said to be "two hundred and forty-five singers, male and female" (Neh
7:67b). It should be noted, however, that the singers are listed after the
assembly and the slaves but before the horses and mules!

---

[17]White, *Christian Worship*, 23-24.
[18]White, *Christian Worship*, 52-55.

Choirs or groups of singers separated from the congregation do not appear in the early decades of the church. To the contrary, the faith community itself was likely the choir. In his letter to the Ephesian church, Ignatius of Antioch writes poetically:

> And now you all become a choir, that being harmonious in love, you may receive the pitch of God in unison, and you may with one voice sing to the Father through Jesus Christ, so that He may both hear you, and perceive by your works that you are indeed the members of His Son.
>
> *(IgnEph* 4.2)[19]

By the middle of the third century there were separate choirs, male and female. From the fourth century on, boys' choirs became customary for medieval churches.

After the Reformation, choir music and choirs eventually developed in most Protestant churches. Some groups still utilize the singing of the total congregation. We think of the Amish, the Hutterites, older Mennonites, and Brethren. The worship effect of the total congregation singing can hardly be overestimated. One thinks, for example, of marvelous music at Methodist campgrounds or a Mennonite congregation singing its identity song, "Praise God from whom all blessings flow" ("Doxology").

Anthem music will vary widely from church to church. Ideally the theme of the choral music presented will be in accordance with the text and sermon for that day. This requires considerable coordination between pastor and musical director, or ideally among committees that work with both.

A time for children. Most Free Church-type congregations will have a special time or story with the children who are called forward.

> Let the little children come to me; do not stop them; for it is to such that the kingdom of God belongs.   (Mark 10:14)

The pastor may lead this time or there may be a designated narrator or storyteller who works with children. There are no set patterns, though there are significant variations. Obviously the story should reflect the morning theme if at all possible. A text should be mentioned, perhaps even read, followed by a dialogue with the children or a story told.[20]

---

[19]See above, pp. 34-35.

[20]There is any number of helps. For example, Deborah Raney and Vicky Miller, *More Children's Sermons to Go: 52 Take-Home Lessons about God* (Nashville: Abingdon, 2001).

Some storytellers read from a children's book that has a biblical theme. Dramatizing, or reenacting, a biblical story offers even more rewards. Prior to the worship service, the storyteller meets with the children involved. Given sufficient time to practice the children might act out the story. Failing sufficient time, the storyteller could narrate the passage and the children walk through it with a minimum of verbal expression. Costumes can be created from scarves. Dramatization of biblical stories can be incredibly educating. The children learn the story better this way than by listening, and the adults normally become more involved than if the story or scripture is simply read.[21]

In the case of a dialogue with the children, it is common for the pastor or leader to bring an object and teach an object lesson related to the text, keeping in mind the ages of the children. Often, Children's Time ends with a short prayer in which the children are invited to participate. In the Free Church the children may go to Sunday school classes following this time in worship. In some churches, they may be seated with their families, share a hymn, place their offerings on the plate, and then leave for their classes. It is good if the Sunday school lessons can reflect the same topic being addressed in the sermon. This way, children and their families may continue the dialogue together after returning home.

Children and adults together must be present in at least the first part of the worship service. The signal must be clear that the entire family of God gathers to worship. The church is not the church if all ages are not represented.

Pastoral prayer. Though not without traditional language, in the Free Church the pastoral prayer will be delivered extemporaneously. This is not difficult if the pastor follows a general, flexible pattern or format and is able to vary the contents according to either the biblical theme for the day, the season of the year, or special circumstances. The leader also adjusts the format and style of the prayer according to the needs and mood of the congregation.

The pastoral prayer will open with an invitation for the congregation to enter the presence of God. The prayer proper should include silence, praise, thanksgiving, confession (not necessarily every week), and supplication on behalf of needy individuals, for the life of the community, and for peace and justice in community and world.

---

[21]Though intended to help the minister reenact the text, some help for performance can be found in Jana Childers, *Performing the Word: Preaching as Theatre* (Nashville: Abingdon, 1998) 15-35.

Through the centuries of Christian history the public prayer has remained much the same:

Address to the divine parent (adoration)
Thanksgiving
Supplication (confession and pardon)
Intercession
Prayers for the faith community (blessings)

Several commonly accepted elements will be found missing in the Free Church opening prayer. While there may be some general form of confession, the pastor will not offer pardon. The pastor cannot speak for God. In mainline churches there will likely be a prayer for the well-being of the nation (even its industries), a prayer for defense against enemies, and a prayer for the national leader and other officials. Because of the historic separation of church and state those prayers will not likely occur in a Free Church worship.

Gestures of prayer. Signs and symbols precede action and thought.[22] Gestures can include clothing (costume), body language, and experience of signs particular to the space in which it is used (for example, dancing or marching). As the use of drums or other kinds of rhythm created community in the opening hymns, so gestures create the context in which community can be experienced. Paul routinely knelt down and prayed (Acts 20:36; 21:5; and see Phil. 2:10). At the fig tree incident Jesus indicated the disciple would stand and pray (Mark 11:25). We may assume the early church followed either pattern—kneeling or standing. The author of 1 Timothy urges the readers to pray with hands lifted up (1 Tim. 2:8), though he makes no mention of the body position. Worshippers also must have bowed their heads, a gesture not often mentioned (Heb. 11:21).

As for clothing, a woman was to pray with her head covered, though Paul's reasoning in 1 Corinthians 11:2-16 regarding headship leaves something to be desired. Likewise a man dare not wear a covering for fear of dishonoring his relationship to God. One suspects both regulations are cultural: most women in the Mediterranean world wore a covering in public. So Christian women did not break the accepted pattern, lest they appear to be prostitutes. Roman priests wore a head covering, so Christian men who

---

[22]Thomas A. Sebeok, *Signs: An Introduction to Semiotics* (Toronto: University of Toronto Press, 2001) 4. Imre Gráfik, *Signs in Culture and Tradition* (Szombathely: Savaria University Press, 1998) 13-15.

prayed needed to disassociate themselves from their non-Christian counterparts.

Gestures signify community. Many religious actors can be identified by costume. In the Free Church tradition, Amish, Hutterites, and some Mennonites and Old Order Brethren can be identified by buttoned coat and broad brim hat for the men and head coverings for the women.[23] That sense of dress identity may be critical for the continued life of these groups. Almost all Christians in the Western world bow their heads in prayer. In the Free Church, head bowing has likely replaced kneeling, which seldom occurs, and standing, which is sporadic. Quakers would not bow or remove their hats before human authority. Free Church types generally dislike any show of obeisance.

Lifting hands is yet another matter. While there is little indication of hand lifting in the post-New Testament church, it has come back. In many churches of all types one can find lifted hands during prayer. It only becomes a communal gesture in more "Spirit-led" congregations.

Prayer hymn. Following the pastoral prayer the congregation may affirm the prayer with a hymn that expresses corporate involvement. Charles Wesley's "Help us to help each other" expresses it well. More recently, Ken Medema has written a very satisfactory response hymn:

> Lord listen to your children praying,
> Lord, send your spirit in this place.
> Lord, listen to your children praying,
>   send us love, send us pow'r, send us grace!
>   (CH #305; HWB #353)

Presentation of the text. For People of the Book, no part of worship could be more important than the reading of the Word of God. While not every text is equally applicable to all times and seasons, still Jews and Christians believe every scriptural selection has some ultimate significance. Once the text of the Hebrew Scriptures was written, we hear of its being read. Following the accidental (?) discovery (2 Kings 22:8) of the "Book of the Law" (that is, Deuteronomy) at the time of King Josiah, the Scripture was read to all the people (2 Chron. 34:30). The result was a great reform in Judah (2 Chron. 34:31-33). When the Jews returned from Exile, the scribe Ezra read the law of Moses (Torah) before all the people as they stood—four hours at a time (Neh. 8:3-5; 9:3). Out of that reading came the

---

[23]Esther Fern Rupel, *Brethren Dress: A Testimony of Faith*, 4-15.

new, postexilic Judaism. The prophets conveyed the Word of God, but when prophets were absent the written text conveyed their real presence.

By the time of Jesus, reading from the Scripture was standard procedure in the synagogue. As we see in Luke 4:16-30 Jesus was given the scroll to read. It was the scroll of Isaiah. We cannot assume the text from Isaiah 61:1-2 caused the ensuing riot, but the interpretation did. Followers of Jesus continued to read the Hebrew Scriptures in their worship (1 Cor. 14:26). The text brought with it the presence of God (2 Tim. 3:15-16) and was to be read when the first Christians met (1 Tim. 4:13).

At some time, no longer clear to us now, the words of Jesus and Acts were added to the reading of the Scriptures. The author of Colossians admonished the congregation to let the "word of Christ" dwell richly in them (Col. 3:16). Perhaps the congregation already possessed a copy of the Gospel of Mark?

In any case, reading from the Hebrew Scriptures, the Gospels, and the apostolic letters became a central part of Christian worship (Justin Martyr, *Apology* 65, 67; *Apostolic Tradition* 4). Eventually, however, the biblical texts were intertwined with the liturgy in such a way that the Scripture as such was no longer central.

Among the Reformation churches, reading the Scripture and preaching the Word replaced liturgically based worship. For the most part Free Churches have not altered that radical shift. That means the reading of Scripture lies at the heart of the worship service. Prior to the reading, the presence of the Spirit (call to worship, singing, greeting, blessing, praying) has prepared the congregants to accept the selected text as the inspired Word. As we noted, it is the inspiration of the congregation that creates the importance of the biblical text. The text itself, apart from the congregation, cannot be considered inspired. Its authority or functionality lies in its applicability to the listeners.

Given this theology, presenting the Scripture cannot be taken lightly. On the one hand, an authoritarian reading denies the role of the congregation. While clarity is demanded, a reading with ponderous voice and overly severe diction will stress more that God is speaking than that the congregation is receiving. Most Free Churches do not ask the members to stand while the Gospel is read. Again that overly stresses authority.

Logically the congregation should be more involved in the reading of the text. Ideally there could be several readers who represent the faith community in its receiving of the text. Readers should include young persons as well as adult women and men. Unfortunately congregational readers do not always articulate the text appropriately. Inability to pronounce difficult words or to emphasize key words and phrases can distract from the reading—even create misunderstanding. Some gracious coaching ahead of time may be necessary.[24]

The reader needs to have practiced, but even more must have studied the meaning of the text sufficiently to convey its intent for the congregation.[25] In some congregations the Scripture is presented by readers who stand in the aisle or even remain at their seat to emphasize that the Word is the possession of the people.

Sermon. The sermon will be an application of the text to the situation of the faith community in whatever context it finds itself. The context may be that of the congregation or it may be that of world conflict. In any case the sermon does not exist in a vacuum. It does not allow indecision. In Free Churches decision making tends to be communal and ethical rather than theological and spiritual. That may be a fault. There could be less confusion in the Free Churches if pastors spoke more often about the meaning of such events as baptism, marriage, communion, and death, or spiritual matters such as prayer and sacrifice.

Still, the sermon is not to be a pronouncement by the pastor or a learned disquisition about a difficult text. The one speaking will have discussed the implications of the text with members of the congregation (called collaborative preaching). The sermon reflects that conversation. The speaker will also be aware that a response will occur. As for the preaching itself, there is no set pattern. There are many examples that are fruitful to consider.[26] Though no developmental pattern can be discerned, there are some essential characteristics of Free Church preaching:

1. Congregation-centered. The sermon addresses the concerns of the gathered community. While apparently obvious, the speaker may have other objectives: arguing an abstract theological issue, raising money,

---

[24]Help in articulation and pronunciation can be found in books like Clayton J. Schmit, *Public Reading of Scriptures: A Handbook* (Nashville: Abingdon, 2002).

[25]Richard F. Ward, *Reading Scripture Aloud* (Nashville: Discipleship Resources, 1989) 8-9.

[26]Some favorite sources include Thomas H. Troeger, Fred B. Craddock, David L. Bartlett, Barbara Brown Taylor, Richard Ward, and Earle Fike, to name only a few. Among African-Americans Henry H. Mitchell would be a frequently used example. The musical or rhythmic response to a sermon, as found in African-American churches, has been aptly described by Evans E. Crawford and Thomas H. Troeger, *The HUM: Call and Response in African American Preaching* (Nashville: Abingdon, 1995). For sermon characteristics see 67-71.

chastising backsliders, or making an addition to the present edifice. All of us who preach have voices behind our back that tell us what to say. Such outside pressures need to be set aside. The sermon applies the text to the congregation.

2. Inspiration. The sermon culminates a worship process that intends to make present the Spirit of God. The sermon cannot abort that process. Even if the subject of the text has a dark side or the congregational context points to community pain, still the sermon reflects the freedom and fervor of the worship itself.

3. Communal. The sermon not only addresses the whole congregation, but it creates a community bonding. If possible, the sermon might reflect the rhythm of the preceding music. In any case the sermon invites communal response by means of gesture, eye contact, or even words.

4. Deep-rooted. The Free Church sermon will not deal with trivia or superficial topics. The speaker has heard the concerns of the congregation and will address their issues, their needs, their laments, and joys.

5. Sending. The genius of the Free Church sermon comes at the end. There is a climax, a call to service, a sending, and invitation to act.[27]

In the next chapter we will offer some examples of Free Church congregational preparation, preaching, and response.

Giving (offering). In most congregations, not only Free Churches, it is understood that the offering is far more than raising funds for the program of the church. Independent financial existence does mark the Free Church. A local congregation cannot receive continued support from the state or from a denomination. The offering maintains that independence.

No member of a Free Church can ignore the fact that the existence of the local congregation depends on individual giving. Still, other considerations probably override the sense of sheer support. Most think of giving to God, or giving back to God. God gave to us all that we have, so we return part—sometimes even all—to God. One can call it praise of God, or more likely a tithe. In the Hebrew Scriptures the tithe refers to giving a tenth back to God. The tenth can imply almost anything (Deut. 12:17; 14:22-23, 28; 26:12).

More pertinent to a congregational-type church is the fact that contributions to the life of the church are absolutely essential. Contributing marks belonging. Persons who do not contribute will, to their detriment, eventu-

---

[27] Arthur van Seters, *Preaching as a Social Act* (Nashville: Abingdon Press, 1981) 13-19.

ally leave the faith community. Of course, contributing includes giving of
self in many ways other than financial: teaching, participation in the
worship, committee membership, maintenance, visitation, and other important functions in the life of the congregation. While a financial collection
must be taken, the church ought also to recognize these other forms of
giving.

As the offering, or giving, marks community involvement, so it also
signals the willingness to sacrifice. It would be very difficult for a person
to remain healthy without the willingness to make a self-sacrifice. While
sacrifices may support an institution, they are also necessary for personal
and corporate existence.[28] In the Hebrew Scriptures we find the use of
animal sacrifice as atonement for sin or guilt, though sacrifice for well-
being was also possible (Lev. 1–7). Eventually the sacrificial system came
under severe attack from the prophets. God preferred moral self-sacrifice:

> I hate, I despise your festivals,
>   and I take no delight in your solemn assemblies.
> Even though you offer me
>   your burnt offerings and grain offerings,
>   I will not accept them;
> and the offerings of well-being of your fatted animals
>   I will not look upon.
> Take away from me the noise of your songs;
>   I will not listen to the melody of your harps.
> But let justice roll down like waters,
>   and righteousness like an ever-flowing stream.   (Amos 5:21-24)

There was no place for animal sacrifice in Christianity. By cleansing
the temple, Jesus signaled the unacceptability of such rituals in the house
of God. For some early Christians, Jesus on the cross destroyed altogether
the need for such sacrifices (Heb. 9:11-14). For Christians, animal sacrifice
is not the issue. The offering creates community, supports religious
institutions, aids the needy, makes food available, and references one's
relationship to God.

Like sacrifice, the tithe plays little role in the New Testament and early
church.[29] Offerings of money were taken (1 Cor. 16:1-4). Giving in the New

---

[28]René Girard, *Violence and the Sacred* (Baltimore: Johns Hopkins University
Press, 1977) 1-18.
    [29]Lukas Vischer, *Tithing in the Early Church*, trans. R. C. Shultz (Philadelphia:
Fortress Press, 1966) 9-11.

Testament occurred primarily in the sharing of goods (Acts 2:45), and providing food for the corporate meals. Early Christian potlucks required members to bring more food than they needed so that the poor, inside the church and out, could be fed (Acts 2:46). In a sense we can see this in a negative way. Paul chastised some Corinthians for not sharing at the Agape (1 Cor. 11:20-22). The author of Jude makes the same complaint about greedy church members (Jude 12). On the positive side the Feeding of the Five Thousand (Mark 6:30-44) clearly reflects the intent of the early Christians to have food available for the poor. The excess baskets of bread occur over and over again in early Christian portrayals of the miraculous feeding and of early church Agape meals.[30]

Given the double importance of giving—identity with the faith community and self-sacrifice—the actual offering certainly is fraught with issues. It is absolutely essential that the offering be understood as a faith act rather than financial support. This can be made clear in year-round education about stewardship by way of preaching, newsletter, forums, and such. Some Free Churches make public the giving, or least make public who gives. That shows who is in and who is not—a very dangerous procedure. Public recognition of giving will almost surely be destructive of the community. At the same time some trusted members of the faith community (not the pastor and staff) should be aware of members who are failing to participate. Such failure is a serious signal, and one of the trusted members (deacon?) should know whether the member needs assistance or has problems with community participation.

The presentation of the offering is often accompanied by a hymn. In many Free Churches it is the same hymn every week, such as,

We give thee but thine own,
    whate'er the gift may be.
All that we have is thine alone,
    a trust, O Lord, from thee.   (CH #382; HWB #384)

Another example might be this doxology, words by Thomas Ken (1637–1711) and most often sung to the tune of "Old Hundredth":

Praise God from whom all blessings flow;
praise him [God] all creatures here below;

---

[30]Bo Reicke, *Diakonie, Festfreude, und Zelos* (Uppsala: Lundequistska, 1951) 21-50.

praise him [God] above ye heav'nly host;
praise Father, Son, and Holy Ghost. Amen.(CH #46, [#47]; HWB #119)

With the move to inclusive language, a number of new variations on the above are being offered. Here below are three examples:

Praise God from whom all blessings flow;
praise Christ, all creatures here below;
praise Holy Spirit evermore;
one God, triune, whom we adore.   (CH #48)

Praise God from whom all blessings flow.
Praise Christ; the savior's love we know.
Praise to the Spirit moving free,
the three in one and one in three.

Praise God from whom all blessings flow;
in heav'n above and earth below;
one God three persons we adore.
To God be praise forevermore.   (HWB #119)

All of these stress giving as returning to God some of what God has given us. Following the hymn a designated person offers a prayer of Thanksgiving:

For the gift of your presence we give thanks.
We bring to you our offering of thanks and praise
    for all your gifts.

Most Protestants will not speak of the offering as sacrifice. If sacrifice itself creates community, then Free Church people, who avoid it, are in dire danger of losing a critical element in community formation. Actually we do sacrifice more than we care to admit. One form of sacrifice is to give up something of yourself in order to have something more important. If a person gives up a prestigious job for a more steady job, that person has sacrificed fame for security. It is a sacrifice. Another form is to give up something important for another. If parents move from a house and neighborhood they like in order to enroll a child in a special school, then they have sacrificed an aspect of their happiness for a child. It is a sacrifice.[31]

---

[31]M. F. C. Bourdillon, ed. *Sacrifice* (London: Academic Press, 1980). See p. 10 in his introduction (1-28).

We have lost the conscious act of sacrifice in Protestant worship. Perhaps the loss comes as a reaction to the sacrifice of the Mass—the sacrifice of the real body and real blood of Christ. In any case no recognition of a real sacrifice has replaced the Mass. Liturgical sacrifice can be quite simple in form. We would argue that most Free Churches do have a sacrificial act, but do not express it consciously. These parts are needed: praise of God, consecration of the gift, giving of the gift, and celebration of the ensuing community.[32] As we have seen, the offering starts with a praise song. That is followed by a prayer of consecration for the gifts:

> All things are thine; no gift have we,
> Lord of all gifts, to offer Thee;
> and hence with grateful hearts today
> thine own before Thy feet we lay.　　(John Greenleaf Whittier, 1872)

Following the consecration prayer, an usher places the collection plates on the communion table. The sacrifice has been made. At that point the congregation recognizes the sacrifice and celebrates the new community that has been established. There are not many hymns, but one is "Is your all on the altar?":

> Verse 4: Who can tell all the love
> 　　　　He will send from above,
> 　　　　and how happy our hearts will be made,
> 　　　　of the fellowship sweet
> 　　　　we shall share at His feet,
> 　　　　when our all on the altar is laid.

> Refrain: Is your all on the altar of sacrifice laid?
> 　　　　Your heart does the Spirit control?
> 　　　　You can only be blest,
> 　　　　and have peace and sweet rest,
> 　　　　as you yield Him your body and soul.　(Elisha Hoffman, 1900)

Sending. In most, but not all, of the congregations in the Free Church tradition a formal benediction will not be used. Pastors are not the CEOs of the congregation. Pastors do not speak for God. In the Free Church tradition a pastor does not bless the congregation either by words or by gestures. There must be a closing moment, a sending. If a blessing is desired, then the congregation will receive it from each other. Singing a blessing hymn,

---

[32]Victor Turner, "Sacrifice as Quintessential Process: Prophylaxis or Abandonment?" *History of Religions* 17 (1977): 189-215; see esp. 189.

praying a corporate or antiphonal prayer, can do this. There are many favorites: "Lord dismiss us with thy blessing" or "God be with you (till we meet again)." One based on Isaiah 55:12 has become a favorite with many:

> You shall go out with joy
> and be led forth with peace.
> The mountains and the hills
> will break forth before you.
> There'll be shouts of joy
> and all the trees of the field
> will clap, will clap their hands.
> And all the trees of the field
> will clap their hands,
> the trees of the field
> will clap their hands.
> The trees of the field
> will clap their hands,
> while you go out with joy.   (HWB #427)

More important than the blessing is the commissioning or sending. It is in these words that the congregation is sent out into the world to advance the Reign of God and to do God's work in the world. A closing hymn might achieve this:

> Savior, again to your dear name we raise
> with one accord our parting hymn of praise.
> We give you thanks before our worship cease;
> then, in the silence, hear your word of peace.   (HWB #656)

Or a sending response:

> Leader: Gentle God,
>   you have come near to us
>   and have shown us your patience,
>   compassion, and love.
>
> Congregation: As we go, O God,
>   give us patience when people
>   are indifferent to your Word,
>   give us compassion for the needs of the world,
>   and give us love that reflects
>   your forgiveness and grace,
>   through Jesus Christ, our Savior. Amen.   (HWB #765)

Response. A number of congregations have instituted an opportunity for some kind of response to the text and the sermon. It usually occurs after the sending. At that time the members of the congregation may seek further clarification from the pastor, as well as discuss the meaning and implications among themselves. The response is the logical conclusion to Free Church worship. Some congregations also make the response a part of a coffee time after the worship, or, when the service is held at an early hour, in an after-worship adult class. Even when there is not an official time designated for responding to the text and sermon, the community's gathering for a coffee or social time is in itself a way of responding. The congregation, following worship, will desire to linger, to be together and inquire of one another's joys, sorrows, and needs. The people will use this time to learn in what ways the faith community might respond to the challenges presented in the sermon. They will also want to continue to be united in spirit while parted. One thinks of the third and fourth verses of the hymn "Bless'd be the tie that binds":

> We share each other's woes,
>   each other's burdens bear,
> and often for each other flows
>   the sympathizing tear.
>
> When we asunder part,
>   it gives us inward pain,
> but we shall still be joined in heart,
>   and hope to meet again.
>
> (HWB #421; see also CH #433)

The worship will have met its goal when the congregation is able not only to respond to worship in social action but by continuing to be together in spirit, to maintain its identity as the Body of Christ while out in the world.

Chapter 6

Preaching
on Free Church Issues

The sermon lies at the heart of Free Church worship. Prior to the sermon a study group will have reflected with the pastor on the meaning of the text—variously called Bible study, roundtable, or collaborative preaching. In the worship itself the reading of the text precedes the sermon. A congregational response follows the sermon, at the end of the worship service or in the next Bible study. In order to illustrate this procedure we are offering as samples four sermons on key Free Church topics: Creation, Creeds, Inclusiveness, and Community Formation. We will give a sample of the reflection on the text before the sermon and then a sample of questions involved in the response.[1]

On Creation and re-Creation

Bible study

> In the beginning when God created the heavens and the earth, the earth was a formless void and darkness covered the face of the deep, while a wind from God swept over the face of the waters. Then God said, "Let there be light"; and there was light. And God saw that the light was good; and God separated the light from the darkness. God called the light Day, and the darkness he called Night. And there was evening and there was morning, the first day. . . .
> So God created humankind in his image,
> > in the image of God he created them;
> > male and female he created them.
> God blessed them, and God said to them, "Be fruitful and multiply, and fill the earth and subdue it; and have dominion over the fish of the sea and over the birds of the air and over every living thing that moves upon the earth." . . .

> The man gave names to all cattle, and to the birds of the air, and to every animal of the field; but for the man there was not found a helper as his partner. So the LORD God caused a deep sleep to fall upon the man, and he slept; then he took one of his ribs and closed up its place with flesh.

---

[1]John S. McClure, *The Roundtable Pulpit: Where Leadership and Preaching Meet* (Nashville: Abingdon, 1995) 73-108.

And the rib that the LORD God had taken from the man he made into a
woman and brought her to the man. Then the man said,

> "This at last is bone of my bones
>   and flesh of my flesh;
> this one shall be called Woman,
>   for out of Man this one was taken."

Therefore a man leaves his father and his mother and clings to his wife,
and they become one flesh. And the man and his wife were both naked,
and were not ashamed.   (Gen. 1:1-5, 27-28; 2:20-25)

The text in its context. The creation narrative occurred in the context of
a seven-day worship festival. The congregation of Israel gathered together
to celebrate and reenact God's gift of a meaningful and orderly world.
Described by a writer very interested in the festivals of Israel, the so-called
Priestly writer, this celebration must have occurred for the first time about
600 BCE as Jerusalem and the Jewish people of God were threatened with
extinction by the power of Babylon, one of the great empires of the Near
East. At such times the Israelites sang songs in which they praised the
creator God:

> You divided the sea by your might;
>   you broke the heads of the dragons in the waters.
> You crushed the heads of Leviathan;
>   you gave him as food
>   for the creatures of the wilderness.
> You cut openings for springs and torrents;
>   you dried up ever-flowing streams.
> Yours is the day, yours also the night;
>   you established the luminaries and the sun.
> You have fixed all the bounds of the earth;
>   you made summer and winter.   (Psa. 74:13-17)

But they were also aware that creation was an ongoing matter. The
world in which they lived would be a watery chaos if the Spirit of God did
not hover over the void and constantly create the world as we know it. They
experienced that continuing creation as they gathered for corporate worship. The Spirit hovered over the congregation and the organizing Word
was heard. In the New Testament the ultimate order of God also was yet to
come. God would make all things new (Rev. 21:5a).

In 600 BCE the forces of Babylon had taken the great city of Ninevah.
The destruction of Jerusalem and perhaps the extinction of the Jewish
people seemed inevitable. The congregation that celebrated the creation
story did not meet to affirm order. They met to call for a re-creation, for

God once more to speak to the chaos, control the seas, establish a right calendar, and put animals as well as humans and nations in their rightful place. Despite their prayers, Jerusalem was overrun. Jewish people were taken into exile. A few decades later they started again under the leadership of Nehemiah. Re-creation had been granted.

The Priestly writer described the simultaneous creation of man and woman (Gen. 1:27), but an earlier writer, called the Yahwist because he called on God as LORD (*Yahweh*), spoke of separate creations of man and woman. Woman was created out of man, or Adam, as a companion. Unfortunately, perhaps, the two companions grew up to be adult individuals. The adult couple wanted to know the difference between good and evil—a euphemism in the Hebrew Scriptures for maturation or wisdom (see Isa. 7:15-16). Because in adulthood each person may (or is it will?) seek his or her own self-fulfillment rather than that of a companion, there became an alienation between man and woman. There was no choice but to leave the garden of childhood innocence (Gen. 3:22-24).

The creation story has been a theological watershed from the very beginning. Is the life of faith based on what has been or what is yet to come? Even in the Hebrew Scriptures the creation story itself was written later (the Priestly narrative) than the description of human beginnings (the Yahwist writer). Without making too sharp a distinction, those denominations that support a national church tend to hark back to the creation, while those groups that are separated from the state tend to envision the future. The mainline churches normally seek order and wish to preserve the public good (*bonum publicum*) as ordained by God. So, if God established a Natural Law, then we should obey it. Free Churches tend to ask how the end-time will of God impacts our present time. If God wills peace, what should we do? If God wills justice, what should we do? If Free Church people have to choose between obeying the law of the state or being a disciple of Jesus, they will often decide to follow the Master.

Even more divisive is the nature of sin. From Augustine on, many Christians have supposed Adam and Eve were created sinners. They had no choice but to seek their own self-fulfillment at the expense of their partner. It was "original sin." And it is sexual in nature. For that reason infants need the sacrament of baptism. For that reason society, populated by persons who cannot do other than sin, must be made orderly, even if by force. On the other hand, Free Church people do not believe in original sin. They believe in the goodness of creation, the goodness of Adam and Eve and the goodness of newborn children. As we have noted, Free Church types are essentially Pelagian rather than Augustinian. So, for heirs of Augustine, divine grace makes a good life possible despite human sinful nature. Grace may be received through baptism as an infant. The possibility of goodness is restored. For followers of Pelagius, grace enables persons to act appropriately even though they have reached that critical age of adult self-centeredness (as did Adam and Eve). That grace may be received through baptism as an adult. God's purpose for our life is not yet finished.

The text in your context. Read as much of Genesis 1–4 as possible. Have a designated person clarify the origin of the book of Genesis, especially the several sources found in this passage. Use the following discussion questions as a guide for the group study. Discussion questions:

1. Do you live according to the created order, or do you live in anticipation of a coming new world? How does that work out? Do you tend to reject alterations to the created order: biotech food, cloning, stem cell research? Or are you willing to embrace anything that promises to make life better?
2. You see children doing mischief in your community. Some may even cause problems in your church. Are they sinful? Should they have been baptized? If they are not sinful, when does mischief turn to sin?
3. Some people take the Genesis text to prove "Creation Science"—that is, that God created the world in recent times. Others take it to mean God was in charge of the evolutionary process. Does it really matter to you? Is re-creation (the future) more critical than creation (the past)?
4. In the places where you live and work, are women equal with men? Is the Bible used to defend the subordination of women? What does it mean to you that the Yahwist story is always used and the Priestly story is not? What does that mean for the authority of these passages?
5. What do you want the pastor to say to the congregation about creation? What do you expect to happen?

Sermon on Creation and Re-Creation

It has almost come to be a joke that, when asked about their life, career, or faith journey, most people begin with the words "Well, I was born in the little town of. . . . " This usually means we are about to launch into a long-winded and possibly boring diatribe about how our humble beginnings led to our present glory.

Still, these opening lines also indicate that most of us are willing to acknowledge that we began as God's very humble creation, helpless, dependent, and without recognized attributes or abilities. Although we do not remember a thing about the first year or two of our lives, we do want everyone to know how and where this marvelous miracle of birth occurred.

There are two creation stories with which most of us are familiar: that of the world's creation, so far back of course that no human could have written of it—usually imagined by us through the narratives of Genesis—and that of our own personal creation—our birth in that little town where no one but our parents and a few friends or relatives even cared what was happening. In fact, the Book of Genesis actually has two creation stories of its own, and there are other creation stories in the Bible. The first creation story ends at Genesis 2, verse 3, where a second rather different story of creation begins. That second one was actually written earlier.

Like our own creation stories in which at least our mother cared, the Genesis story (1:1–2:3) is about God who cares a lot, God who brings order out of chaos. Here we hear about God's careful and systematic creation of the world step by step, day by day, separating land from water, light from darkness, all for the purpose of the culmination of the project: to create us in God's image and then to pronounce us "good."

This first-in-the-Bible creation narrative teaches that all life and all that exists are under the power of a loving God who made these things—not by accident, but intentionally. We learn from this that no amount of evil can ultimately overcome God's plan of good for us. Another lesson here is that God makes a space for us, this world, a place to call home. Chaos has been routed and order will prevail.

This message must have been badly needed at the time of the Babylonian exile. We can hardly imagine the suffering. The Israelites were taken out of their homes, away from their means of making a living, and were brought by force into a foreign land. Their temple was destroyed, so even their holiest of places had been lost to them. They must have been asking, "Where is God?" As the years in exile passed the hope for a return to their homeland grew dim.

Even if we have not personally experienced anything like exile, we see suffering all around us. Too often we believe chaos is winning. Even though we may not have lost a loved one on September 11, 2001, our hearts break for those who did. Even though we do not live in the midst of the troubles of the Middle East, or suffer the hunger or AIDS epidemic in Africa, surely we need to hear again that God routs chaos. We must hear again too that not only were we created "good" but also we were created to experience a good life.

Undergirding the Genesis opening is the message that life has a purpose. God is pictured here, back at the beginning of history, guiding and separating, creating and directing.

I once was given a gift. A poster, mostly plain white. On it were pictured only two things: a megaphone and a tall director's chair with a name on the back—*GOD*! That poster presented a clear message. I am not in control of everything. God is the director. A good message. Still, there is something the poster did not say. And this is also found in the Genesis creation stories: we have a job to do! We humans are appointed *stewards* of creation. God may be the director, but we are involved in the enterprise.

In the second creation story, beginning at Genesis 2:4, we are told that God did not just make generic humans. No. We are unique: styled, formed, or sculpted by the hand of God. Unfortunately, this second creation story, the one written first, also sets man and woman in contention with each other due to their curiosity and self-centeredness. Each individual seeks his or her own self-fulfillment and only the grace of God will make a person be altruistic.

You may be surprised to know, however, that these Genesis creation stories as understood by Jewish people do not include anything like what we Christians call "The Fall." The couple in and out of the garden are never removed from God's grace and no one is ever a sinner by birth. Rather, in eating from the tree of the knowledge of good and evil, they are gaining wisdom and maturing into an adulthood that includes responsibility for their actions. This is necessary because, if we only obeyed God without question and did not think for ourselves, we would be puppets, not humans. The great joy of living is that when one human meets with another, when we are face to face and in community, God's grace can and does happen. We see again that our creator is not haphazard. In grace, our human relationships can be selfless. God made us for each other, to cleave to one another, and to find our true identity in human-to-human relationship. We were not meant to be alone.

How wonderful that the world's creation happened. But how much more wonderful that it continues every day. The middle section of the Book of Isaiah, written during the Babylonian Exile, includes what might be called "re-creation stories." The enemy king, Cyrus of Persia, turns out to be the very unlikely candidate who makes it possible for the Israelites to return to their homeland and rebuild their lives, their temple, and their community. Yes, God is able, even through the most unlikely candidates—even us!—to *re*-create. The message of Isaiah here again is that chaos will not win, because God has the ultimate power. Even a power-mongering enemy in the process of his own selfish deeds, such as King Cyrus, can be used by God for bringing about good.

We live in a very troubled world right now. We know too much. The downside of all the great technology is that too much of the suffering of the world is laid on our doorsteps daily. The Bible may be telling us God is in charge, but what about the Holocaust, child slavery, today's power-hungry despots, terrorism, and our deep undercurrent of fear? In addition to all this, each of us lives with personal troubles, illness, loneliness, or hurt. We have a perfect right, like Job, to cry out to God asking, "Where are you?"

In times like these we come to realize how wonderfully our Bible is integrated and how deeply it meets our needs for today. When we start heading toward despair, we need only remember that God has not only created, but also promises to re-create and to include us and our work in making a better world. The book of Revelation completes the Bible, telling us that a time is promised when God will wipe away every tear from our eye and there will be no more pain. We can trust these promises even when we have no proof, because we are people of the promise: living in the hope provided by the church's stories of creation in Genesis, of re-creation in Isaiah and Revelation, and, of course the best of all, the message of Jesus' resurrection in the Gospels.

We trust in the Bible's messages also because they are the words of the church. This community, this church, that we share today is an heir of every Christian community that has been birthed and re-created up to this time. As the Body of Christ gathered, we can say in the face of any kind of chaos that the biblical words are true. We believe in creation, re-creation, and resurrection. Here's why.

Our own people, down through the ages, bear witness! Believe it or not, all of this happens regularly right here in our own church. Creation! Think of the many children who have been brought into our community by their parents over the years. Re-creation! Now, take a few minutes and remember back to a time when you thought there was little or no hope for yourself, a friend, or even for this church. (We've all had some difficult days in the past.) Or maybe you remember a time of war when it seemed the world was in grave danger? You see. We came through. We were reborn. Re-creation!

Yes, it was God who got us through the tough times. But I'm sure when you remembered, there came to mind also the people and the community that helped re-creation to happen. God does it, but it is through our relationships with each other that God's work gets done! Along with God, we re-build life out of dust and ashes. We have been re-created more than once.

Yes, your creation story begins with "I was born in a town or a city called . . . " but my guess is you also have a re-creation story or two! Are you the exact person you expected or planned to be when you were younger? Or did things happen that changed that plan? Maybe you didn't have a specific course of action but along the way someone or some series of events pushed you in a particular direction. This is true of many people who have done great things beyond what they ever imagined. Think of it. Most people who are advocates for the cure or understanding about particular diseases are either afflicted with that disease themselves or have a family member with it.

Christopher Reeve was a sterling example. As a handsome and healthy young actor he played Superman. Then suddenly after a horseback accident he became a paraplegic. Reeve became an advocate for research in this area. He gave hope to every person who has dreamed of walking again. "We will do it!" he said, and he was believed because of the hope that was in him. He could so easily have given in to despair, and no doubt he did. But Reeve said that his family's love and his own faith gave him strength beyond himself. He found a direction, a calling, and a purpose above what he ever could have imagined. Before his terrible accident, he was an actor, and a good one. Then he became another kind of superman. God did not cause his accident, but God can and does re-create, bringing new life even out of death. And God does this work through us and by way of our relationships.

Creation and re-creation are needed more than ever in our broken world. Jesus spoke constantly of the Kingdom or Reign of God, saying it was coming but also that it is in the midst of us. To be human is to know want and suffering of some sort or another, and anyone who is sensitive suffers for the pain of others. So many are unloved. So many are sick and lonely and troubled. The world is and always has been filled with wars and rumors of wars, pestilence, earthquakes, and death. The creation stories teach us that we are called to respond to each other with grace and to act on the behalf of those who suffer. We are stewards of creation. "It's too much!" we might quite fairly say. Yes, but remember we were created good and were created for doing good! Surely then we will be given grace and strength to work on behalf of good.

The creation narratives also remind us that God is moving in history. The creator who is described in Genesis as, in the beginning, hovering over the waters of chaos and with a word bringing the world into being, even now continues to see us as good and to direct our ways, guiding us in good paths, lifting us when we fall, and bringing us, male and female, face to face with one another.

This is accomplished as we live together in community. In each other we see the face of the Creator. Here, right now, in this place, God's re-creation is happening. Just like that day when we ourselves were born, there was a time God began to create this church community, to breathe it into being. Everything was set into motion through and by love. Think of it. It may indeed have been a great and glorious day when we were born. But if our parents and community had not continued to nurture us with both love and food, we would not be here now.

Creation happens once and it is the work of God. Re-creation happens all the time and we are privileged to be a part of it. God works with us. We need only participate. We, our church, and our world have a new chance every day. There is a wonderful Bible passage In First John that says: "Beloved, now we are the children of God and we know not yet what we shall be." This is true right now. We do not know what we will be and that's O.K. We need only to know that the God who created us is working with us: directing, guiding, protecting, forgiving, and urging us on toward goodness. We participate in recreation in one primary way: by manifesting love toward each other. In doing so, we will truly know that when God created us, it really was *good*.

Only God can create, but together with God we are privileged to participate in *re*-creation. Together we can begin to bring order out of chaos.

A perfect world? Well, maybe not yet. We very likely will see no perfect world in our lifetime. But, good people of the promise, all we need to know is that it's on its way.

Postsermon discussion. (Can occur after the sermon, at a coffee time, or the beginning of the next presermon Bible study.)

1. Did the sermon interpret the text as you expected?
2. Did the sermon speak to you in your context? At what point?
3. In times of trouble and turmoil does it give you comfort to know that the world, living things and humans were created according to God's will (the Word)? God is in charge?
4. In times of trouble and turmoil does it give you hope and energy to know that all things (Adam-Christ, Eve-Mary, old Jerusalem-new Jerusalem, old heaven-new heaven, old earth-new earth) will eventually be recreated? God's promise will be fulfilled?
5. What changes does/should this sermon and study make in your life?

* * * * *

On confession of Faith

Bible study

> Hear, O Israel: The LORD is our God, the LORD alone. You shall love
> the LORD your God with all your heart, and with all your soul, and with all
> your might. Keep these words that I am commanding you today in your
> heart. Recite them to your children and talk about them when you are at
> home and when you are away, when you lie down and when you rise. Bind
> them as a sign on your hand, fix them as an emblem on your forehead, and
> write them on the doorposts of your house and on your gates. . . .
>
> (Deut. 6:4-9)

> Just then a lawyer stood up to test Jesus. "Teacher," he said, "what
> must I do to inherit eternal life?" He said to him, "What is written in the
> law? What do you read there?" He answered, "You shall love the Lord
> your God with all your heart, and with all your soul, and with all your
> strength, and with all your mind; and your neighbor as yourself." And he
> said to him, "You have given the right answer; do this, and you will live."
>
> (Luke 10:25-28)

The text in its context. When one thinks of essential Judaism, the
Shema (the so-called Jewish "confession of faith") and the Ten Commandments immediately come to mind. The Shema speaks of loving God. The
Ten Commandments speak of a lifestyle that will solidify one's covenant
relationship with God and with neighbor: love (or trust) and obedience.

There is practically no faith statement in the Hebrew Scriptures. Jews
did not believe in descriptions (words) about God and the created world.
Words are like idols. They cannot act; they cannot speak; they are immo-
bile. Martin Buber, in his famous book *I-Thou*, makes the personal God-
relationship the heart of Judaism. When I-Thou becomes I-It then the
Jewish faith has been disastrously altered. As Isaiah says of idols:

> Bel bows down, Nebo stoops,
>   their idols are on beasts and cattle;
> these things you carry are loaded
>   as burdens on weary animals.
> They stoop, they bow down together;
>   they cannot save the burden,
>   but themselves go into captivity. . . .
> They lift it to their shoulders, they carry it,
>   they set it in its place, and it stands there;
>   it cannot move from its place.

If one cries out to it, it does not answer
or save anyone from trouble.

(Isa. 46:1-2, 7)

Written words can be idols. Jews were action oriented. Out of their covenant relationship with God they followed God's commands. Through the centuries the Shema, specifically Deuteronomy 6:5, has become the cornerstone of Jewish faith, a statement usually repeated in Jewish worship.

Jesus affirmed the Jewish Shema. A lawyer asked what he should do to share in the end-time. Jesus asked him what was written in "the law" (that is, in Torah, the Pentateuch, the first five books of the Hebrew Scriptures, Luke 10:26). The lawyer repeated the Deuteronomy 6:5 Shema with the additional extension of loving your neighbor as yourself (Lev. 19:18b). Jesus approved.

As in the Hebrew Scriptures, there is no "statement of faith" in the sayings of Jesus. In fact, the author of the Gospel of John never uses "faith" as a noun; it is always a verb (for example, 12:44). Paul also usually spoke of faith as an activity and attitude (for example, the well-known Romans 1:17). In contrast to Jesus, however, Paul can articulate a more formal faith statement such as 1 Corinthians 8:6, though obviously Paul has simply adapted the Shema to his new faith in Jesus Christ:

[Y]et for us there is one God, the Father, from whom are all things and for whom we exist, and one Lord, Jesus Christ, through whom are all things and through whom we exist.   (1 Cor. 8:6)

As nascent Christianity moved more and more into the Hellenistic world, faith came to be defined in terms of statements and creeds. The narrative style of Jewish thought shifted to rhetorical affirmations. It became possible to identify Christians more by the creedal statement they affirmed than by the love of neighbor they lived. So, for the first time, various confessions (for example, 2 Corinthians 13:13) and events from the New Testament (often called the "kerygma" or summary message) were placed in a composite statement of faith called the "Apostles' Creed" (origin uncertain):

I believe in God, the Father almighty,
    creator of heaven and earth.
I believe in Jesus Christ, his only Son, our Lord.
        He was conceived by the power of the Holy Spirit
            and born of the Virgin Mary.
        He suffered under Pontius Pilate,
            was crucified, died, and was buried.

He descended to the dead.
On the third day he rose again.
He ascended into heaven,
     and is seated at the right hand of the Father.
He will come again to judge the living and the dead.
I believe in the Holy Spirit,
     the holy catholic [universal] church,
     the communion of saints,
     the forgiveness of sins,
     the resurrection of the body,
     and the life everlasting. Amen.   (CH #359; HWB #712)[2]

While the Reformation churches kept and used creeds, the Free Churches rejected the notion that faith was a statement about belief. And while many Free Churches do have creedal-type statements, they are not often used in worship. Nor are they used to determine whether a person is a believer or a heretic. In some Free Churches it is impossible to define heresy because words do not signify faith. Put another way, in some mainline churches deviation from creeds can be cause for divisions and excommunication. That is much less likely in Free Churches. If divisions or excommunication occur in the Free Church it will be because of community alienation or lack of trust.

The text in your context. Read as much of the two texts as possible. Have a designated person clarify the meaning of the Shema in Deuteronomy and its use by Jesus. Use the following discussion questions as a guide for the group study. Discussion questions:

1.   Does your church include a faith statement in its worship service? If so, where? Can you repeat it? If faith statements are not used, do you know why not?
2.   Do you judge what is Christian by what is believed or by how people act? That is, do you feel best when what is Christian can be defined? Or are you more comfortable with lifestyle expectations?
3.   If your faith community does not use a confession of faith or creed, are there still some basic affirmations? Jesus is the Son of God? The

---

[2]The version quoted here is that of CH #359, "Apostolic Affirmation of Faith." See the slightly different version at HWB #712, and see "Nicene Affirmation of Faith" at CH #358. For variations of this ancient creed and its historical development see "The Apostles' Creed" in *Documents of the Christian Church*, 2nd ed., ed. Henry Bettenson (London/New York: Oxford University Press, 1963) 23-26; 1st ed. (1943) 33-37.

Bible is divinely inspired? Can people be excluded from your church because of these expectations?

Sermon on Confession of Faith

Let me begin with a story. A young girl was visiting with friends in another city. The family took her to church on Sunday morning. On her way out the door she noticed a plaque on the back wall with a long list of names. When it was her turn to shake hands with the pastor she asked a question: "What is that list of names?" The pastor answered, "Those are the names of members of our church who died in the service."

On their way home the young girl's friends asked her how she liked their church. "I think it's really nice," she said, "but I don't think I'd like to join. Did you see how many people never made it out of worship? There must have been over a hundred who died in the service."

This brings me to the question: Have you visited any other churches lately? It's always good to be involved in ecumenical and interfaith activities. Still, there are many of us who seldom get to churches other than our own, except for a wedding, a funeral, or maybe a shared Thanksgiving service. Of course, we want you here on Sunday but it's good for everyone occasionally to venture out and worship with other people. When we do, we often return home with a sense that we have much in common with other worshippers, even though our styles may be different. We can experience some of the variety of what we might call "ways of worship."

Worshipping with groups other than our own also gives us a chance to think about how our church and our traditions differ. This may lead to questioning and then hopefully we can learn more about why we of the Free Church tradition are the way we are. The traditions that shape our Sunday services do not come by accident. What we choose to do and not do in worship is directly related to our history, values, and theologies. It may be that you went to a church that had music quite different from what we are used to. Differences are often related to style, but also to the accepted liturgy and, more specifically, to the amount of ritual involved.

Depending on the place you visit, participation from the congregation will vary. The garb of the leaders and the number of lay participants may be different. The service may be longer or shorter—not that I'm suggesting our profound love for the "one hour or less" service has any deep theological underpinnings. One thing you will experience if you visit an orthodox church, (and also many mainline protestant churches) is the weekly repetition of a creed by the entire congregation, most often the Apostles' Creed.

We visitors from the Free Church tradition may choose to read along with the rest. After all, there is probably nothing in the creed with which we disagree theologically. I suspect that, should we choose to join in and recite the creed aloud, some of us may experience some sense of discomfort and not be sure exactly why we feel that way. It is not likely to be the claims about the identity of God, Jesus, and the Holy Spirit that are bothering us so much as the fact that we are being asked to repeat a specific set of words as proof of our belief system. Although some of our own churches do include statements of faith as part of worship, we Free Church people generally like to choose our own words and our own proclamations about the identity of God.

An additional reason for our discomfort may be that we see our faith to be reflected in action rather than words. We tend to believe our relationship with God does not rest on having the exact faith formula. To go further, we suspect that God is less concerned about the right words and much more interested that we live and love in a way that honors God. This is not to say that people of creedal faiths do not also choose to love and honor God. It's just that in the Free Church we are exactly that: free—free to proclaim God in a way that comes out of our own scriptural interpretation, our own relationship with Jesus, and our own personal decisions.

First-century Judaism consisted of many groups. In the time of Jesus there were some groups within Judaism (just as in Christianity today) that had become so law-oriented that they were burdening the people with far too many rules. Jesus argued with their leaders by reminding them there were only two precepts to follow. You know them. "Love the Lord your God with all your heart (your mind) and with all your soul (your whole being) and with all your might (your strength). And love your neighbor as yourself (action)." Jesus knew people would understand that all the requirements of Torah (the Law) are covered by these simple statements: love God and love each other.

Jesus was not saying anything new. He was reminding the people of what they knew from their Hebrew Scriptures, our Old Testament. In the book of Leviticus, laws of love are mentioned twice, at Leviticus 19:18 and again at 19:34. Neither text refers to loving God, however. Both are admonitions to love our fellow humans.

Next, Jesus spoke of the words from Deuteronomy that have become the watchwords of Judaism:

Shema Yisrael. Adonai Elohenu. Adonai Echad.
Hear, O Israel: The LORD our God, the LORD is One.

The passage goes on to say: "You shall love the LORD your God with all your heart, and with all your soul, and with all your might." The Jewish people view these words as the pivotal point of scripture. These words encompass everything that scripture is about—loving God. For this reason the Jewish people never needed creeds. Obedience to God is what is important, rather than identifying or making statements *about* God.

There is some confusion about the Hebrew word *echad* in Deuteronomy 6:4. It may mean that there is only one God: God is one. Or it may mean that God is unique. But the writer of Deuteronomy is less concerned about who we think God is, and more interested in the relationship with God—one of love. The word "love" (Hebrew *aheb*) means much more than an emotion here. It represents giving of self without expectation of return.

We of the Free Church can be satisfied with this biblical understanding of faith. God is one, and we see God in Jesus. Jesus teaches love and service which is the natural outcome of genuine love. It is the simplicity of it and yet the completeness that make it so beautiful. Love is the key to our relationship with God and each other. Our human relationships are to reflect our love of God. In ancient Chasidic writings the Jewish people came to understand that the only way we can really demonstrate our love for God is through loving each other and loving what God has created.

Because we of the Free Church are creedless, we as individuals feel called to a higher responsibility. Although we are not expected or required to recite particular creeds that remind us about the nature of God, we come to know and proclaim God through loving service within family, faith community, and the world.

Those churches requiring the recitation of creeds do so for many good reasons. The purpose of a creed is to spell out and maintain the basics of the faith; what is believed *about* God, so that these tenets will not be lost to future generations. This is of course a worthy enterprise. It is just that creeds can easily turn from being testimonies of faith into being tests of faith. The required recitation of creeds can deliberately or inadvertently point out who is "in" and who is "out" of a given community. People's inclusion in community will tend then to be related to what they believe rather than to who they are or what they do.

It has been vital in our Free Church tradition neither to be defined nor confined by faith statements. Proclamations and decrees that are given from any hierarchical position are not automatically accepted. Only God. Only Christ. Only scripture. Like our predecessors in ancient Israel, the words ring true: The Lord our God is one. Let us love the Lord our God and let us love our neighbor as ourselves.

Ultimately, you see, we affirm that it is not what we believe *about* God that counts. God is a God of love and forgiveness, a God who calls us to action. Out of this love from God freely given, we feel called to loving actions toward one another. This action, then, is the way we show what we know about God and that we love the Lord our God with all our heart and soul and might.

In many ways, having creeds can make things easier. When a congregation is not fed with the exact words, individuals will have to determine for themselves the specifics of their relationship with God. Free Church means free choice, but with freedom comes responsibility. Those who have gone before us in this tradition found that it was worth the extra work. This way of believing works for us. When we don't have to answer to hierarchy, we are less apt to pass the buck. People seem more likely to do what is right for the circumstances and the particular community. Individuals are more willing to share individual ideas, and to be tolerant of others because they realize every faith journey has its own twists, turns, and directions. Each of us accesses God and would describe God in our own way. When individual ways of believing are respected, then community becomes all the more precious, and consensus can happen without being forced.

Visited any other churches lately? Needless to say, God was there. Ultimately I suspect God is not concerned so much about the details of how we worship as the fact that we do worship. Visiting another church is always your gift to that community and they will surely also be a gift to you. But, should you choose to go, don't stay away too long. In this, your home church, your individuality is respected and encouraged—but your presence is expected! Why?

Your presence is important to all of us, because it is here that what we believe about God begins to get put into action. Your presence is important because we need each other to expand our experience and grow in faith.

Ultimately, it is in our ways of being together (sharing in worship and sharing our lives with its sorrows and joys) that we know what love is. It is also through our interactions that we can really begin to know who God is.

Postsermon discussion. (Can occur after the sermon, at a coffee time, or the beginning of the next presermon Bible study.)

1.   Did the sermon convey the meaning of the texts as you expected?
2.   Did the sermon speak to your own issues about faith?
3.   Is this your home church because of family circumstances or by personal choice? What actions do you take here to demonstrate your

love for God and your thankfulness for God's love, grace and
forgiveness?

4. If you were to write a personal creed, what would you say?
5. How do your beliefs *about* God affect your behavior toward others
and your world? Or do they at all?
6. In what ways might a creedless church demonstrate to the world its
beliefs about God?

* * * * *

On inclusion of others

Bible study

> From there he set out and went away to the region of Tyre. He entered
> a house and did not want anyone to know he was there. Yet he could not
> escape notice, but a woman whose little daughter had an unclean spirit
> immediately heard about him, and she came and bowed down at his feet.
> Now the woman was a Gentile, of Syrophoenician origin. She begged him
> to cast the demon out of her daughter. He said to her, "Let the children be
> fed first, for it is not fair to take the children's food and throw it to the
> dogs." But she answered him, "Sir, even the dogs under the table eat the
> children's crumbs." Then he said to her, "For saying that, you may go—
> the demon has left your daughter." So she went home, found the child
> lying on the bed, and the demon gone.
>
> (Mark 7:24-30)

The text in its context. The Jewish people were not mission-minded. It
is difficult to find even minor traces of Jews who traveled outside Palestine
for the purpose of converting Gentiles. Other than Palestinian Jews there
were surely many Hellenistic Jews who shared their faith with neighbors.
At least we find throughout the Mediterranean world not only Jews by
birth, but "god-fearers" who wished to associate with Judaism—whether
or not they converted (Acts 13:16, 26). Still, there is little to indicate that
Jews sought out even these Gentiles. Apparently some Gentiles recognized
the theological and moral superiority of Judaism and wished to be included.

To be sure, one word of Jesus gives us pause: "Woe to you, scribes and
Pharisees, hypocrites! For you cross sea and land to make a single convert"
(Matthew 23:15). Yet, there is little evidence for such missionary activity.
Certainly Jesus did not seem to share that concern.

To the contrary, and somewhat to our surprise, Jesus enjoins his
disciples not to leave Palestine:

> These twelve Jesus sent out with the following instructions: "Go nowhere among the Gentiles, and enter no town of the Samaritans, but go rather to the lost sheep of the house of Israel."   (Matt. 10:5-6)

Given this command we are not surprised, though somewhat dismayed, perhaps, to see a reluctant Jesus recoil when the Syrophoenician woman asked him to heal her daughter. On the other hand, the Jesus tradition is not that simple. Earlier, in the same Gospel, Jesus heals the slave of a Roman centurion and praises his great faith, greater than any in all Israel:

> When he entered Capernaum, a centurion came to him, appealing to him and saying, "Lord, my servant is lying at home paralyzed, in terrible distress." And he said to him, "I will come and cure him." The centurion answered, "Lord, I am not worthy to have you come under my roof; but only speak the word, and my servant will be healed. For I also am a man under authority, with soldiers under me; and I say to one, 'Go,' and he goes, and to another, 'Come,' and he comes, and to my slave, 'Do this,' and the slave does it." When Jesus heard him, he was amazed and said to those who followed him, "Truly I tell you, in no one in Israel have I found such faith. I tell you, many will come from east and west and will eat with Abraham and Isaac and Jacob in the kingdom of heaven, while the heirs of the kingdom will be thrown into the outer darkness, where there will be weeping and gnashing of teeth." And to the centurion Jesus said, "Go; let it be done for you according to your faith." And the servant was healed in that hour.   (Matt. 8:5-13)

To further confound the issue, the greatest missionary statement of the Gospels comes from the mouth of the resurrected Jesus in the same Gospel (Matthew) that recorded the severe restriction:

> And Jesus came and said to them, "All authority in heaven and on earth has been given to me. Go therefore and make disciples of all nations, baptizing them in the name of the Father and of the Son and of the Holy Spirit. . . .   (Matt. 28:18-19)

Whatever we say about Jesus, Matthew, and the Syrophoenician woman, early Christians did carry the good news, as the author of Acts says, to "all Judea and Samaria, and to the ends of the earth" (Acts 1:8).

The first major conversion of a Gentile came when Peter visited and baptized a centurion of the Italian legion (Acts 10:23b-48). More to the point was Paul's commission to go to the Gentiles (15:22-35). According to Acts, and the letters, Paul did indeed carry the Gospel to Asia Minor and Greece. According to Paul's own words, he was called to go as far as Spain (the ends of the earth, Romans 15:28). We suppose that did not happen.

Instead Paul may have sent Phoebe, the pastor of the church in Cenchreae. According to tradition, other apostles also were called to Gentile lands: Peter to Rome, Andrew to Scythia, Thomas to India, Mark to Egypt, Philip to Hieropolis, and John to Ephesus.

By the fourth century, it became prudent for the Roman Emperor, Constantine, to declare Christianity the state religion. Gradually, from that time on, through the Middle Ages to the establishment of the Holy Roman Empire under Charlemagne, conversion became more a territorial involvement than a decision to follow Jesus Christ.

Even after the Reformation, allegiance to Christ remained geopolitical, that is, connected to the religion of the prince: Lutheran, Calvinist, or Catholic. Only the Left Wing of the Reformation broke that national attachment.

The Left Wing first attracted only adult Christians who had been baptized in the state system. Mainline Protestants themselves were not mission-minded. Catholics, on the other hand, did tend to carry their faith where Catholic nations (France, Spain, and Portugal) were expanding. Consequently South America and the Philippines became Catholic. In addition to these national interests the Jesuits did establish missions in Japan, China, and India.

By the eighteenth century Protestants finally became involved in the expansion of their faith along the lines of national colonization. One thinks primarily of the British and Dutch involvement in southern Africa. In the nineteenth century Free Churches also became engaged in missions. Baptists like William Carey, Robert Moffat, and David Livingstone are often credited for proposing programs to carry the Gospel to the whole human race.

Free Church missionaries had no national structure to take with them, though all too often, they did carry a Western culture. The missionary movement eventually became an enormous enterprise—even to this day. As a result, in some places Free Churches are growing at a very rapid rate. They are often independent and therefore express more the culture of the people involved than the culture of the missionaries. We have yet to see the end of this story.

The text in your context. Read the story in Mark 7:24-30. Have a designated person reflect on the meaning of the passage. Use the following questions as a guide for the presermon discussion:

1. Why do you think Jesus was reluctant to help the Syrophoenician woman? Why did he instruct his disciples to carry his message only to those within Israel?

2. Was Jesus bound to people of his "own kind," or was there a reason why Israel should be first in the fulfillment of God's will?
3. When did that reluctance change and who was responsible for a mission to all people?
4. How does your congregation deal with mission and evangelization?
5. Does your congregation tend to include only certain people, or are you open to all? If people join your church, must they "become like you"? What do you receive from "new people"?
6. Do you support missions and evangelism? How can you "go to all the world" without destroying the many cultures of the world? That is, was it necessary to destroy the Syrophoencian culture before Jesus could help her? Or was her faith sufficient? And what did she teach Jesus?

Sermon on Inclusion of Others

Most, although not all, of the Bible stories about Jesus tell about how perfect he was, how correct, kind, and gentle. Today's story of Jesus' encounter with the Syrophoenician woman, on the other hand, is one of the few narratives that presents Jesus in what appears to be less than a complimentary light—at least to begin with.

Jesus seems to be tired and maybe a little out of sorts. He has come to "a place apart," away from his own people and country. The text tells us that he wants to be left alone. We might guess he is planning to pray and reflect, perhaps find a few hours or days of peace, and maybe even make plans for the direction of his ministry. Whatever the reason, Jesus has removed himself from the crowds.

But, as happens to so many of us so often, his quiet time is disrupted and things do not go the way he planned. The needs of the world will not allow him his time of peace. Jesus is accosted by an agitated woman. She is said to be a Syrophoenician—not one of his own people. She has come with a specific request and will not take No for an answer. She wants healing for her daughter. She makes demands and, in her quest to get her needs met, she seems to challenge his way of thinking about himself and his mission.

Jesus and this foreign woman engage in a good old-fashioned argument and, surprisingly, both come out winners, though it doesn't look too promising as it goes along. Jesus seems unwilling at first to heal her daughter, and he speaks to her in a way unlike the Jesus we know. He says he is called to his own people. He can't take the bread for the children (meaning the Children of Israel) and throw that bread to the dogs (meaning the Gentiles).

Our first reaction to this story is likely to be shock. To throw something to the dogs reminds us of the expression "going to the dogs"—a phrase with very negative connotations. Jesus seems to be treating this woman as if she is less than human. The original Greek for the term "the dogs" in this passage refers to something more like little beloved pet doggies, rather than ravenous angry outdoor curs. Still, one gets the impression Jesus is talking to this woman as if she somehow doesn't "qualify" for her daughter to be healed. She's an outsider.

It would appear Jesus had decided he could only help so many people. If his own are not even cared for, how can he reach out to the stranger? This is one of the very human pictures we have of Jesus. Such human images of Jesus in the Bible are very precious to us, because they bring him closer to our own experiences in life.

One might expect the woman to leave Jesus immediately, to give up on him. What happens instead is that this foreigner stands up to Jesus. (She is actually engaging in what might be considered good rabbinic argument. She was not Jewish, but the writer of this gospel was.) Yes, children get fed, she says, but little dogs under the table are fed as well. Dogs are entitled to the scraps and nourishment is nourishment.

This powerless woman, talking back to Jesus, is not only an outsider, but she is also what today we would call *pushy*! (Pushy! You know what that is? That is a description of the behavior found in women which, when found in men is often spoken of as "commanding.")

This woman is clearly less than polite. But her cause, the healing of her daughter, is too important for her to back away. She can't afford to be polite. Her child's health, perhaps even her child's life, is at stake. This unnamed woman bombards Jesus until she gets what she needs by arguing him down. (There are echoes here of Jesus' parable about the woman who nags the judge until she gets what she wants and needs.) She holds onto him verbally, like a wrestler in a stranglehold.

This brings to mind also the famous passage of Hebrew scripture in which Jacob wrestles all night with a stranger (an angel?) and will not let go until he receives a blessing. When Jacob wakes the next morning, he finds he has a pain in his thigh that will never go away. But Jacob also awakens changed because of his encounter. He has received the blessing. Every encounter we have with each other and with God, be it a struggle or a stranglehold, carries within it the possibility that both will leave with a blessing.

Think about it. In their encounter, both Jesus and the Syrophoenician were changed. It happened because neither of them walked away too soon. They both stayed in the encounter—and were blessed by it. The woman had her precious daughter healed. And Jesus received something really important too—his message from God on that particular day through this outcast woman—that God the Creator is creator of all people. By way of her reprimanding words, Jesus was clearly and strongly reminded that the God who renews and re-creates, the God who rebuilds lives, is not just for any one group of people.

Healing and wholeness are for *all* people. They are not the result of having the right theology. They are not the result of the correct amount of piety or stewardship or attitude or creed or anything else. Could Jesus have come out to this Gentile territory in order to pray about his ministry? Might he even have been discouraged, maybe wondering how he would be able to reach even his own people? And now he was reminded through this woman's plea that God's healing is not just for a chosen few. Jesus' mission was bigger, greater than just to his own people.

As you know, it is John the Baptist who announces that Jesus is the one sent by God. Well, it is this Syrophoenician outsider woman who is first to announce that Jesus is for *all* people. In this respect she too is a prophet. She actually proclaims it to Jesus himself and, through her story, to those of us today who will listen. Jesus can bring us hope for a new way of living—yes, whoever we are. An encounter with the Body of Christ can bring about radical change in our situations. A connection with the Christian community can make us see that even we are worthy, because God loves *all* the people God has made, no matter our race, gender, social location, financial situation, sexual identity—whatever!

Dare we go even further—and say that God also loves us whatever our attitude or understanding of religion or even of God? Just think of it. This woman who knows little or nothing of the "official" and acceptable finer points of religion, is chosen as the one to proclaim God's love and purposes. She makes it plain that God's love overrides all patriarchal and cultural barriers (even the dogs). She understood even in the midst of her rejection and pain and need, that the kingdom or reign of God is radically inclusive. Her story points out as well how much we all need to stay with each other and stay open. A community of people that knows its struggle is for justice, for those who are seen as outsiders, will have behind it the power of the living God.

When we remember that Jesus' mission was also to the Gentiles, we too feel called to mission. Christians have always responded in an attempt to follow Jesus' command in Matthew to "Go therefore and make disciples of all nations, baptizing them in the name of the Father and of the Son and of the Holy Spirit, and teaching them to obey everything that I have commanded you" (Matt. 28:19-20).

The ways we have gone about that mission, however, have not always brought as good news as we had hoped. The reason for this is that too often we have deliberately or unwittingly brought or even forced our culture along with our Christian message. Too often Christians have confused culture and message—and in so doing have caused all manner of suffering among those they wished to evangelize.

Today missionaries are beginning go out into the world with a different focus: going into new places (Gentile territory, so to speak), looking to see the ways that other cultures manifest the love we already know in Christ, and seeking to be willing to learn from them as well as give to them.

What we glean for mission from today's message is invaluable. It is that those (outsiders?) to whom we choose to carry our message have much to teach us about the love of God, as well as about healing, wholeness, and clarity. If we really believe that God is God of all people, then we need to recognize that God is already in the midst of them before we arrive. We must be ready to open ourselves to both teach and learn from those who are different from ourselves.

Often it is not from those who are like us that we learn the most important things about God. It is from those who are different. We need to ask ourselves regularly whether we are hearing their voices and recognizing and receiving their gifts. It is one thing to go out and deliver the good news. But maybe even more importantly, we have to be ready to make space in our faith community for outsiders to enter and become family. And when they do come to us, it is our challenge to do more than just expect them to become like us. We need to be open to the possibility that through them we may be the ones that change for the better.

God sends us to each other. Too often we think the Reign or Kingdom of God is a place exactly the way we would like to be. God is bigger than our ideas of God. There is so much we can learn and do. Look what happened even to Jesus, just because his little trip to get away for a while didn't turn out the way he planned.

It is in the unexpected moments and with those unexpected people that miracles and healings happen and we find evidence of God's unending love. Thanks be to God for the "Gentiles" and thanks be to God for the surprises.

Postsermon discussion questions.

1. Has my life and my community become too homogeneous?
2. What kinds of healing and learning and clarity for mission might I or this community find by opening ourselves up to diversity?
3. Who are the outsiders (the "Gentiles") in the area where we live? Why are they such? What would it mean if we began a dialogue with them, or shared a social occasion, or even a mission of some kind? Would I feel comfortable with this? Would this faith community feel comfortable? Do you even need to feel comfortable?
4. What are some examples of how you have already learned from the "outsider"?

* * * * *

On the faith community

Bible study

> For by the grace given to me I say to everyone among you not to think of yourself more highly than you ought to think, but to think with sober judgment, each according to the measure of faith that God has assigned. For as in one body we have many members, and not all the members have the same function, so we, who are many, are one body in Christ, and individually we are members one of another. We have gifts that differ according to the grace given to us: prophecy, in proportion to faith; ministry, in ministering; the teacher, in teaching; the exhorter, in exhortation; the giver, in generosity; the leader, in diligence; the compassionate, in cheerfulness. (Rom. 12:3-8)

The text in its context. Paul wrote this letter to the Christians of Rome about 65 CE. Most readers would assume he had never been to Rome. That makes the Book of Romans different because obviously Paul had been in Thessalonica, Corinth, and Philippi. Yet Romans 16 does indicate he had many friends among the house churches of Rome.

Since Paul had never been to Rome he spends practically no time on their problems and issues. Instead he expounds his faith in a way we find in no other letter. Romans is quintessential Paul. Some would call it the most important document of the New Testament, perhaps even in early Christianity.

Romans might be looked upon with suspicion by many Free Church types. It is true that the letter contains sections that Free Church readers have found difficult to interpret (the author of 2 Peter had the same problem: 2 Peter 3:15-16). But, for example, Romans 1:17 has been the source of the Augustinian/Lutheran teaching of grace alone (*sola gratia*):

> For I am not ashamed of the gospel; it is the power of God for salvation to everyone who has faith, to the Jew first and also to the Greek. For in it the righteousness of God is revealed through faith for faith; as it is written, "The one who is righteous will live by faith."   (Rom. 1:16-17)

Free Church people stress discipleship, following Jesus, more than divine grace.

Even more complex is Paul's admonition to obey the governing authorities:

> Let every person be subject to the governing authorities; for there is no authority except from God, and those authorities that exist have been instituted by God.   (Rom. 13:1)

This passage has been used to support the divine right of kings and even today gives credence to those who believe the church should be in a subordinate relationship to the state. As such, this passage calls into question the biblical basis for a Free Church.

Romans 9–11 (regarding the certainty of God's purposes toward Israel) has been a difficult passage for all Christians. Of late, it has been picked up, even, by very conservative American Christians as a reason to support Israel, politically and financially, and to reject the cause of the Palestinians:

> So that you may not claim to be wiser than you are, brothers and sisters, I want you to understand this mystery: a hardening has come upon part of Israel, until the full number of the Gentiles has come in. And so all Israel will be saved; as it is written,
> "Out of Zion will come the Deliverer;
>   he will banish ungodliness from Jacob."
> "And this is my covenant with them,
>   when I take away their sins."
> As regards the gospel they are enemies of God for your sake; but as regards election they are beloved, for the sake of their ancestors.
>   (Rom. 11:25-28)

Most Free Church types could not support Israel in a conflict with Palestine. They would find the intense support of any country a violation of separation of church and state. Despite these several difficulties, there are many passages in Romans dear to Free Church readers. The Radical Reformation resonated with Paul's words about suffering with Christ:

Who will separate us from the love of Christ? Will hardship, or distress, or persecution, or famine, or nakedness, or peril, or sword? As it is written,

"For your sake we are being killed all day long;
        we are accounted as sheep to be slaughtered."

No, in all these things we are more than conquerors through him who loved us. For I am convinced that neither death, nor life, nor angels, nor rulers, nor things present, nor things to come, nor powers, nor height, nor depth, nor anything else in all creation, will be able to separate us from the love of God in Christ Jesus our Lord.   (Rom. 8:35-39)

Even more dear to the Free Church is chapter 12. It ends (vv. 9-21) with words that echo the sayings of Jesus, even to the point of returning good for evil. The first verses of chapter 12, using the Exodus motif of sacrifice (Exodus 13:11-16), call on followers of Jesus to offer their faith community (bodies) as a sacrifice for the world. Then Paul describes how that "body" is formed. For the Free Church this passage on the Body, along with 1 Corinthians 12:4-39, constitutes a paradigm for the function of the faith community.

The Body in the Romans 12 and 1 Corinthians 12 passages refers to the resurrected Body of Christ. It is the new community, the new Israel, the new temple promised by Jesus. (Jesus told the Jews they could destroy "this temple" and he would raise it up again in three days, John 2:19.)

The disciples and followers of Jesus constituted this new faith community. Jesus was not their leader. They understood themselves as the risen Jesus. The body parts, such as arms or ears, referenced the functions of the church. Some were teachers, some were ministers, some were exhorters (speakers), some were healers, some interpreted the scriptures (prophets). Some offered space for the group to meet. Some prepared the food for the potluck (Agape). Some arranged the seating. Some cleaned up afterward. All were members of the body.

These were not necessarily skills people had. The Holy Spirit guided people to carry out the necessary tasks. Perhaps someone skilled in selling produce was asked to lead in the morning prayer. It was something that needed to be done. The Spirit led them.

Eventually this commonality faded away. By the time Colossians was written Jesus Christ was the head of the body (Col. 1:18). By the time of Ignatius of Antioch, it was possible for him to say the church could be found wherever he the bishop was (*IgnEph* 1.3). The communality of the church first expressed by Paul began to disappear. Unfortunately there seems to be no choice. Most of us would agree that any given group of people will eventually grant leadership to someone. It was inevitable.

After the first century a strong hierarchy developed. The power of the bishops, the cardinals, and the pope became nearly sacrosanct. The Reformation broke the hierarchical tradition, but kept strong leadership. Again it was the Radical Reformation and the Free Church that sought a communality among the believers. Such communality has been essential to the Free Church, but as in the first century it can quickly disappear.

The text in your context.

1. Read aloud Romans 12:3-8 and possibly 1 Corinthians 12:4-31.
2. Have a designated person explain the writing of Romans and the background for the "body" analogy.
3. Is the body analogy a useful way to describe the faith community?
4. Is everyone in the church some part of the body? If not, why? Can you describe some of those roles: song leader, usher, deacon, and others? Are they all "body parts"? Is there anyone who is not a "body part"?
5. Is the pastor a member of the body? What part? Did you notice there was no head in the Corinthians passage?
6. Can you speak of Christ as the Body? Or is it strange language to you? What seems most important to you: Christ as the Body or Christ as the Head of the Body? What difference would it make?
7. How do we become certain parts of the Body? Were any of you an ear or an eye before you became a member of this congregation? Or did you become an eye or an ear after you joined this church?
8. Being an eye or an ear is a gift of the Spirit. How does that gift happen?
9. What steps are necessary to keep the faith community as the Body of Christ?

Sermon on the Faith Community

It may well be built right into our DNA, this profound desire to be a part of something bigger and better than ourselves. It could be some kind of response that goes back to days when we lived in caves. It may derive from a deep-seated inner knowledge that for the survival of the individual it is necessary for each of us to be part of a larger family, community, tribe, or nation.

Whatever the reason, we humans, who begin with the desire to have only our selfish needs met, eventually come to realize that with others we are safer, stronger, wiser, and better. Within a family one member could find food while the other kept safe the dwelling and provided a warm fire, clothing, and nurture. In dangerous times, communities gathered for mutual protection. In better times, they met to share food, experiences, stories, and wisdom. And ultimately, it is only in mutual relationship and in community that we find real fulfillment.

Even though all this is the case, there came a time when we began to lose sight of such wisdom. We stressed the great importance of the individual. This was also true. Every person is valuable, talented, and to be treasured.

With both of these paradigms in place, an issue arises. Which takes precedence: the will and the good of the community or that of the individual? In America the answer has seemed clear. Our constitution reads that each person has the right to "life, liberty"—not only that but also "the pursuit of happiness."

The autonomy of the individual is also a basic premise of our Free Church tradition. Every person has the right to decide how to be a Christian. Every individual can read and interpret scripture. Every local church also holds the power to choose a pastor, to decide how it will be governed, and what action it will take or not take in the larger community. In no other church is the individual held in such high esteem.

Yet, strangely, it is also the Free Church that holds most dear to its heart the importance of community. I once heard an interesting statement about the Free Church. Speaking lovingly about his church, a friend said to me "I can believe what I choose. I can be in disagreement with everyone in my church. This is not a problem; but if I don't bring my tuna casserole to the potluck, that would be a serious theological breach!" You see, Free Church theology is profoundly connected with the vital importance of the individual in conjunction with the value of the community.

What is this? Don't we have to place the importance of one over the other—individual or community? Paul, in his letter to the Romans, explains. We must remember that Paul's letter to the Romans is not like his letters to individual communities. When writing 1 and 2 Corinthians for example he is especially addressing the house-churches in Corinth. For this reason, what he says may likely be a response to particular issues. With Romans we can assume his words are intended more for Christian communities in general.

In Romans, as in 1 Corinthians, Paul lists various talents or gifts that members of the community possess, but he is careful in Romans to begin with this disclaimer: "Do not think of yourself more highly than you ought." Many have balked at that suggestion, believing this is only included to keep us in our place, but Paul completes the thought by telling us why.

We are to think "with sober judgment, each according to the measure of faith that God has assigned" (Rom. 12:3)

All our gifts and talents are not our own, just as our lives are not our own. They have been given by God. For this reason, we should be grateful for the opportunity to possess and use our gifts. You see, Paul is helping the people to better understand the gifts that are about to be identified.

Next, words are offered to prepare the reader for the list of gifts:

> For as in one body we have many members [parts], and not all members have the same function, so we, who are many, are one body in Christ, and individually we are members one of another. We have gifts that differ according to the grace given to us.   (Rom. 12:4-6)

Here, Paul is reiterating his words to the church at Corinth. He is also clarifying the meaning of the term "Body of Christ." This has profound implications for the church. If we, who are many, are one body in Christ then the "Body of Christ" is present when, in unity, we use our diverse gifts to do the will of God.

For this reason the communion service has a much different meaning in the Free Church than in, for example, Roman Catholicism. When the bread and the wine are presented and the leader says "The Body of Christ," the Catholic Church is pronouncing that transubstantiation has taken place; that the actual bread and wine have turned into the physical body and the real blood of the risen Christ.

When we Free Church people receive the bread and the wine, it is in the sharing together that the "Body of Christ" becomes a reality. We the people, together, in communion *become* the Body, exactly because we are eating and drinking together, in unity, with a common purpose to do God's will.

Paul goes on to list some of the talents individuals bring to the church. Depending on the translation, the talents are something like this: vision, service, teaching, giving, leading, and compassion. The list seems to go back and forth between what we moderns might call the talents of "process people" and those of "order people." It has been noted over the years that people usually fit into one of these two very general categories, and the two types do not always get along too well. If there is a controversy in a church setting (or an office or home for that matter) it may be because these two types have difficulty understanding each other.

The so-called "process people" like to move forward, making decisions as they go along and using what works best. They are comfortable with changing their minds in midstream if something isn't working. These people rarely sit long in the present. They are always looking to the future and pushing us on to get ready for it.

The "order"-type people are sometimes negatively known as the bean counters, but what would we ever do without them? They keep continuity. They balance budgets. They make sure everything is in the right place at the right time. They keep the furnace running and the lightbulbs burning. They make sure there is enough food at the potluck, teachers for the Sunday school, ushers at the door. We would be lost without them.

Needless to say, some people have aspects of both the process and order types. Paul's list of course is longer and more complete: vision, service, teaching, giving, leading and compassion. (I'm sure each of you can recognize your own gifts in such a list.) It is clear that should we remove any one of these the body would not be complete.

There are churches that suffer, for example, from lack of leadership, others that may not have enough caregivers, or enough people who are passionate about stewardship. These churches may be in trouble because they have made the mistake of holding up the importance of certain gifts above others. Paul is writing to prevent such a problem. The most important thing he says is that "Individually we are members one of another."

This means that, in order to function, every person is vital to the working of the community—that is, the Body of Christ needs you! This would include the little children whose very presence brings joy to all. It includes the elderly who may even be homebound but are with us in spirit and take the time to pray for the church daily.

Do you see what happens when we understand this? Yes, the community is uplifted and able to function. The individual is also celebrated because of the opportunity to use the gifts, and because of the security and sense of well-being that community affords.

I think most would agree that Communism as it was practiced in the USSR in years past has been an experiment that failed. We often think this because we believe our own system is the only one that can work. My family visited the USSR in 1982. I'm not sure what we expected to see but the negative results of such a system were manifold. There seemed to be what I would describe as a distinct lack of color! Because there was no free enterprise, there was no need to strive for creativity and quality. Result? Grey!

There was also a distinct lack of enthusiasm for work. People took time off work to stand first in the breadline and then in the milkline. These lines never seemed to be moving. Why? My guess is that, when gifts are not celebrated, there is little reason to work at all!

As an ideal, communism purports that all people are equal and ought to share their work and wealth. Sounds good for community, in principle at least. Somehow, however, the community ideal had pushed the individual right out of the picture. Individual gifts were not being used and celebrated.

Hear this story about gifts. George was a retired construction engineer. He had looked forward, upon retirement, to sharing his talents in this field with his church family. He even filled out the "Recognizing your Gifts/ Time and Talent Survey" to let his church know that he was now ready. Greatly disappointed that there were no openings on the "Buildings and Grounds" committee, he decided he would get to know some of the committee members better. So he would take them out to lunch or dinner and give them advice. Over the last three or four years he had taken the time to make himself aware of the various repairs the church needed. The committee members seemed not only not to be interested in his ideas but almost annoyed by his efforts to get involved.

George began to feel the committee members did not appreciate his gifts, but he kept his feelings to himself. As months went by, it seemed nobody even remembered that he had spent his life in this kind of work and that he was clearly the local church buildings and grounds expert.

In the meantime, however, a lot of other things were happening to George. He had begun spending more time with his grandchildren who were also members of the church. As a result, the youth group had invited him to participate as a leader on a couple of trips. Before long he was teaching Sunday school to the older youth.

The years passed and George got more and more involved with the young people of the church. There were often times he even found himself telling them about the work he used to do. The kids enjoyed his presence with them for a lot of reasons. He took the time. He had a warm and welcoming demeanor. When he talked about Jesus' being a carpenter he seemed to really understand what that meant. Besides, he was different from the other teachers. Instead of entering the class with one of those professional teacher-type attitudes, George came to the task of teaching with all the authenticity of someone who had lived a life and sincerely wanted to share his faith.

It took a while, but eventually George came to realize that what had happened to him was very good. You see, it was not George himself but his church community that had determined what gifts were needed, and the Spirit had given him the ability and the opportunity to meet those needs.

His earlier talents which had taken him through forty years at work were not the ones needed in this particular time and in this particular place.

To tell it in terms like those of the apostle Paul, we could say that George had thought he was an "arm" and turned out to be a "leg." Even when he had been feeling disgruntled, the Spirit had known best. If George had been chosen for the buildings and grounds committee, very likely none of these wonderful opportunities would have arisen. Some kind of resurrection had happened here, both for George and for his church.

Besides, those who were on that committee were the ones who needed to be on it. Not only might their new ideas have been stifled but their hard work may have been diminished. It is not the individual but the community that determines what gifts are needed and who will provide them. And best yet, George came to realize that in his faith community it was not what he did that was so important, but who he was.

Another vital issue about gifts is that there can be no strings attached. A gift is always freely given or it is no gift at all. The gift George thought he needed to give would have provided a way for him to continue on as if he had not retired at all. He had determined in advance, either intentionally or not, that people would respect and admire him if he were on that committee. Little did he know that all he had to do was allow himself to become the part of the body his church needed and everything else would fall into place. One cannot help but think of the old-hat phrase, "Let go and let God!"

"Do not think too highly of yourself," says Paul. But this does not mean our individual gift are not valued. We only need to remember our gifts have a much greater purpose than self-aggrandizement. I belonged to an organization when I was a young adult whose motto was a difficult one for me to understand at the time. The motto was: "The only right we have is the right to be useful." I eventually came to appreciate the importance of usefulness. But Paul has clarified and expanded this concept. It's not just that we have the right to be useful but that being useful affords us the opportunity to be what Paul so beautifully describes as "members one of another."

Today's passage of Romans is a particularly important one in the Free Church. In embracing this passage of Romans, the Free Church has chosen pure gold. We don't choose between individual and communal. It is part of God's plan that these be intertwined. Without our faith community we may miss giving our best gifts. And, without our gifts, the faith community will not be whole. As the old song about love and marriage goes, "You can't have one without the other."

The gifts our church chooses to glean from us are for the upbuilding of the faith community, but they also turn into a gift for us. Do you see how wonderful it is? We—all of us whatever our age or expertise—are able through these kinds of gifts (freely given us by a loving God and determined by our faith community) to actually participate in the building of the reign of God. We are working, with God's help and the leadership of Jesus, toward bringing into being the world as God would have it: a world of justice, peace, and joy.

It is time right now to ask ourselves in what ways we are being a part of the Body of Christ. It is also time to look around and ask, "Have I been aware of and celebrating the gifts of others?" and then begin to do so.

Most of all, it is time to thank God for the incredible variety of gifts that exist and are used within this faith community.

God is generous. God has given us the opportunity to truly be individuals, and also the capacity to live together in community, not just for survival but for true happiness.

Let us pray.

Great God, you are the giver of all good gifts. Guide us to use our talents for the upbuilding of our families, community, and world. We ask this in the name of Jesus who shows us the way. Amen.

Postsermon discussion questions.

1. In what ways are you used in the life of the faith community?
2. Are you more likely to use your known skills in the church or do you do what the community needs?
3. Do you think you might have gifts to share that have not been requested? Do you wish they would be?
4. How do you know what the church needs? Can you see it, or do people need to talk about it?
5. How do the gifts you "receive" at church affect your daily life outside the church?

Chapter 7

Governance in the Free Church

Because to worship is more than simply attending a service once a week, Free Church people desire to extend their worship into the ways they work together. Governance in the Free Church reflects directly the fact that the people of the worshipping community understand their community as the body of Christ. The norm, a self-governing system, refers to a faith community in which various boards and committees participate in all decision making. Unlike hierarchical church systems from which the Free Church has removed itself, no single church official or official group holds ultimate power. While in hierarchical systems both responsibility and blame can be laid on another individual or body, in the Free Church all members share accountability for what happens.

Corporate responsibility makes awareness of self-governing a constant factor in church life. Major decision making will often take the form of a congregational vote. Some Free Churches will hold congregational votes regularly and on almost every issue. In others, such a vote will only be called for when the church council has come to an impasse or the issue has major import. Either way, a full congregational meeting will take place at least once a year to vote the approval of an annual report, the budget for the upcoming year, and an election of officers.

This congregational or self-regulating method of governance has deep theological roots as well as sociological implications. Sociologically speaking, most societies have started as self-regulating groups.[1] Because of increased size, because of outside threats, because of food and supply crises, a self-regulating group will almost surely shift to a hierarchical structure. Theologically speaking, Free Church people believe they should carry out the will of God; they believe the Holy Spirit leads them in that journey; they believe Jesus Christ is both the model and the form for their task. So, though it may go contrary to sociological axioms, congregational types believe the people of God were from the beginning self-regulating, and can, with considerable determination, remain so.

---

[1]Victor Turner, *The Ritual Process: Structure and Antistructure* (Ithaca NY: Cornell University Press, 1969) 132.

Of course, from the beginning there were fathers of the tribes who directed the people in the name of God (Abraham, Isaac, Jacob). Some leaders, chosen by God, like Moses, spoke to the Jews on behalf of God. But once the tribes entered Palestine, leadership by a single father disappeared. Decision making was congregational—for example, the destructive revenge taken on the tribe of Benjamin:

> Then all the Israelites came out, from Dan to Beer-sheba, including the land of Gilead, and the congregation assembled in one body before the LORD at Mizpah. The chiefs of all the people, of all the tribes of Israel, presented themselves in the assembly of the people of God, four hundred thousand foot-soldiers bearing arms.   (Judg. 20:1-2)

We don't know who, if anyone, led the tribes against wayward Benjamin. We do know under similar threatening circumstances the Lord called out unlikely leaders like Gideon (Judges 6:11-14). Such judges arose in Israel, but attempts to establish a monarchy, by men like Abimelech, resulted in catastrophic failure (Judges 9:50-57). During stable times tribal/family leaders led the Jews. If necessary, these leaders, called elders, made important decisions (Ruth 4:2ff.). They advised, but had no means of enforcing a decision or creating a military force. The early people of Israel were self-regulating, guided by natural leaders such as elders, judges and prophets. That situation did not satisfy the people of Israel. Again speaking sociologically, we have an insoluble conflict. People want to have self-rule; at the same time they want to be guided and protected by powerful figures. The early Jews were no different. Sometime around 1000 BCE, they insisted on having a king. The prophet/judge Samuel warned them a king would destroy the kind of life they knew and loved:

> So Samuel reported all the words of the LORD to the people who were asking him for a king. He said, "These will be the ways of the king who will reign over you: he will take your sons and appoint them to his chariots and to be his horsemen, and to run before his chariots; and he will appoint for himself commanders of thousands and commanders of fifties, and some to plow his ground and to reap his harvest, and to make his implements of war and the equipment of his chariots. He will take your daughters to be perfumers and cooks and bakers. He will take the best of your fields and vineyards and olive orchards and give them to his courtiers. He will take one-tenth of your grain and of your vineyards and give it to his officers and his courtiers. He will take your male and female slaves, and the best of your cattle and donkeys, and put them to his work. He will take one-tenth of your flocks, and you shall be his slaves. And in that day you will

cry out because of your king, whom you have chosen for yourselves; but the LORD will not answer you in that day."

But the people refused to listen to the voice of Samuel; they said, "No! but we are determined to have a king over us, so that we also may be like other nations, and that our king may govern us and go out before us and fight our battles."   (1 Sam. 8:10-20)

In whatever way one chooses to evaluate the reign of Saul, David, Solomon, and their successors, Samuel was correct—the self-governing way of life vanished. After the conquest by Babylon and the Exile, the Jewish monarchy disappeared. After the Jews returned to Palestine once more, God called out temporary leaders like Ezra, Nehemiah, and the Maccabees. By the time of Jesus the Jews again followed the advice of sociologically natural leaders—elders and scribes/rabbis (Mark 14:53). The elders were respected members of diverse groups. The scribes (rabbis by the end of the first century CE) updated the Law for new times and new issues.

The Jesus movement arose in this self-governing, self-adjusting ethos. The first communities consisted of members who shared the necessary tasks and assignments. The Spirit led them in this shared ministry. No final authority existed in the early church. Remarkable! The powerful Apostle Paul chastised (excommunicated?) someone in the Corinthian church (1 Cor. 5:1-5). His power move failed. He had to back off and enter a process of reconciliation (2 Cor. 1:23–2:11).

The revered author of the Johannine letters (John the Elder?) discovered to his dismay that the church leader Diotrephes would not submit to his authority (3 John 9). The author of the church manual *Didache* (ca. 100 CE) gives us a remarkable insight into leadership. Itinerant apostles, prophets, and teachers did have some authority, but they could stay with the congregation only three days (*Didache* 11-13). Permanent outside authorities were not welcome. The congregation appointed its own natural leaders (elders?) to be bishops and deacons (*Didache* 15).

Only after the end of the first century did hierarchical authorities appear. About 96 CE, Clement, the bishop of Rome, attempted, with a letter, to settle factionalism in Corinth. He wrote with the assumption that Rome had the right to interfere with other city churches, but he made no power threats. In the second decade of the second century Ignatius, bishop of Antioch, made clear his authoritative position (see above, p. 100). Though Ignatius was something of a maverick, from that time on the power of bishops began to override the self-governing style of the congregation.[2]

---

[2]Several scholars see this as the Fall of the early church. Most famous is

Through the centuries, in opposition to increasing hierarchical rule, populist movements constantly appeared, but it took the Radical Reformation of the sixteenth century to once more make self-governing congregations a norm (see above, pp. 9, 19).

Self-governing defines the Free Church. It determines the nature of the worship service from greeting, to seating, to architecture, to participation of members, to authority of the leader, to the expected results. While self-governing may define the Free Church, we dare not make Free Church and self-governing equivalent entities. Some churches we have identified as Free Church do indeed have bishops with power to make decisions (Methodists, for example). Many Free Church congregations have opted for a more hierarchical local organization: the pastor (or moderator) makes the decisions, supervises committees, and may even do the banking. The presence of such a hierarchy can prevent the spread of congregational dissension. Nevertheless, many mainline churches yearn for and spawn self-governing congregations. There is no lack of populist activists and congregations that refuse to follow denominational policies and procedures. The sociological drive for self-rule exists everywhere. The Free Church differs from other denominations only in that it started with the self-governing premise and continues to define itself that way.

So any discussion of Free Church governance maintenance, ipso facto, also references any organization, religious or secular, that wishes to maintain a self-governing style. We will discuss here only the church, of course, but we are aware that we are speaking of important sociological issues.

1. How do we enculturate children and interested adults in a self-governing life style?
2. What role should natural leaders play?
3. What elected positions are needed and what role should they play?
4. What is the function of the ex-officio leaders?
5. How does the local congregation relate to denominational decision making?

Rudolph Sohm who said at this point *Das Kirchrecht steht mit dem Wesen der Kirche in Widerspruch* ("Church organization stands in contradiction with the essence of the church"). See his *Kirchenrecht* (Leipzig: Duncker & Humboldt, 1892) 1:1. Also Snyder, *Inculturation of the Jesus Traditon*, 81-84.

Enculturation

Because the members of a Free Church share responsibility, they need to be educated and informed. Because the world in which they live will usually not be self-governing, it takes considerable effort to generate a lasting instinctive feeling for congregationalism. While such enculturation takes the form of special classes, actual experience provides the only format for absorbing a sense of participative worship and church life. Classes for children dare not constantly consist of teacher-dominated instruction and religious propaganda. Children must take part in class dialogue, give reports, and express their opinion. If a conflict arises, the teacher needs to demonstrate how differences of opinion can be resolved in a congregational structure. As soon as possible (see above, pp. 133-34) children should be included in the main worship service.

New adult members also can assimilate Free Church polity by reading and taking membership classes. Guests and new members are not attracted to a Free Church because of its overwhelming theological acumen or its stunning architecture. They are attracted by the friendliness of the members, the joy of the worship, enthusiastic music, and the opportunity to participate in vital work for the reign of God. New people can sense the friendliness as the community gathers for worship or special meetings. But soon—not too soon—they should be included in the governance. It may simply be a volunteer task to meet with one of the elected committees, to learn from others who are already experienced. The need for every member of the church, especially youth and recent adherents, to serve in governance is taken seriously in the Free Church. Many Free churches intentionally include voting youth members on all committees or select youth delegates at state and national denominational synods and gatherings.

Natural leaders

Any group of people will have natural leaders. For centuries Jews and Christians have benefited from the natural guidance of elders and then, later, deacons. They exist and then the community finds a way, by election or appointment, to recognize their leadership roles. The deacons or elders primarily respond, along with the pastor, to the spiritual needs of the congregation. This responsibility can take any number of forms. Some of these forms are as follows:

   •Deacons, along with the minister, may make the decisions related to all services of worship.

•Deacons often serve or supervise communion.
•Deacons may also be in charge of the décor, appointments, or appearance of the meetinghouse or sanctuary along with other worship-related materials such as communion elements, candles, and floral arrangements.
•If there is not a separate membership committee, the deacons aid the pastor in educating and in welcoming those who will join the church.
•Another vital responsibility shared among deacons and with the pastor is that of pastoral care or visitation.

Equality between the sexes has recently become an issue in the recognition of natural leaders. The traditional roles of deacon and deaconess have been consolidated into one role for both women and men in most Free Churches. In most Free churches both male and female deacons now serve communion. The result of the blending of deacons and deaconesses in many churches is that the women, now serving alongside men as deacons, have simply added new commitments to their traditional helper roles of caretaking, doing kitchen duties, beautifying the church house. There is, as yet, no satisfactory resolution to this issue, except that some churches are making social activities committees completely separate from that of deacons.

Elected Positions

Church committees and their titles vary widely but will usually include trustees, a mission or Christian service committee, and a Christian education committee. These may be divided into any number of subcommittees with individual responsibilities. Either the chairperson or a selected member of each of these will normally constitute the church council. The power for decision making on issues that do not require a congregational vote rests in the council, although this can vary widely from church to church. Because a church council generally represents all the groups in the church, the council makes decisions that relate to issues affecting the whole congregation. Ultimately, in the Free Church, each individual congregation will find its own way of self-governing.

In order to keep a self-governing church "Free," some regulations or bylaws must be adopted. While it seems self-defeating for a non-authoritarian group to have bylaws, some simple rules can prevent or discourage the establishment of latent hierarchies.

The bylaws and church constitution are agreed upon by a vote of all church members. Any changes to these documents must be voted on as well, in order that all members are afforded the opportunity to participate in the decision. A general rule is that any proposed changes to these documents must be in the hands of every member two weeks in advance of a congregational vote.

For our purpose the primary issue in the bylaws has to do with length of office. In most Free Churches, committee members are voted into office for either two or three years. In some, lay leadership positions are extendable for a second term. In yet others, a person must remain out of office for one or two years and then can be returned for a second term by way of a congregational vote. Too many rules would be inappropriate for the Free Church. These election rules, however, serve the purpose of providing opportunities for more people to participate and thereby make shared leadership a reality. They also discourage individuals and small cliques from taking too much control. Ideally they provide openings for every person to participate in church governance.

The bylaws also provide for committees, or servant groups, to expedite the functions of the church. The bylaws give direction to each committee. At the same time, the bylaws limit the authority and scope of each committee. In the Free Church some leaders can become autocratic and so can some committees.

Trustees. Trustees are church administrators who oversee appropriate gathering and dispersing of the church's assets; supervise the annual budget; care for endowment funds; allocate special funds; and care for the church's buildings and grounds. Though no longer true, at the time of Paul trustees would have been the bishops of the church. The English term "bishop" translates the Greek *episcopos* which means "overseer." Many assume the Hellenistic church adapted some of it's organization from the Roman world, so the *episcopos* would have been a Greco-Roman city official. The few New Testament references make the administrative role clear. We see the list of qualifications in 1 Timothy 3:1-7:

> The saying is sure: whoever aspires to the office of bishop [overseer] desires a noble task. Now a bishop must be above reproach, married only once [Greek: the husband of one wife], temperate, sensible, respectable, hospitable, an apt teacher, not a drunkard, not violent but gentle, not quarrelsome, and not a lover of money. He must manage his own household well, keeping his children submissive and respectful in every way— for if someone does not know how to manage his own household, how can he take care of God's church? He must not be a recent convert, or he may be puffed up with conceit and fall into the condemnation of the devil. Moreover, he must be well thought of by outsiders, so that he may not fall into disgrace and the snare of the devil.   (1 Tim. 3:1-7)

These people must be good administrators in their families and must have good relationships with outside business people.

Just as the authoritative development of the bishopric eventually altered the self-governing faith community in the second century, so today no other committee poses as much of a hazard to congregationalism as the trustees. Competent people, who do banking, make investments, contact contractors, oversee maintenance agreements, are special people. Once in place they tend to be permanent—both because of their skill and because of their involvement with the outside business world. On the other hand, this committee has such broad responsibilities it can also become an ideal place for member participation. The elected trustees should supervise the work of several subcommittees or groups of volunteers (banking, maintenance, care of the offering). In this way self-governing can be maintained. The term on the trustee committee needs to be staggered so that new blood constantly appears while some experienced persons remain.

Education and worship

This education and worship committee makes all decisions related to the education of children and adults in the congregation, and aids the pastor in creating a participative worship. It will arrange for teachers at all levels, and will choose and purchase appropriate curriculum materials. While educational programs vary widely among individual congregations, it must be repeated that church school and/or Bible study are almost as much a mark of the Free Church as self-governance.

It is surprising that we know so little about education in the early church. We know that wealthy Romans could send their children to three levels of school: primary, beginning at age seven; secondary, at age twelve; and advanced, from fifteen to about twenty. While nothing is absolutely clear, apparently many children in the Hellenistic world would have attended the primary school and therefore could read and write. As far as Judaism is concerned synagogues and schools were first established during the Exile. Many Jewish children also must have learned to read and write, though they, of course, used the Hebrew Scriptures rather than Greek classics. In any case, for Jewish children education was closely associated with worship and festival occasions. They heard the scriptures and could repeat some from memory:

> Give ear, O my people, to my teaching;
>> incline your ears to the words of my mouth.
> I will open my mouth in a parable;

> I will utter dark sayings from of old,
> things that we have heard and known,
>> that our ancestors have told us.
> We will not hide them from their children;
>> we will tell to the coming generation
> the glorious deeds of the LORD, and his might,
>> and the wonders that he has done. (Psa. 78:1-4)

Families and groups reenacted the events of the Exodus (the seder service during Passover) so that the children could learn by participation the basic tenet of their faith:

> You shall tell your child on that day, "It is because of what the LORD did for me when I came out of Egypt." It shall serve for you as a sign on your hand and as a reminder on your forehead, so that the teaching of the LORD may be on your lips; for with a strong hand the LORD brought you out of Egypt. You shall keep this ordinance at its proper time from year to year. (Exod. 13:8-10)

Responsibility for education or enculturation at the time of Jesus belonged to the family or family group, as seen in the Jewish examples. The early church inherited the family model:

> And, fathers, do not provoke your children to anger, but bring them up in the discipline and instruction of the Lord. (Eph. 6:4)

As the Jesus movement entered the Hellenistic world the process of education shifted. While the church continued faith education, children were educated in the Roman system. Despite the idolatry of Greco-Roman education, even hardnosed Tertullian agreed to its use (*Idol.* 10). Even much later Augustine complained about the obscenity and idolatrous nature of "public education." Soon thereafter all education was provided by the medieval Catholic church, especially for clerics and monks.

After the thirteenth century, with the establishment of universities, educational opportunities expanded greatly. Following the Reformation schools were established by each new denomination. It was not until 1830 that the United States established public schools for all children (in theory, not in fact). We had gone full circle—back to the first centuries of the faith community. Some Free Churches did continue private education, but most congregational types, believing as they did in separation of church and state, offered intensive Christian education to supplement the secular education of the public schools. And most Free Churches insist that the public schools remain secular.

Given our historical situation, nothing is more crucial than the integration of children into the life of the church by means of worship and classes. That integration will be kept alive by offering adult church school, education, and periods of Bible study.

Missions and witness

As we have seen, Christian Education supplements public education and creates the ethos necessary for a self-governing congregation. The mission committee directs the congregation toward the end-time reign of God. By and large, Free Churches position themselves more toward the end-time than back to the creation. The Free Church looks for the day when there will be "a new heaven and a new earth." They do not consider protection of past structures and traditions to be a major function of the church. They understand themselves in light of biblical prophetic traditions. They can resonate with the words of Amos:

> I hate, I despise your festivals,
> > and I take no delight in your solemn assemblies.
> Even though you offer me
> > your burnt offerings and grain offerings,
> > I will not accept them;
> and the offerings of well-being of your fatted animals
> > I will not look upon.
> Take away from me the noise of your songs;
> > I will not listen to the melody of your harps.
> But let justice roll down like waters,
> > and righteousness like an ever-flowing stream.   (Amos 5:21-24)

The words of Micah could be a motto for most congregational types:

> [W]hat does the LORD require of you
> > but to do justice, and to love kindness,
> and to walk humbly with your God?   (Micah 6:8)

Despite the words of the prophets, much of Judaism sought to preserve past ways and to obey the commands of God. We may look askance at their 613 regulations, but we should remember such laws were formulated to keep Jews from actually violating a vital commandment (like a warning sign prior to a stop light: see *Pirqe Aboth* 1.1).[3] Despite the value of these

---

[3]*Pirqe Aboth* [Sayings of the Fathers] 1.1: "Moses received the Torah from Sinai, and he delivered it to Joshua, and Joshua to the elders, and the elders to the

regulations Jesus continued the efforts of the prophets to redefine Judaism. He stressed more the ultimate purpose of the people of God. Jesus scolded his own people, the Jews, for valuing kosher laws over personal integrity (Mark 7:14-23), or for making Sabbath laws more important than healing a crippled person (Mark 3:1-6). Jesus not only called the Jews to the service of others, but according to Matthew 28 gave us the great commission:

> And Jesus came and said to them, "All authority in heaven and on earth has been given to me. Go therefore and make disciples of all nations, baptizing them in the name of the Father and of the Son and of the Holy Spirit, and teaching them to obey everything that I have commanded you. And remember, I am with you always, to the end of the age."
>
> (Matt. 28:18-20)

Jesus preached (Greek, evangelized) the coming of the reign of God. He called for a repentance that expected history to change:

> Now after John was arrested, Jesus came to Galilee, proclaiming the good news of God, and saying, "The time is fulfilled, and the kingdom of God has come near; repent, and believe in the good news."
>
> (Mark 1:14-15)

It was Paul, though, who carried out the great commission by proclaiming the good news of Jesus Christ, Christ crucified (1 Cor. 1:23) to the ends of the earth (Rom. 15:20-28). He, like Jesus, tried to break through the exclusivity of the Jews by altering kosher laws (Gal. 2:11-14), Sabbath proscriptions (Gal. 4:10-11) and circumcision (Gal. 5:12).[4] The early church grew rapidly, not only because of the preaching, but because Christians cared for the sick, the disabled, and the abandoned.[5]

Through the centuries the church has grown and developed by sharing the good news and helping others. The missions/witness committee, sometimes known as the Christian service committee, takes responsibility for the many ways church members reach out to others. This committee will evaluate the various possibilities for sharing and then choose whatever will satisfactorily express the interests the congregation. Many will support

---

prophets, and the prophets delivered it to the men of the Great Synagogue. They said three things: Be deliberate in judgment; and raise up many disciples; and *make a fence [safeguards] to the Torah*" (italics added). (*Pirqe Aboth* is part of the Mishnah—a Jewish commentary on the Torah written shortly after the time of Jesus.)

[4]Snyder, *Irish Jesus, Roman Jesus*, 42.
[5]Stark, *The Rise of Christianity*, 13-21.

services like Heifer International, Christian Rural Overseas Project, and Church World Service—all of which derived from earlier Free Church projects. Understanding that the call of Christ means to build the reign of God by sharing tangible goods, this group will make possible hands-on opportunities to engage in activities that help the needy (such as food pantries, clothing distribution, legal and medical advice, and financial consultation).

A missions committee will also provide openings for social action, for the people to be a part of social justice work that brings about systemic change. Although one may find a great sense of warmth in giving the proverbial can of beans to a food pantry, the church is called to even larger work: helping people to become self-sustaining and to find real self-esteem, and working for worldwide-justice issues. Like all Christians, Free Church congregations will express solidarity with the oppressed. Ultimately, the work of a mission/witness committee helps both those who receive and those who give.

A church growth or evangelism committee might be chosen or voted in as an ad hoc committee by the church council, the entire congregation, or it might be a subcommittee of the missions committee. In recent years, many new ideas have emerged about evangelism and church growth. It is generally agreed that a church that is not growing is probably dying. Although committees exist for this purpose, in the Free Church it is understood that evangelism is part of being a member of the body of Christ. So while some Free Churches may hold special services of evangelism, growth normally occurs when members create small groups in their homes or invite friends, family, and neighbors to events at the church.

Ex officio leaders

The moderator or president. As one would expect, in the early church certain persons seemed most responsible for the local congregation. They had no title, but we can sense their presence. We can imagine, perhaps, they owned the house in which the faith community met. Prisca and Aquila would be prime examples (Rom. 16:3; 1 Cor. 16:19). Nympha in Laodicea would be another (Col. 4:15). Despite the problem with Onesimus, one suspects Philemon was such a leader in a house church in Asia Minor (Philem. 1-2). Gaius may have been the moderator of the house church that received 3 John, though Diotrephes and/or Demetrius seem involved in a leadership conflict (3 John 9, 12).

In most Free Churches, though not all, there will also be a person who holds the title of moderator or church president. ("Moderator" is much preferred as "president" has the suggestion of power and responsibility which in the Free Church is to be shared by all.) This leader will be carefully chosen by the members of a nominating committee or the church council and then voted on by the entire congregation. Such a person's leadership term will generally be the same as that of the other members of committees: anywhere from one to three years, and possibly renewable for up to a maximum of six years.

The work of a church moderator or president varies widely according to the traditions of the particular church and the style of that individual. Primarily the moderator chairs the congregational meetings. Such a leader needs to keep in mind that he or she is not the sole decision maker in any matters whatsoever. Most often the moderator or president, like the pastor, does not even have a vote. This way, pastor and moderator will be able to serve all members of the congregation with equality. Pastor and moderator, in other words, are facilitators of the will of the people. The moderator assures that all voices are heard and that congregational meetings are kept moving and focused. The moderator may also be a spokesperson along with the pastor, representing all the members of the church, in wider church, community, ecumenical or interfaith settings.

The pastor. As we observed in the discussion regarding deacons, there were natural leaders who became pastoral-type leaders in the New Testament churches. We cannot precisely define the roles played by such persons. As suggested (above, pp. 18, 99-100), the Spirit guided believers into whatever the faith community needed (1 Cor. 12:4-11, 28-30). One such function indicated by the Greek word *diakonos* sometimes is transliterated simply as "deacon" (Phil. 1:1). It is a role or office. More often though, because the deacon plays a pastoral role, modern translators use the English term "minister." There are two major functions of these ministers. They teach and make known the Gospel:

> This you learned from Epaphras, our beloved fellow servant. He is a faithful minister [*diakonos*] of Christ on your behalf, and he has made known to us your love in the Spirit.   (Col. 1:7-8)

In the same chapter of Colossians, Paul speaks of his own activity as a proclaimer while serving as a minister (Gk. *diakonos*, NRSV "servant") of the Gospel (Col. 1:23). The second function reflects the root meaning of *diakonos*: service to the faith community, as seen, for example, in the well-known description in Ephesians:

> The gifts he gave were that some would be apostles, some prophets, some evangelists, some pastors and teachers, to equip the saints for the work of

ministry [*diakonia*], for building up the body of Christ, until all of us come to the unity of the faith and of the knowledge of the Son of God, to maturity, to the measure of the full stature of Christ.   (Eph. 4:11-13)

For many of us there is no greater description of ministry than Paul's reflection on both the message and the action:

From now on, therefore, we regard no one from a human point of view; even though we once knew Christ from a human point of view, we know him no longer in that way. So if anyone is in Christ, there is a new creation: everything old has passed away; see, everything has become new! All this is from God, who reconciled us to himself through Christ, and has given us the ministry [*diakonia*] of reconciliation; that is, in Christ God was reconciling the world to himself, not counting their trespasses against them, and entrusting the message of reconciliation to us.

(2 Cor. 5:16-19)

Through the centuries of church history, the pastor or minister has always played an important role in the life of the church. That role might differ from time to time and place to place, but it remains.

The place of the pastor in a Free Church system of governance is most often as a nonvoting ex officio member and advisor to each committee. This way, the pastor can be present at meetings, available to offer an overview of the general needs of the church, and can serve as a troubleshooter to avoid any possible conflicts of interest.

Throughout this book, it is continually and strongly affirmed that the power of the Holy Spirit at work in the church resides in and is moving among the people who make up the body of Christ. In a nonhierarchical community of people who equally share responsibilities, what is the authority of a pastor? At first it seems there is none. The pastor in the Free Church carries no special or final authority. The pastor is not to be obeyed as a parent figure. The pastor holds no special charisms for vision, has no God-given authority to consecrate the elements of communion, and may even be considered just one of the group in Bible study. In some Free Churches the pastor is chosen out of the congregation and not even specially educated or prepared for the work. However, the pastor who clearly understands the nature of the Free Church is priceless and can contribute invaluably to the spiritual growth and the appropriate functioning of the church.

To begin with, the pastor is a faith leader and guide. This does not mean that the pastor tells people what to believe or how to do things. Rather, the pastor is simply recognized as the person who has been chosen by them—set apart, so to speak—to guide people in directions that will help them continue to grow in the faith and, together, live out Christian life. While others in the congregation will likely have to spend much of their time doing other tasks, it is the pastor (in most but not all cases) who has had theological education and who is employed to spend time focusing on issues of faith and the church.

It is the pastor who (in all cases) has been chosen by the congregation for the purpose of giving direction to this particular group. The pastor will often be required to act as a spokesperson for this faith community in larger settings. At all times the pastor will understand that it is not his or her personal opinion being sought by the outside community but rather that of the people that constitute this particular church.

Although in the Free Church every member (ideally at least) will be engaged in pastoral care, the pastor is the one person who is expected to be available to the people of the church in their times of need. It is the responsibility of the Free Church pastor to facilitate the engagement of the church community in continuing care for those in need. The pastor will also perform baptisms, marriages and funeral services.

Practically speaking, the pastor is also very likely to be the one person in the church who has a larger picture of what is going on with all the groups and committees. This makes the pastor an automatic choice for the role of troubleshooter. It is the pastor who can explain to one committee what it needs to know about the others in order to avoid overlapping of activities, calendar problems, or misunderstandings. Although it is the responsibility of every member to know how the Free Church operates, the pastor is a teacher, urging people to greater faith and reminding them what it means to be the Free Church, as the day to day activities, meetings, and worship take place.

The Free Church pastor may not always be the preacher. In many Free Church settings that person can help to make room for lay leaders to preach or even for groups (such as drama groups or discussion panels) to offer the gospel message during worship.

In many respects the Free Church pastor serves as an overseer: guiding, uplifting, cheering people on, balancing, advising, instigating, prodding, and helping. The pastor needs to know when to lead and when to follow, keeping in mind the welfare of the church as the people of God. Like Paul, the pastor needs to know when to move into a given situation and when to back away, when to speak up and when to remain silent, when to educate and when to be educated by others. The Free Church affords opportunities for this to be a reality.

In other church traditions, the pastor may officially at least be given authority and respect. In the Free Church, authority resides with the people and respect is earned. The Free Church is an experiment in living out the reign of God, an attempt in one community to live out in the world a time and a place where people do not wield power over other people.

As Jesus said to his disciples when his Mother and family came to him "Who are my mother and my brothers? . . . Here are my mother and my brothers. Whoever does the will of God is my brother and sister and mother" (Mark 3:33-35). Jesus was not rejecting his family. He was teaching that there can be a kind of community where there is no hierarchy and in which everyone is family.

The Free Church cannot begin to live out its mission unless the pastor understands that goal clearly. The pastor must continually guard against the classic dangers of egoism and power seeking. The relationship between pastor and people will become much more than that of supervisor and worker, teacher and student, or rule-giver and obeyer of rules. The relationship will be that of mutual friends. Jesus said: "I do not call you servants any longer, because the servant does not know what the master is doing; but I have called you friends . . . " (John 15:15).

The pastor will be respected for the hard work, the love, and the caring he or she gives to the people. The respect the pastor will receive from the people will then be genuine, earned, mutual, and holy.

Denominational authority

In many Free Churches there are also responsibilities and opportunities in relation to larger entities of the greater church. In the United Church of Christ, for example, the local church relates to and interacts with mission boards (groups of local UCC churches), associations (larger groups of local UCC churches), statewide conferences of the UCC, and the national bodies of the UCC. It is vital that all of these bodies maintain focus on the fact that their relationships are nonhierarchical. This means that they are mutually responsible and mutually accountable. Each individual member, local church, or church body listed above is called to assist the others, and to provide opportunities for interaction and the upbuilding of the larger church. Each is also called to admonish the other should that be needed and appropriate. This means that these church entities, ideally at least, are self-correcting. None therefore should fall into the kinds of problems of power wielding that can occur in churches with hierarchical formats.

State or national bodies of the Free Church often hold annual or biennial synod-type meetings at which decisions or determinations are made. It is not required that such decisions or proclamations be accepted by either local church bodies or even, perhaps, individual church members. This is a primary example of what it means to be a Free Church. Local church bodies remain absolutely free to make their own decisions in all things related to their Christian faith. The disadvantage of such a system can be that there is no place where the proverbial "buck" stops, that is, no final authority. The advantage is that any individual, being absolutely free to make individual faith-based decisions, will perhaps be more likely to stand by and live by those decisions. In this respect, the Free Church form of governance represents an attempt to model the reign of God.

Chapter 8

Conclusion

Although there were earlier attempts to establish independent churches, we have defined the Free Churches as those that stem from the sixteenth-century Radical Reformation (Left Wing). Inspired by the courage and success of their continental brothers and sisters, soon thereafter British separatists also formed Free Churches. Many British and continental Free Church groups immigrated to North America, where, encouraged by laws separating church and state, they multiplied at a rapid rate.

We have described the Free Churches as those faith communities with the following characteristics:

(1) they believe in the separation of church and state;
(2) because of that separation they practice adult baptism;
(3) because an adult decision is required, they dare not be forced into a religious community against their will;
(4) disconnected from state aid and support, Free Church members take care of each other (mutual assistance) as far as possible;
(5) because they broke with much of prior church tradition and relate on a voluntary basis to the state, they avoid oaths of allegiance and are cautious about creeds;
(6) only a few groups practice community of goods, but all share in decision making and corporate responsibility;
(7) in making communal decisions they work at discerning what the Spirit would have them do;
(8) they find it important not to place wealth and material gain above their allegiance to Jesus Christ.

The Free Church people first met in homes, halls, or simple meeting houses. When builtforms occurred they were simple and constructed to increase community participation. The people are holy, but the building is not. The interior of Free Church buildings remains rather simple without much artistic enhancement. On the other hand, music blossomed. The communal nature of these groups resulted in enthusiastic congregational singing. The music not only expressed their praise to God, but also, with rhythm, increased bonding in the faith community.

Theologically speaking, Jesus of Nazareth is the source of Free Church faith and action. Jesus' words and deeds comprise the center of the New Testament. Jesus spoke of life in the coming reign of God. He sidestepped rules that might exclude some people and healed those who could not fully

participate in the new community. Failing to give allegiance to the state—
the Roman Empire, eventually he was crucified on a cross. Resurrected, his
followers then formed the Body of Christ, a community led by the Holy
Spirit. The Spirit not only called out various ministries, but led the community as it studied the Hebrew Scriptures, the words of Jesus, and his
actions. Along with regular worship that Bible study became a mark of the
Free Church.

Free and open Bible study has many parallels with modern approaches
to the Bible. It shares the postmodern freedom from the historical-critical
method. It recognizes that much of biblical interpretation through the centuries has been determined by major dominating (colonial) powers. It
agrees that everyone studying the Bible should have a voice in interpreting
the text.

Besides regular worship there are occasions in the life of the Free
Church that mark the involvement of the member in the faith community.
Affiliation begins with baptism when a person of appropriate age leaves the
blood family and becomes one of the faith family. Eating together (the
Agape), sharing the breaking of bread, and partaking of the wine/Spirit constantly renews participation in the faith community. When two people wish
to start a new blood family, the original blood family gladly hands them to
the faith community.

In the faith family there are many opportunities and tasks. Led by the
Spirit the faith community selects appropriate people for these offices. Of
course, there are problems: conflicts, inappropriate actions, and illnesses.
The faith community, again led by the Spirit can, over time, heal these
wounds. The ultimate pain occurs when one of the members passes away.
The faith community comes together, with the blood family, to celebrate
the life of the one now missing, and anticipates a spiritual return to the
Body of Christ.

In most Free Churches, as in all Christian groups, members of the faith
community gather at least once a week to praise God, express their unity as
disciples of Jesus, and let the Holy Spirit lead them into fresh understandings of the faith and new directions in a rapidly changing world.

We have shown the variety of ways in which every church member in
the Free Church is called to be a worshipping and acting entity in the body
of Christ. This active participation is a primary premise of the working
reality of the Free Church. Free Church members cannot sit back and
choose not to participate, while expecting others to do the work of the

church in their place. From biblical study and interpretation to church meetings and potluck dinners, everyone participates.

Everyone is also valued. This aspect of the Free Church tradition has appealed to many over the years. It has the advantage of bringing together faith perceptions with the realities of life. Every person who participates in such a living and vibrant community will have genuine and practical experience in a living Christianity. Every person will experience validation and a sense of equality. The church will be less likely to see itself as only a self-centered institution and will exist, instead, as "the body of Christ" active in anticipating the reign of God.

We have written about the progeny of the Radical Reformation in Europe. Those offspring are many. There is yet a more serious matter. In this post-Western Christian world the most growth is occurring in Asia and Africa. While Catholicism remains the largest Christian group, the independent churches comprise the second largest. Given the fact that many of the third largest group, Protestants, will include what we call Free Churches, then in this book we have described a theology, a pattern of worship, and a system of governance that could be the mark of millions of Christians in the coming generation.[1]

---

[1]Philip Jenkins, *The Next Christendom: The Rise of Global Christianity* (Oxford: Oxford University Press, 2002) 60.

Bibliography

Adam, A. K. M. *What Is Postmodern Biblical Criticism?* Minneapolis: Fortress Press, 1995.

Biesecker-Mast, Gerald, and Susan Biesecker-Mast. *Anabaptists and Post-modernity*. Telford PA: Pandora Press, 2000.

Basden, Paul, and David S. Dockery, editors. *The People of God: Essays on the Believers' Church*. Nashville: Broadman Press, 1991.

Bender, Ross Thomas. *The People of God: A Mennonite Interpretation of the Free Church Tradition*. Scottdale PA: Herald Press, 1971.

Chalice Hymnal. St. Louis MO: Chalice Press, 1995.

Davies, Horton. *The English Free Churches*. Home University Library of Modern Knowledge 220. Oxford: Oxford University Press, 1952. Second edition: Westport CT: Greenwood Press, 1963; repr. 1985.

Durnbaugh, Donald. *The Believers' Church: The History and Character of Radical Protestantism*. New York: Macmillan, 1968.

Eller, Vernard. *In Place of Sacraments: A Study of Baptism and the Lord's Supper*. Grand Rapids MI: Eerdmans, 1972.

Garrett, James Leo, Jr., editor. *The Concept of the Believers' Church*. Scottdale PA: Herald Press, 1969.

Gottwald, Norman K., editor. *The Bible and Liberation: Political and Social Hermeneutics*. Maryknoll NY: Orbis, 1983.

Grout, Donald J. *A History of Western Music*. Revised edition. New York: W. W. Norton, 1973.

Hymnal. A Worship Book. Elgin IL: Brethren Press; Newton KS: Faith and Life Press; Scottdale PA: Mennonite Publishing House, 1992.

Jones, Cheslyn, Geoffrey Wainwright, Edward Yarnold, and Paul Bradshaw, editors. *The Study of Liturgy*. New York: Oxford University Press, 1992.

McClure, John S. *The Roundtable Pulpit: Where Leadership and Preaching Meet*. Nashville: Abingdon, 1995.

McKnight, Edgar. *Jesus Christ in History and Scripture: A Poetic and Sectarian Perspective*. Macon GA: Mercer University Press, 1999.

Payne, Ernest A. *The Free Church Tradition in the Life of England*. London: S.C.M. Press, 1944.

Payne, John B., editor. *Reformation Roots*. Living Theological Heritage of the United Church of Christ, volume 2. Barbara Brown Zikmund, series editor. Cleveland: Pilgrim Press, 1997.

Redekop, Calvin. *Mennonite Society*. Baltimore: Johns Hopkins University Press, 1989.

Segovia, Fernando F., and Mary Ann Tolbert, editors. *Teaching the Bible: The Discourse and Politics of Biblical Pedagogy*. Maryknoll NY: Orbis, 1998.

_____, editors. *Reading from This Place*. Two volumes. Minneapolis: Fortress Press, 1995.

Skoglund, John E. *Worship in the Free Churches*. Valley Forge PA: Judson Press, 1965.

Snyder, Graydon F. *Ante Pacem: Archaeological Evidence for Church Life Before Constantine*. Revised edition. Macon GA: Mercer University Press, 2003; 1st ed. 1985.

Strege, Merle D., editor. *Baptism and Church: A Believers' Church Vision*. Grand Rapids MI: Sagamore, 1986.

Sugirtharajah, R. S., editor. *Voices from the Margin: Interpreting the Bible in the Third World*. London: SPCK, 1991.

White, James F. *Introduction to Christian Worship*. Third edition. Nashville: Abingdon Press, 2000.

_____, *A Brief History of Christian Worship*. Nashville: Abingdon, 1993.

_____, *Protestant Worship and Church Architecture*. New York: Oxford University Press, 1964.

Williams, D. H., editor. *The Free Church and the Early Church: Bridging the Historical and Theological Divide*. Grand Rapids MI: Eerdmans, 2002.

Williams, George H. *The Radical Reformation*. Philadelphia: Westminster Press, 1962.

Wink, Walter. *Transforming Bible Study*. Nashville: Abingdon Press, 1989.

Yoder, John Howard. *The Politics of Jesus*. Grand Rapids MI: Eerdmans, 1972.

Index

Scripture Index

(Only those scriptures quoted, not just cited, in the text are indexed.)

Old Testament/Hebrew Scriptures

New Testament